Unless Recalled Earlier
Date Due

AUG 29 1990			
ILL 7-23-92			

An Artificial Intelligence Approach to Legal Reasoning

Artificial Intelligence and Legal Reasoning

L. Thorne McCarty and Edwina L. Rissland, editors

An Artificial Intelligence Approach to Legal Reasoning
Anne von der Lieth Gardner, 1987

An Artificial Intelligence Approach to Legal Reasoning

Anne von der Lieth Gardner

A Bradford Book
The MIT Press
Cambridge, Massachusetts
London, England

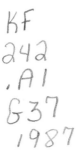

This book was set in Palatino by DEKR Corporation and printed and bound by Halliday Lithograph in the United States of America.

Library of Congress Cataloging-in-Publication Data

Gardner, Anne von der Lieth
An artificial intelligence approach to legal reasoning.

(Artificial intelligence and the law: processes and models of legal reasoning series)
"A Bradford book."
Bibliography: p.
Includes index.
1. Information storage and retrieval systems—Law—United States. 2. Law—United States—Methodology. 3. Artificial intelligence. I. Title. II. Series: Artificial intelligence and the law.
KF242.A1V36 1987   025′.0634   86-10469
ISBN 0-262-07104-5

For my father, who has always
encouraged and never pushed

Contents

List of Figures

Series Foreword

The law, with its diverse modes of reasoning, provides a rich area for the study of both human and artificial intelligence. The reasoning can involve cases, rules, or text. Cases can be real or hypothetical; rules, well- or ill-formulated; text, free or highly structured. And the reasoning can be deductive, inductive, or analogical. It is a perfect arena in which cognitive scientists and artificial intelligence researchers can merge interests.

Although jurisprudence has traditionally grappled with problems of legal reasoning, it has not been able to describe them at the level of specificity that artificial intelligence and cognitive science strive for. Armed with new techniques of knowledge representation, procedural specification, and the like, artificial intelligence researchers now believe that a more detailed analysis of legal reasoning is possible. But artificial intelligence, which has had some practical successes in areas like medicine and geology, has not yet had much empirical experience in a domain with such hybrid modes of thought as the law. The law challenges AI on all fronts, from natural language processing to computational architectures combining rule- and case-based paradigms.

A joint endeavor in artificial intelligence and law will strengthen and inform both disciplines.

L. Thorne McCarty
Edwina L. Rissland

Acknowledgments

This book is a revision of a dissertation submitted to the Department of Computer Science of Stanford University in June 1984. For the opportunity to pursue the dissertation, I owe thanks to many people. I am grateful to the members of my reading committee, Terry Winograd, Bruce Buchanan, and Doug Lenat. As my principal adviser, Terry provided good advice, encouragement, and freedom to explore in the directions that seemed to me most important.

Helpful advice and a supportive working atmosphere were available both within and without Stanford's Heuristic Programming Project (now the Knowledge Systems Laboratory). Besides the members of my committee, I wish to thank Ed Feigenbaum, Mike Genesereth, John McCarthy, and Richard Weyhrauch. For guidance through undocumented mysteries of Maclisp and MRS, special thanks to Dick Gabriel and Andy Freeman. Outside Stanford, I have received valuable comments from Jerry Hobbs, Thorne McCarty, and Edwina Rissland.

Members of the Stanford Law School faculty have also been of great help in the course of this work. The late Joseph Leininger was one of the first to see the potential for law in AI. J. Keith Mann, who knew me as a law student, has helped pave the way for many things. Currently Paul Brest, Tom Heller, and Bob Mnookin are making Stanford an exciting place to work on computers and law.

Financial support for this work was provided, during 1979–81, by a fellowship from IBM's Thomas J. Watson Research Center in Yorktown Heights, New York. Support during three summers was provided through a grant from IBM to the Stanford Law School. The revised version of the dissertation was prepared at Stanford's Center for the Study of Language and Information, through the courtesy of John Perry and Terry Winograd.

1   Introduction

Legal reasoning is a major topic in the philosophy of law, but it is only beginning to receive widespread attention in artificial intelligence. The challenge, for AI, is to produce a description of legal reasoning that reflects its characteristic features and is, at least for appropriate subproblems, computationally well defined.

Jurists have long given noncomputational descriptions of legal reasoning. How far the accounts could be made computational has been the subject of deep, if inexplicit, debate. Some computer-oriented work, on the other hand, has produced models made computational by suppressing just those aspects of legal reasoning that jurists think important.

The objective of this study is to create a model of the legal reasoning process that makes sense from both jurisprudential and AI perspectives.

1.1 Some Aspects of Legal Reasoning

As a task for AI programs, legal reasoning brings together two areas usually treated as distinct. One is research on expert systems (Feigenbaum 1977; Buchanan 1982; Hayes-Roth, Waterman, and Lenat 1983); the other, natural-language understanding and commonsense reasoning (Schank and Abelson 1977; Winograd 1980a; McCarthy 1984; Hobbs and Moore 1985).

The expert-systems area is obviously relevant since a legal reasoning program requires substantial professional knowledge. But a good computer model of the legal domain will need several capabilities not provided by previous work on expert systems. These include (1) distinguishing between questions the program has enough information to resolve and questions that competent professionals could argue either way, (2) using incompletely defined technical concepts, and (3) combining the use of knowledge expressed as rules and knowledge expressed as examples. All are important in other domains besides law, but past AI research has left them largely unexplored.

The natural-language aspect of the project is present partly because of the particular legal subdomain selected: the formation of contracts by offer and acceptance. In problems about offer and acceptance, the data to be interpreted consist mostly of reported dialogue.

But there is a deeper reason for the natural-language aspect of legal analysis. This reason is the incomplete definition, or open texture, of many legal predicates. More accurately, *open texture* refers to the inherent indeterminacy of meaning in the words by which fact situations are classified into instances and noninstances of legal concepts (see Hart 1961, pp. 121–132). It applies equally to legal subdomains such as assault and battery (Meldman 1975), corporate taxation (McCarty 1977; McCarty and Sridharan 1982), and manufacturers' product liability (Waterman and Peterson 1981, 1984), as well as contract law. Although the work described here deals only with open texture in law, the concept has much wider importance. The term was coined in philosophy and used originally of words like *dog* and *gold* in pointing out that most empirical concepts are not delimited in all possible directions (Waismann 1945).[1] Recent analyses of such natural-kind words, and other sorts of words too, have involved closely related observations (Putnam 1975; see generally Schwartz 1977). There is at least a kinship with Wittgenstein's idea of family resemblances (1958 ed.). In AI, Winograd's discussion of the word *bachelor* (1976) is an exploration of open texture.

In this book I will propose a framework within which to provide for open texture and for the other capabilities listed. I will also describe a program based on this framework. The design of the program is intended to reflect lawyers' own understanding of the nature and uses of legal materials—in other words, to accord with a legally plausible conceptualization of the domain. The result is a conceptual analysis of legal reasoning, not a psychology. In terms of a contrast drawn by Newell and Simon (1972, p. 55), the focus is on the structure of the legal task environment, as distinguished from the psychology of a problem-solving agent. The environment has the following distinctive features.

First, legal rules are used consciously by the expert to provide guidance in the analysis, argumentation, and decision of cases. In this respect the rules are unlike those used in most expert systems or the rules of a grammar, which seek to describe behavioral regularities of which the expert or native speaker may be unaware. Legal reasoning might thus be classified as a *rule-guided activity* rather than a rule-governed activity.

Second, and as a consequence, the experts can do more with the rules than just follow them. In a field like contract law, where the rules have been developed mainly through decisions in individual cases, lawyers can argue about the rules themselves and can propose refinements, reformulations, or even newly formulated rules to adapt the law to a particular case at hand. Sometimes, it is true, the rules may be taken as fixed. In a case law field, like contracts, they can become fixed by long acceptance; in a statutory field, like taxation, they are fixed by legislative enactment. Even with the simplification of fixed rules, lawyers are free to argue about what counts as following the rules in a particular case.

Third, lawyers are not merely free to disagree; on hard questions of law they are expected to do so. Unlike other domains, in which writers of expert systems hope for consensus among the experts, the legal system makes institutional provision for expert disagreement—for instance, in the institutions of opposing counsel, dissenting judicial opinions, and appellate review of lower court decisions.

Fourth, since lawyers are expected sometimes to disagree, the following question arises: Is there any class of cases as to which all competent lawyers would reach the same conclusion? In the legal literature, the problem is stated, but not solved, in terms of whether a dividing line between hard cases and clear cases can be found (Hart 1958; Fuller 1958; M. Moore 1981). Despite the lack of a theoretical solution, most cases are in fact treated as raising no hard questions of law. (Whether they raise hard questions of fact is another matter.)

Fifth, when hard legal questions do arise, their basis is quite different from the sources of uncertainty usually described in connection with expert systems. They do not generally involve insufficient data, for example, or incomplete understanding of the workings of some physical process. Instead, an especially important source of hard questions is the open texture of legal predicates.

Finally, there is the task of resolving legal questions, hard or easy. How does the judge carry out this task? How should the task be done? Once it is done, how should the judge justify the results in a written opinion? These questions—often not distinguished from one another—are central in legal philosophy. Different writers, all intimately familiar with the judicial process, paint rather different pictures of it (Cardozo 1921; Levi 1949; Llewellyn 1960; Hart 1961; Dworkin 1977a). They agree on this much: in a well-developed, relatively stable field of law (like contracts), at least two distinct knowledge sources must be brought to bear. Legal rules are one; and rules exist even in a nonstatutory field (like contracts) where they lack official wording. (For an influential unofficial attempt to state the rules of contract law, see Restatement of Contracts, 1932, and Restatement of Contracts, Second, 1981.) Second, there are decisions in previous cases. There is no tidy consensus about how the rules and the precedents are used together.

These domain characteristics dictate the main features of the program. The overall objective is not a program that "solves" legal problems by producing a single "correct" analysis. Instead, the objective is to enable the program to recognize the issues a problem raises and to distinguish between those it has enough information to resolve and those on which competent human judgments might differ. Toward this end a heuristic distinction between hard and easy questions is proposed. The distinction in turn draws on ideas about how rules and examples interact and how their interaction allows for open texture.

1.2 Choosing a Legal Reasoning Task

1.2.1 The Input

To provide a definite context for studying legal reasoning, this study uses materials classically taught by the case method in law schools and classically tested by asking the student, given the facts of a new case, to analyze their legal consequences. The specific legal topic is a standard one for first-year law students, the formation of contracts by offer and acceptance. A typical examination question is the following:

On July 1 Buyer sent the following telegram to Seller: "Have customers for salt and need carload immediately. Will you supply carload at $2.40 per cwt?" Seller received the telegram the same day.

On July 12 Seller sent Buyer the following telegram, which Buyer received the same day: "Accept your offer carload of salt, immediate shipment, terms cash on delivery."

On July 13 Buyer sent by Air Mail its standard form "Purchase Order" to Seller. On the face of the form Buyer had written that it accepted "Seller's offer of July 12" and had written "One carload" and "$2.40 per cwt." in the appropriate spaces for quantity and price. Among numerous printed provisions on the reverse of the form was the following: "Unless otherwise stated on the face hereof, payment on all purchase orders shall not be due until 30 days following delivery." There was no statement on the face of the form regarding time of payment.

Later on July 13 another party offered to sell Buyer a carload of salt for $2.30 per cwt. Buyer immediately wired Seller: "Ignore purchase order mailed earlier today; your offer of July 12 rejected." This telegram was received by Seller on the same day (July 13). Seller received Buyer's purchase order in the mail the following day (July 14).

Briefly analyze each of the items of correspondence in terms of its legal effect, and indicate what the result will be in Seller's action against Buyer for breach of contract.

To define an adequate internal representation for such questions is itself a substantial research task. The representation used will be discussed in chapter 5. The encoding of English into this representation is done by hand. Giving an algorithm to encode questions automatically would involve further difficulties, some of which will be mentioned in chapter 5.

The Choice of Offer and Acceptance Problems

As the legal area to be studied, offer and acceptance problems have several features in common with Meldman's (1975) choice of assault and battery: the law is reasonably well settled; it is taught early in the first semester of law school, so that not much other legal knowledge is prerequisite; and it is an area dominated by case law, not statutes, so that legal reasoning is used in its most traditional and most studied forms.

It might seem that a statutory field, like taxation, would be easier for an AI program to handle. In such a field, reasoning can begin from explicit rules enacted by a legislature. In contrast, fields based on case law, or *common law*, develop their rules gradually through decisions in individual cases, and whatever rules there are are not officially tied to any fixed form of words.

The task of statutory interpretation, however, raises many special problems of its own (see Dias 1979, chap. 7). Further, once there have been decisions interpreting the statutes, one must then be concerned with interpreting the decisions too. It would be unrealistic to try to work with statutes to the exclusion of case law. Beginning from statutes therefore seems likelier to add a layer of complication than to remove one.

There are also some special features of offer and acceptance that make it an attractive subject. From an AI point of view, it differs from assault and battery in being centrally concerned with interpreting what people have said to one another. On the legal side, several major writers on jurisprudence have also had a special interest in the law of contracts (Llewellyn 1938, 1960; Fuller 1969; Fuller and Eisenberg 1981; Gilmore 1974, 1977). In much writing about legal reasoning in general, then, it is often fair to take reasoning about contracts cases as a prototype.

The Choice of Law Examination Problems

As a vehicle for studying reasoning about contracts cases, law examination problems have several advantages. First, they are at a reasonable level of difficulty for an AI program to undertake. In one sense they are toy problems, since they do not present real cases. They are not, however, toy problems made up by the programmer. And although they may be more straightforward to analyze than many real cases—for example, the Supreme Court cases that McCarty considers (McCarty 1977; McCarty and Sridharan 1982)—it will be correspondingly easier to get a consensus as to the adequacy of whatever analysis the program produces.

In another sense examination problems are very real: the careers of would-be lawyers depend on being able to answer them satisfactorily. The skills they require, therefore, are those that all lawyers can be expected to share. In contrast, many other legal skills—such as interviewing clients, drafting documents, negotiating agreements, and trying cases—are developed mostly by apprenticeship and only as one's practice requires.

Law examination problems have some conveniently simplifying features. One is that all the relevant events have already occurred; there is no question of legal reasoning as planning in an uncertain world. The program need not find a plan of action to bring about a legal consequence, like keeping one's taxes low or ensuring that a prospective transaction will have the desired effect, but need only consider the consequences of actions already taken.

In their focus on past events, examination problems are like lawsuits. Unlike most lawsuits, though, there are no conflicts in the evidence. The problem states what happened; one need not decide which witnesses to believe. There may still be questions that in a trial would be treated as questions of fact for the jury, as well as questions of law for the judge. For example, whether a particular response to a particular offer has been made within a reasonable time is considered a question of fact (see Restatement of Contracts, Second, sec. 41). In extreme situations, however, a judge might conclude that a reasonable jury could decide only one way. Whether a case presents such an extreme counts as a question of law.

1.2.2 The Output

General Considerations
The main task of a student faced with a problem like the one presented earlier is to recognize the issues the problem raises and to indicate the ways they might be decided. Discussing why an issue should be resolved one way or another is desirable but secondary. On some questions—those whose answers are obvious and those that make no difference to the outcome of the case—extensive discussion should be avoided. Above all the student should avoid assuming that a question has an obvious answer when in fact it does not.

A characterization of law examination problems, similar to the one just given, appears in a book describing the experiences of a first-year Harvard Law School student:

The typical law-school test is what's usually referred to as an "issue spotter." A long narrative is presented, involving a complicated series of events and a number of actors. The exam generally instructs the student to put himself in the position of a law-firm associate who has been asked by a senior partner for a memo describing the legal issues raised.

Inevitably, the narrative has been constructed in such a way that its facts straddle the boundaries of dozens of legal categories. A varying interpretation of a single detail can produce a Merlin-like change in the issues, and often the outcome of the case. For the student, the job is to sort quickly through the situation to try to name the endless skein of applicable rules and also to describe the implications of using one rule rather than another. Like a good lawyer, the student is expected to be able to argue both sides of each choice.

Issue spotters obviously place considerable weight on detailed mastery of the predominant common-law rules—the ones followed by the courts of most states and sometimes referred to as "black-letter law". . . . (Turow 1978, pp. 169–170)

Turow goes on to say that many law students object to such questions because they place too little weight on an important part of class discussion: "those philosophical, political, economic, and other pragmatic concerns which justify the rules and usually pass under the name of 'policy'" (p. 170). For law students this criticism may be well taken. For an experimental AI program, however, the narrowness of the issue spotter is a helpful limitation.

In the problem stated in section 1.2.1, issue spotting should lead to at least four analyses of the case:[2]

1. The first telegram is an offer and the second an acceptance. Hence a contract was formed, which Buyer later repudiated. Seller wins.

2. The first telegram is an offer, but it expired before Seller replied to it eleven days later. Or, with the same net result, the first telegram is only a preliminary inquiry. But the second telegram is an offer and the purchase order an acceptance. Buyer repudiated the resulting contract. Seller wins.

3. As in (2), the second telegram is an offer and the purchase order an acceptance. But the final telegram operated to revoke the acceptance and reject the offer. So there is no contract, and Seller loses.

4. As in (2), the second telegram is an offer. The purchase order, proposing a change in the terms of payment, operated only as a counteroffer, which the final telegram withdrew. Again, Seller loses.

Deciding among these analyses would require resolving questions like the following:

1. Are the terms of the (possible) offer reasonably certain?

2. Does the (possible) offeror seem ready to be bound to a contract without doing anything more?

3. Was the (possible) acceptance sent within a reasonable time?

4. If you mail an acceptance and then change your mind and wire a rejection, which prevails?

5. Can you accept an offer and propose a change in the terms at the same time?

The examinee is not in a position to say definitely how these questions would be resolved. A judge (or, on appropriate questions, a jury) could go either way; this is what makes the questions significant. Others analyzing the case can at most make arguments as to why the questions should be decided one way or another. Such arguments may draw on, among other things, the general human store of commonsense knowledge, the precedents set in earlier cases, and ideas about what is just. Much of this is beyond the present capacity of AI. Some of it, particularly justice, may remain so forever.

For that reason the present program is limited to finding the significant issues in a case. This task alone turns out to pose significant theoretical difficulties. A later version of the program may be able to make some arguments about how the issues should be decided, but these will remain an insufficient basis for rendering the decision.

This way of dividing things up receives some support from jurisprudence. Karl Llewellyn saw the just decision as a member of the larger set of technically defensible decisions:

[W]hile it is possible to build a number of divergent logical ladders up out of the same cases and down again to the same dispute, *there are not so many that can be built defensibly.* And of these few there are some, or there is one, toward which the prior cases pretty definitely press. . . . It is [the judge's] job to decide which ladder leads to the *just* conclusion, or to the *wise* conclusion—when he sees two clear possibilities. (Llewellyn 1930, p. 73)

The program's task, then, is to find only the set of technically defensible decisions. Again in Llewellyn's language, it is to accept as input a set of "trial facts" (that is, facts as found at the trial or as stated in an examination question) and to produce as output the set of "technically perfect cases" on those facts. Llewellyn states some "ABC's of appellate argument":

First, and negatively, *the Insufficiency of Technical Law: it is plainly not enough to bring in a technically perfect case on "the law"* under the authorities and *some* of the accepted correct techniques for their use and interpretation or "development." Unless the judgment you are appealing from is incompetent, there is an equally perfect technical case to be made on the other side, and if your opponent is any good, he will make it. . . . The struggle will then be for *acceptance* by the tribunal of the one technically perfect view of the law as against the other. Acceptance will turn on something beyond "legal correctness." It ought to.

Second, the Trickiness of Classification: a "technically" perfect case is of itself equally unreliable in regard to the interpretation or classification of the facts. For rarely indeed do the raw facts of even a commercial transaction fit cleanly into any legal pattern; or even the "trial facts" as they emerge from conflicting testimony. No matter what the state of the law may be, if the essential pattern of the facts is not seen by the court as fitting *cleanly* under the rule you contend for, your case is still in jeopardy. . . .

Per contra, and *third*, the *Necessity of a Sound Case "in Law": Without a technically perfect case on the law*, under the relevant authorities and some one or more of the thoroughly correct procedures of their use and interpretation, *you have no business to expect to win* your case. (Llewellyn 1960, p. 237)

Data Structures

Examination problems normally call for essay answers. The general structure of an answer, however, can be given by generating an appropriate graph. In the program the output graph consists of two levels, comparable to the distinct abstraction levels used in hierarchical planning (Sacerdoti 1974, 1980). The upper level is a decision tree, such as the one shown in figure 1.1. Here each node corresponds to the question of what legal characterization to attach to a particular event—in light of the characterizations of any earlier events, as represented along the path from the root to the node in question. When the program terminates, the depth of the tree is equal to the number of events in the problem. The number of terminal nodes is the number of distinct analyses.

On the lower, more detailed level of the graph, a separate tree may be associated with each upper-level node. The detailed tree is con-

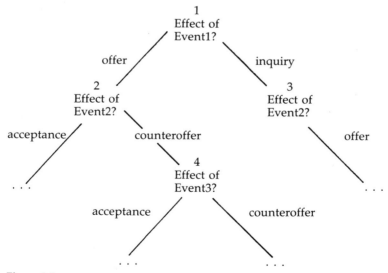

Figure 1.1
Upper level of an output graph

structed in the course of trying to reach a characterization of the event being examined. As the analysis proceeds, conclusions about the event are entered as *new findings* at a node of this tree. Whenever a hard question is encountered, a branch point is created in the detailed tree, with alternative new findings entered at each child. The branch points include both hard legal questions (such as whether the July 13 statement of acceptance could be withdrawn by the final telegram) and computational choice points (in particular, which of several candidate bindings for a variable will turn out to be appropriate).

Whenever a detailed tree is completed, yielding some set of alternate characterizations of the current event, the program summarizes the results in the upper-level tree before going on to the next event. The summarizing step is essential in controlling the combinatorics of the problem.

1.3 A Preview

The rest of this book is concerned with developing a computational model for analyzing legal problems, taking law examination problems as the subset on which to focus. Chapters 2 and 3 develop a general framework from a jurisprudential perspective. The task here is twofold: to identify some aspects of legal reasoning that any truly expert system in law must make a place for, and to suggest a way of decomposing the process of legal analysis that takes these aspects into account. At the most general level, the problem is to reflect both the uncertainties and the (relative) certainties in legal reasoning. The major knowledge base elements and the key aspects of using them are discussed. Chapter 4 then compares the resulting framework with those used by other legal analysis programs.

Chapters 5 and 6 describe the implementation of a program based on this framework. The program is written in Maclisp (Pitman 1983) and runs on a DECSYSTEM-20. Database storage, retrieval, and basic inference capabilities are provided by the representation language MRS (Genesereth, Greiner, and Smith 1980; Genesereth et al. 1984; Russell 1985). In chapter 5 the topic is how to represent the facts of a case to be analyzed. This topic is one that legal theory generally finds no need to discuss, but it is basic to any AI effort at applying legal theory. There are two pervasive problems: to represent the facts in a way that does not beg legal conclusions and to formalize enough general knowledge to support the legal analysis. Chapter 6 takes up the representation and use of legal knowledge. The rest of this chapter presents a brief preview of the resulting program and indicates some of its connections to the framework of chapters 2 and 3. Finally chapter 7 summarizes the program's performance on several problems, and chapter 8 presents conclusions.

1.3.1 Knowledge Sources for Legal Reasoning

In defining the knowledge sources to be used for analyzing legal problems, we begin with a distinction between legal knowledge and general nontechnical knowledge. The distinction is real, but it is fluid. For example, an acceptance cannot exist in the absence of an offer; is that a matter of law or of simple common sense?

In the present knowledge base, knowledge on the borderline between the legal and the general has been allocated to the legal side. Accordingly, the knowledge identified as nontechnical is simple and limited. There is a language in which to state the facts of cases; it uses a propositional format and a lexicon whose elements correspond, for the most part, to the class names and slot names of a frame representation. There is a set of rules, which are universally quantified propositions, that arrange the class names into a generalization hierarchy and permit inferences about the fillers of slots. The language and the rules are described in chapter 5. The rules, called *CSK rules,* are the program's (weak) approximation to general commonsense knowledge. The inferences they support are assumed to be certain unless overridden by technical knowledge. Because the research objective has been to deal with the inconclusiveness of much legal knowledge, there has been no attempt to model uncertainties in nontechnical knowledge as well.

The program's legal knowledge is more varied. The most general knowledge structure is a version of an augmented transition network; it is needed because the sequencing of events is critical in offer and acceptance problems. The nodes of the network correspond to legally distinct types of states of the world; they have labels like "no relevant legal relations exist," "an offer is pending," and "a contract exists." The arcs, corresponding to legal categorizations of events, have labels like "offer," "counteroffer," "rejection," and "acceptance." In addition, each arc has an attached logical expression, such as (*offer x*), for possible matching against the input. Figure 1.2 shows a highly simplified version of the network.

The next knowledge source consists of declarative rules, in an if-then format, which say how to infer that an instance of a legal category is present. The rules are organized into sets, all of whose members lead to the same general conclusion. To make partial allowance for disagreement among lawyers over what the rules are, the rules in a set may be marked as competing. When competing rules are encountered, all must be tried in order to determine whether a choice among them will make a difference in the outcome of the case.

The predicates occurring in the rules—including those in the *if* parts, or antecedents—are understood to be technical legal terms. Some are expanded by additional declarative rules. A few are tested using a procedural representation of legal knowledge. The procedural representation is a matter of convenience, not of principle, and is not viewed as a distinct knowledge source.

All the legal knowledge mentioned so far corresponds to what jurists speak of as rules of law. In legal theory, particularly as applied to case law, there has been enormous controversy over the significance of abstract rules, their status as law, and even their existence. Chapter 2 reviews a bit of the history, with a view to giving readers some sense of how seriously (or nonseriously) any statement of legal rules should be taken. Initially one might expect to judge an AI rule base according to whether it provides an accurate statement of the

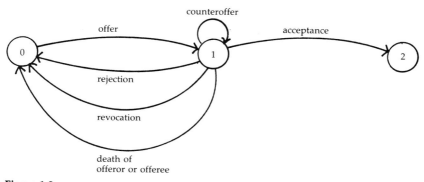

Figure 1.2
Simplified transition network

law; but it turns out that such a criterion can be applied only by giving *accurate statement* and *law* artificial stipulative definitions. A more apt question about AI knowledge bases in law will be how well they compare with traditional knowledge representations such as textbooks and treatises. Such works do speak, to varying extents, in terms of legal rules. The justification for rule-based treatment of case law fields may finally come as much from cognitive necessity as from current legal theory.

If the predicates used in legal rules are all part of a technical language, the question arises what happens when the rules run out. How do technical rules connect with the nontechnical descriptions of fact that appear in an input problem? Chapter 3 develops an answer, which draws on another knowledge source: knowledge of legal cases, both actual precedents and hypothetical examples. The cases are thought of as giving partial extensional or semantic definitions of legal predicates: although we do not know what the predicate's full definition by a formal rule might be, we do know that, under our reading of the cases, the facts in *Armstrong v. Baker* were found to satisfy it and the facts in *Carter v. Dodge* were found not to. As indicated, both positive and negative examples may be included.

Representation of the cases at two levels of abstraction is assumed. At one level, not currently implemented, each case is a separate data structure, and its facts appear in a degree of detail similar to that of an input problem. At the other level, the cases are represented more abstractly, in the form of simple patterns including only the facts relevant to the satisfaction of a particular legal predicate. In this abstract representation, one case may give rise to several patterns pertaining to different predicates, and one abstract pattern may derive from several cases.

1.3.2 Levels of Processing

The framework divides the task of analyzing legal problems into four levels of processing. At the top two levels the reasoning is primarily deductive. At the third level the property of open texture appears, and the program uses heuristics to judge whether it is capable of deciding whether open-textured predicates apply. Whatever issues it leaves unresolved at this stage are viewed as raising hard questions, which only humans can decide. At the fourth level, which remains for future development, the task is to find arguments on both sides of the hard questions.

The legal knowledge used at the four levels corresponds to the knowledge sources mentioned above. At level 1 the task is to process the events of the input problem through the augmented transition network. Thus, the outermost loop of the program is roughly as follows: Given a data structure called a *context*, which contains (1) a list of events not yet accounted for, (2) the conclusions reached about any events already processed, and (3) the current configuration of the transition network, find the best legal characterization of the next event. In general, hard questions may arise in characterizing the event, making it impossible to settle on one best characterization. The result is a tree of contexts, such as that shown in figure 1.1. For a trivial problem, however, like "Joe made an offer and Bill accepted it"—in which the "facts" are stipulated legal conclusions—the program would find the relevant characterizations, and conclude that there is a contract, using only the network of level 1.

In nontrivial problems, the legal characterizations of events will not be stipulated. Level 2, then, is the application of legal rules to decide whether an arc of the network can be followed. If the rules fail at all available arcs, the conclusion is that the event is legally ineffective. There is one exception to the deductive character of the reasoning at level 2: if competing rules are encountered and yield different characterizations of the event, the choice between rules is considered to raise a hard legal question.

Level 3 is reached repeatedly in the course of trying legal rules. It comes into play whenever the rules run out—that is, whenever the program needs to test a predicate that occurs in the antecedent of some legal rule but whose meaning is given neither by further rules nor by an attached procedure. These are the predicates that are understood to have open texture. In the program, they are the main sources of hard questions.

Of course not every application of an open-textured predicate raises a hard question; the case at hand may present as clear an instance, positive or negative, as one can imagine. On the other hand, a case may seem to be clear, on a literal interpretation of the predicate, and yet present features that make the literal reading inappropriate. Chapter 3 examines the complications and proposes heuristics for dealing with them. Chapter 6 includes the details.

The objective of the heuristics is to enable the program to resolve quickly those questions whose answers humans would find entirely obvious, while leaving open those questions that could be seriously argued either way. Toward the first part of the objective, two knowledge sources are employed: the CSK rules, as a basis for factual inferences, and the patterns drawn from the cases, as a basis for inferring that the precedents make the answer clear. These knowledge sources may or may not yield an answer. If they do, the program must then look for grounds on which this tentative answer might be defeated. No general model of possible grounds for defeat has been attempted; again the program looks to the precedents, in the form of abstract patterns. As a result of these heuristics, the satisfaction of a legal predicate is treated as an easy question—one within the program's competence to resolve—if an answer can be derived either from the CSK rules or from case knowledge or both, provided that conflicting cases are not found. If the knowledge sources provide no answer or the cases point both ways, a hard legal question has been identified, and a branch point is entered into the output graph.

Since the program's distinction between hard questions and easy questions is a heuristic one, it may make classifications that to human intuition seem wrong. A fully developed program might prove useful, nonetheless, if it finds some significant questions that the human user might have overlooked. In addition, unintuitive results can be thought-provoking. If programs to simulate legal reasoning behave interestingly enough, they may eventually yield a new set of questions, if not of answers, for legal theory.

2

Design I: The Place of Rules

2.1 Introduction

Some AI research makes a strong assumption: that whatever the particular problem domain, traditional, noncomputational treatments of problem solving in the domain contain nothing of value for a computational approach. Sometimes the assumption seems to be justified. In looking at writings about mathematical discovery, for example, Douglas Lenat[1] found mostly maxims on the order of "get a good night's sleep"—hardly useful advice for a computer program. Legal reasoning, however, is not such a domain.

It is true that there has been some useless advice. William Blackstone, author of the first systematic treatment of English law (1765–69), wrote that the common law was based on custom, and customs gained their authority by having been used "time whereof the memory of man runneth not to the contrary." As for how judges could know what the customs were—that is, what rules they were supposed to follow in deciding particular cases—Blackstone spoke of the "nocturnal studies of twenty years" and of judges "being long personally accustomed to the judicial decisions of their predecessors" (Jones, ed., 1973, pp. 49–50).

But two hundred years have passed since Blackstone, and legal reasoning, particularly judicial reasoning, has become a central topic in jurisprudence. The general question has been, What grounds are there for criticizing or commending judicial decisions? The discussion contains a good many lessons for the design of a legal reasoning program—in particular, by pointing up some ways such a program should not be organized. The discussion also indicates some limits on how a legal reasoning program might properly be used—an important topic, in view of suggestions made from time to time that computers might take the place of human judges.

This chapter and the next review some of the previous answers to the general question. In the jurisprudential literature, there are some constraints on the kind of answer desired. First, the decision process is to be understood, so far as possible, as a rational process. Whatever makes the process rational is what distinguishes it from, say, decision by flipping a coin, or decision by the primitive method of trial by ordeal, or decision according to the mere personal preferences of someone who happens to be in a position to enforce them.

For most writers on jurisprudence, rationality is to be sought at a level that might be displayed in a judge's opinion. Some exceptions, not directly relevant here, are concerned with discovery of the proper decision, rather than its justification, or with the psychology of legal reasoning rather than its logic. These include John Dewey (1924) (a logic of discovery), Hutcheson (1929) (the "judgment intuitive"), and Frank (1930) (the judge's personality).

A further constraint, usually present, is that the decision process be described in terms that human judges are capable of following. For if the account requires judges to know the unknowable (such as Blackstone's fictitious customs from "time out of mind"), then it fails both as description and, of greater ultimate interest to most legal theorists, as a possible source of guidance to the conscientious judge. A good deal of writing in jurisprudence has been devoted to showing that other constructs, less obviously fictitious than Blackstone's, are also only idealizations that no one could use even if he tried. On the positive side, one can read much of the literature on judicial decision making as asking how far the process is computable. We will review it in that light. The main conclusions are summarized at the beginning of chapter 3.

2.2 Legal Theories and AI Paradigms

As a standard for evaluating judicial decisions, one might demand more than rational justifiability. A stronger requirement would be that decisions be demonstrably correct. And there is a tradition, in law, that legal questions have correct answers. The tradition has long been out of favor academically; but it may still have currency among laymen, it may still affect judicial practice (Llewellyn 1960, pp. 24–25), and it recently has again raised academic controversy (Dworkin 1977b, 1978).

There is also a tradition that computer programs should produce correct answers to the problems they are given. What would it mean, then, for a program to produce right answers, or at least rational answers, to legal questions? This is, in effect, the problem of system validation for a legal reasoning program. I will begin by reviewing, in oversimplified form, three legal positions.

2.2.1 Mechanical Jurisprudence

The term *mechanical jurisprudence* was coined by Pound (1908). In AI language, it has come to mean a view of law as axioms and legal reasoning as deduction. On this view law is sometimes analogized to mathematics. Holmes, for example, remarked that "judicial dissent often is blamed, as if it meant simply that one side or the other were not doing their sums right, and, if they would take more trouble, agreement inevitably would come" (1897, p. 465). Other analogies are less attractive. Frank referred to "judicial slot-machines, the facts being inserted in one end of the machine and the decision, through the use of mechanical logic, coming out at the other end" (1930, p. 209). Dworkin (1977a) provides convenient, striking descriptions of mechanical jurisprudence and the other positions to be considered. Mechanical jurisprudence is the view that

when we speak of "the law" we mean a set of timeless rules stocked in some conceptual warehouse awaiting discovery by judges, and that when we speak of legal obligation we mean the invisible chains these mysterious rules somehow drape around us. The theory that there are such rules and chains [the nominalists] call "mechanical jurisprudence", and they are right in ridiculing its practitioners. Their difficulty, however, lies in finding practitioners to ridicule. (Dworkin 1977a, p. 15)

Some synonyms for *mechanical jurisprudence* are *conceptualism* and *formalism*.

It is true, as Dworkin points out, that consistent practitioners of mechanical jurisprudence are hard to find. But there is at least a standard example. He is Christopher Columbus Langdell, who became dean of the Harvard Law School in 1870 and who revolutionized legal education by inventing the case method. In contracts, Langdell argued from an abstract concept of contract to particular rules of contract law. He was capable of dismissing, as irrelevant, that the rules derived might be inconvenient for everyone. The following well-known passage illustrates:

It has been claimed that the purposes of substantial justice and the interests of contracting parties as understood by themselves will be best served by holding that the contract is complete the moment the letter of acceptance is mailed; and cases have been put to show that the contrary view would produce not only unjust but absurd results. . . . The true answer to this argument is, that it is irrelevant. . . . (Langdell 1879, pp. 995–996)

That is, on a view of law as fixed rules with deductive consequences, there is no room to ask whether a valid deduction leads to an unjust conclusion. In fairness to Langdell, he did go on to argue that his conclusion was not absurd or unjust.

As for the timelessness of the rules, Langdell invoked not Blackstone's idea of custom but an analogy to the laws of science:

[I]t was indispensable to establish at least two things—that law is a science, and that all the available materials of that science are contained in printed books. . . .
. . . We have . . . constantly inculcated the idea that the library is the proper workshop of professors and students alike; that it is to us all that the laboratories of the university are to the chemists and physicists, the museum of natural history to the zoologists, the botanical garden to the botanists. (Langdell 1886, p. 124)

The data in the library, of course, were the precedents. The rules were to be inferred from some of the cases and then used to test the result in further cases. The inference process, however, was left completely unelucidated. Worse, the selection of cases from which the rules were inferred—in AI terms, the training set—was apparently guided mainly by the conclusions Langdell wanted to draw (Gilmore 1974, pp. 17–18; Gilmore 1977, pp. 47–48).

2.2.2 Legal Realism

The movement called *legal realism* developed as a reaction to mechanical or conceptual approaches to law. So influential was the movement that it still shapes a central research question about computers and legal reasoning: how is it possible for an AI program, or any other computer program, to reason about legal problems without engaging in something deserving to be called mechanical jurisprudence?

A main feature of the realist movement was its downgrading of legal rules. All that counted as law were decisions in particular cases (Frank 1930, p. 128). In an extreme view, rules had no legitimate place in legal discourse at all. Dworkin gives the name *nominalism* to such a position:

In [the nominalists'] view the concepts of "legal obligation" and "the law" are myths, invented and sustained by lawyers for a dismal mix of conscious and subconscious motives. . . . We would do better to flush away . . . the concepts altogether, and pursue our important social objectives without this excess baggage. (Dworkin 1977a, p. 15; see also Hart 1961, pp. 132–137, on varieties of rule-skepticism)

Two of the main writers identified with legal realism, or nominalism, are Oliver Wendell Holmes and Karl Llewellyn. As a description of their actual positions, the paragraph just quoted is false (and Dworkin carefully avoids attributing his version of the theory to anyone in particular). Nevertheless there are some famous sentences in the writings of Holmes and Llewellyn, on the nature of law and the place of rules, that lend support to the description as a caricature:

The prophecies of what the courts will do in fact, and nothing more pretentious, are what I mean by the law. (Holmes 1897, p. 461)

The life of the law has not been logic: it has been experience. The felt necessities of the time, the prevalent moral and political theories, intuitions of public policy, avowed or unconscious, even the prejudices which judges share with their fellow-men, have had a good deal more to do than the syllogism in determining the rules by which men should be governed. (Holmes 1881, p. 5)

What . . . officials do about disputes is, to my mind, the law itself. (Llewellyn 1930, p. 12; footnote omitted)

And *rules,* in all of this, are important to you so far as they help you see or predict what judges will do or so far as they help you get judges to do something. That is their importance. That is all their importance, except as pretty playthings. (Ibid., p. 14)

These passages add up to a view of law as behavior or predictions of behavior. The behavior of interest is the action of judges in handing down decisions (or the action of other government officials). There is skepticism about whether this behavior is controlled by legal rules.

In the teaching of law, Llewellyn wrote later, the extreme realist view led to the attitude that judges "can decide any way they want to, and they do, and then they write it up to suit; and the opinion tells you nothing" (Llewellyn 1960, p. 13). That is, it was common for only two alternatives to be seen: either decisions were dictated by deductive logic, or they were arbitrary, with judicial opinions as mere rationalization. The effect of the legal realist movement, in short, was to destroy the old conceptualist paradigm and to put nothing in its place. One writer is reminded of a quotation: "He led them into the Wilderness and left them there" (in Stevens 1971, p. 481).

If legal realism is right, it appears to make the AI paradigm of rule-based expert systems inappropriate, at least with any simple mapping from legal rules to knowledge-base rules. There are several directions one might go instead. One direction would emphasize the idea that it is individual decisions, not general rules, that have authoritative status as law. With this emphasis, one might look for a method of reasoning from the decisions in past cases to a conclusion in a present case (see Levi 1949). But this cannot be the whole story. If it were, why would present-day law professors, thoroughly aware of the insights of realism, continue to expect their students to know rules? (Compare the quotation from Turow 1978 in section 1.2.2.) Another direction would emphasize the behavioristic side of legal realism. Some such work has been done. It is associated with an offshoot of legal realism called *jurimetrics* (see chapter 4) and, more extensively, with quantitative political science (Schubert 1975; Goldman and Sarat 1978). A third possibility, which this study adopts, is to retain an important place for legal rules but to reinterpret their significance. Rulelike sentences can be understood as useful cognitive constructs, needed to find order in (or impose order upon) an unwieldy mass of individual decisions. Once articulated, they can provide guidance as to how future decisions can be kept in some rough conformance with this order; or, if the articulated rule seems to be a bad rule, it can suggest a way of saying how the course of decisions ought to be changed. Obviously, seeing rules as cognitive tools does not require seeing them either as authoritative statements of law or as adequate descriptions of judicial behavior.

2.2.3 Legal Positivism

Discussion of legal rules does not end with the opposition of realism to conceptualism. Much work has gone into trying to provide a replacement for the conceptual account that realism destroyed. One such alternative is the position called *legal positivism*. It goes back to John Austin (1790–1859), whose negative criticism was directed not at Langdell, of course, but at Blackstone. The fullest modern expression of positivism is Hart's *Concept of Law* (1961), and according to Dworkin, it is "now accepted in one form or another by most working and academic lawyers who hold views on jurisprudence" (1977a, p. 16). Again Dworkin provides a convenient summary. There are three key tenets:

(a) The law of a community is a set of special rules used by the community directly or indirectly for the purpose of determining which behavior will be punished or coerced by the public power. These special rules can be identified and distinguished by specific criteria, by tests having to do not with their content but with their *pedigree* or the manner in which they were adopted or developed. . . .
(b) The set of these valid legal rules is exhaustive of "the law", so that if someone's case is not clearly covered by such a rule (because there is none that seems appropriate, or those that seem appropriate are vague, or for some other reason) then that case cannot be decided by "applying the law." It must be decided by some official, like a judge, "exercising his discretion," which means reaching beyond the law for some other sort of standard to guide him in manufacturing a fresh legal rule or supplementing an old one.
(c) To say that someone has a "legal obligation" is to say that his case falls under a valid legal rule that requires him to do or to forbear from doing something. (Dworkin 1977a, p. 17)

Two points here are of potential importance for an AI program. One is the idea that rulelike sentences are valid legal rules—that they have authority as law—if they are properly pedigreed. If this is right and if the knowledge base of an AI program consisted of properly pedigreed rules, one would have the beginning of an argument that results derived by the program were legally correct—that the program in fact gets right answers.

Unfortunately there is an insuperable problem. Dworkin also says, "These tests of pedigree can be used to distinguish valid legal rules from spurious legal rules (rules which lawyers and litigants wrongly argue are rules of law) and also from other sorts of social rules (generally lumped together as 'moral rules') that the community follows but does not enforce through public power" (1977a, p. 17). Now if lawyers and litigants cannot tell spurious legal rules from valid ones, then neither can a program designer, and a program certainly cannot. Whether or not it is correct to analyze case law in terms of tests of pedigree, the analysis is epistemologically inadequate (McCarthy and Hayes 1969; McCarthy 1977) in assuming that usable tests of pedigree exist. Hart admits as much:

Any honest description of the use of precedent in English law must allow a place for the following pairs of contrasting facts. *First, there is no single method of determining the rule* for which a given authoritative precedent is an author-ity. Notwithstanding this, in the vast majority of decided cases there is very little doubt. The head-note is usually correct enough. *Secondly, there is no authoritative or uniquely correct formulation of any rule* to be extracted from cases. On the other hand, there is often very general agreement, when the bearing of a precedent on a later case is in issue, that a given formulation is adequate. (Hart 1961, p. 131; emphasis added. For a detailed justification of the italicized conclusions, see Stone 1964, pp. 35–37, 267–280.)

There remains another possibility for saying that the rules in an AI knowledge base are correct statements of the law. If, as Hart observes, there is often "very general agreement . . . that a given formulation is adequate," perhaps rules can be validated by consen-sus rather than by pedigree. We will consider that possibility in the next section.

The second important point about positivism is its distinction be-tween cases that can be decided by "applying the law" and cases requiring the exercise of discretion. If such a distinction holds up and can be made precise, it should provide a basis for identifying the significant issues in a case. Cases not requiring discretion on any issue would be clear cases. In clear cases, which by hypothesis would leave no room for expert disagreement about the proper outcome, the program's summary-level decision tree would usually reduce to a straight line—representing the one right answer.

There has been some important criticism of positivism, notably by Lon Fuller (1940, 1969), who rejected the idea that the validity of a legal rule is an all-or-none characteristic, and Ronald Dworkin (1977a), who rejects the idea that judges have discretion in any cases whatever. We will return to the views of these writers.

2.3 Rules for Contract Law

2.3.1 The Positivist Theory and the Restatement of Contracts

It was suggested that there might still be room within positivism for saying that the rules in a program's knowledge base are valid—that they are, in fact, rules of law. The idea was that, even if we cannot tell whether the rules are properly pedigreed, there may still be some set of rules whose validity no one disputes. For the law of contracts, moreover, there is an attractive candidate to fill the role. It is the Restatement of the Law of Contracts, and it looks like an expert-system builder's dream.

The Restatement project began in 1923 with the establishment of the American Law Institute. The organizing committee, and later the institute membership, included many of the country's most distinguished judges, law professors, and other lawyers. The problem that gave rise to such a group was later stated thus:

> The vast and ever increasing volume of the decisions of the courts establishing new rules or precedents, and the numerous instances in which the decisions are irreconcilable has resulted in ever increasing uncertainty in the law. The American Law Institute was formed in the belief that in order to clarify and simplify the law and to render it more certain, the first step must be the preparation of an orderly restatement of the common law . . . . (Restatement of Contracts, 1932, p. viii)

Contracts was one of the topics initially chosen for restatement. Samuel Williston, then the country's leading contracts scholar, was chosen as reporter; it was his function, with a committee of equally able advisers, to prepare drafts for presentation to the institute's executive council and then to the institute as a whole. Nine years and about seventy drafts later, the first Restatement of Contracts appeared. The introduction to the two volumes stated:

> The function of the courts is to decide the controversies brought before them. The function of the Institute is to state clearly and precisely in the light of the decisions the principles and rules of the common law.
>
> The sections of the Restatement express the result of a careful analysis of the subject and a thorough examination and discussion of pertinent cases— often very numerous and sometimes conflicting. The accuracy of the statements of law made rests on the authority of the Institute. They may be regarded both as the product of expert opinion and as the expression of the law by the legal profession. (Restatement of Contracts, 1932, pp. xi–xii)

For each section of the Restatement, the format is a black-letter rule followed by comments and illustrations, as in this example:

Section 60. PURPORTED ACCEPTANCE WHICH ADDS QUALIFICATIONS.

A reply to an offer, though purporting to accept it, which adds qualifications or requires performance of conditions, is not an acceptance but is a counter-offer.

Comment:

a. A qualified or conditional acceptance is a counter-offer, since such an acceptance is a statement of an exchange that the person making it is willing to make, differing from that proposed by the original offeror. A counter-offer is a rejection of the original offer (see section 38 and Comment thereon). An acceptance, however, is not inoperative as such merely because it is expressly conditional, if the requirement of the condition would be implied from the offer, though not expressed therein.

Illustrations:
    1. A makes an offer to B, and B in terms accepts but adds, "Prompt acknowledgment must be made of receipt of this letter." There is no contract, but a counter-offer.
    2. A makes a written offer to B to sell him Blackacre. B replies, "I accept your offer if you can convey me a good title." There is a contract. (Restatement of Contracts, 1932)

The need for such a distillation of the rules of a subject domain has been an enormous stumbling block to AI programmers. Buchanan, Sutherland, and Feigenbaum (1970) and Pople (1977) describe the problems a computer scientist faces in trying to reconstruct the expert knowledge of a chemist or physician. AI approaches to reducing the effort are represented by Davis (1979) (assistance to the expert in communicating rules to the program directly rather than through a programmer) and Buchanan and Mitchell (1978) (discovery of rules by the program itself). Hayes-Roth, Waterman, and Lenat (1983, chap. 5) provide a survey.

Nevertheless, the Restatement is not a document to be adopted uncritically as the final word on contract law. The trouble is not that the Restatement is out of date. It is not. A revision was undertaken in 1962 and completed in 1979 (Restatement of Contracts, Second, 1981, p. vii). But the position we were considering was that there exists a set of legal rules whose validity is undisputed and that the Restatement is such a set. If the Restatement does not qualify, it is hard to imagine (for case law) what would.

The Restatement does not qualify. Some of the objections are relatively narrow, and some may have been cured in Restatement Second. Arthur Corbin, a co-reporter for the first Restatement and the author of a twelve-volume treatise on contracts, says that "there was not enough competence in the nation for the reduction of such a mass of material into the form of accurate, well organized, clearly expressed, and up-to-date generalizations" (1961, p. 198) and that "in some places [the learned doctors] merely restated former rules and principles that were even then substantially moribund or even actually dead" (1964, pp. 186–187). Gilmore reports on the need for compromise between Corbin and Williston (1974, pp. 59–65), possibly with the result that the final version reflected neither of their views; and Corbin confirms that there were "scenes of carnage and mutilation" (1929, p. 31). Henry Hart and Sacks complain that the restaters included only specific rules, not general principles; that even the specific rules were not backed up by the statement of supporting reasons or case authority; and that the persuasiveness of the rules thus rested only on the authority of the American Law Institute (1958, pp. 761–764).

In the second Restatement, explanations and cases have been added. Beyond that change, the first reporter, Robert Braucher, is rather ambiguous: "[T]he main innovations in the revision may be described as stylistic rather than substantive. But it should not be surprising that a stylistic revision may be symptomatic of fundamental shifts in modes of thought" (1964, p. 303). On the whole, then, even though the Restatement of Contracts has been called the best of the restatements and "one of the great legal accomplishments of all time" (Gilmore 1974, p. 59), it does not add up to a set of undoubtedly valid rules.

The Restatement is, nevertheless, as good a starting point as we have for an AI rule base on contract law. What, then, are its limitations?

2.3.2 Absence of Official Wording

Since the Restatement was never adopted by any legislature, the wording of its rules has no official status. This is more an advantage than a limitation. If some other wording of the same general ideas seems preferable, the author of an AI knowledge base is free to use it.

The rules actually used in the knowledge base will be discussed in some detail in chapter 6. Here, though, are two preliminary examples of changes from the Restatement version.

The second Restatement defines an *offer*, in part, as "the manifestation of willingness to enter into a bargain" (section 24). It then defines a *bargain*, in part, as an agreement for an exchange, and an *agreement* as "a manifestation of mutual assent on the part of two or more persons" (section 3). Finally, it is said that "the manifestation of mutual assent to an exchange ordinarily takes the form of an offer . . . followed by an acceptance . . ." (section 22(1)). This is circular. The sections amount to saying that an offer, ordinarily, is the manifestation of willingness to enter into an offer followed by an acceptance. To remove the circularity, section 24 has been treated as if it said, "An offer is the manifestation of willingness to enter into an *exchange* . . . ."

As a second example, the Restatement definition of *acceptance* begins, "Acceptance of an offer is a manifestation of assent to the terms thereof" (section 50(1)). In the program, the corresponding knowledge-base rule looks for a manifestation of assent not directly to the terms of an offer but simply to an exchange. The program's rule then adds that there must be a match between the terms of the offer and any description of the exchange given in the potential acceptance.

The Restatement's acceptance rule was changed mostly for convenience. For example, the change permits factoring out what is common to acceptances and counteroffers rather than, as in the Restatement, giving entirely separate definitions. In addition, the change avoids any suggestion that accepting an offer requires knowing what all its terms are[2] or knowing that the communication responded to is, in legal effect, an offer.[3]

To a contracts scholar, changes like these might or might not seem to be improvements. The point is that the versions encoded reflect just one understanding of how best to write the rules. A rule base for case law will always have to be a personal synthesis, whose quality will vary with its authors. In this respect an AI knowledge base is in the same position as the Restatement, a textbook, or any other secondary source. These can be extremely useful, but they are not ultimate statements of the law.

2.3.3 Disagreement over Rules

The Restatement attempts to state a consistent set of rules for contract law. Legal texts, though, often talk about the majority view, the minority view, and points on which courts have not expressed a view. The Restatement writers made a choice among conflicting views. As a result, lawyers need to know about more versions of the rules than the Restatement tells them. Legal knowledge includes knowledge of inconsistent alternatives.

The first addition, then, to the knowledge base as a Restatement-like formulation of rules is that conflicting rules can be represented. In particular, there can be several different rules all purporting to cover the same ground. Examples will be given in section 6.3.1.

There is a more dramatic kind of disagreement over rules than disagreement over alternatives already formulated. Dworkin points out, as an objection to positivism, that positivism cannot find a place for this kind of disagreement:

In fact, judges often disagree . . . about . . . whether the rule or principle one judge cites should be acknowledged to be a rule or principle at all. In some cases both the majority and the dissenting opinions recognize the same earlier cases as relevant, but disagree about what rule or principle these precedents should be understood to have established. In adjudication, unlike chess, the argument *for* a particular rule may be more important than the argument *from* that rule to the particular case; and while the chess referee who decides a case by appeal to a rule no one has ever heard of before is likely to be dismissed or certified, the judge who does so is likely to be celebrated in law school lectures. (Dworkin 1977a, p. 112)

It is a limitation of the present model that it does not even try to accommodate disagreement over the formulation of a new rule. The possibility that no existing rule is satisfactory, and that a new rule should be formulated on the fly, is not provided for. In a well-explored field like contracts, this limitation seems to be reasonable. The program may never become celebrated for its creativity, but neither do most judges.

2.3.4 Change in the Rules

Another ground on which the Restatement has been criticized is that its representation of the law makes no allowance for change in the rules. Dworkin's example, of the judge who is celebrated for introducing a new rule, is the extreme case. The announcement of an entirely new rule, perhaps with direct overruling of earlier decisions, is exceptional. More often the change is gradual, as apparently relevant precedents are distinguished away or are extended to cover new situations.

One interpretation that can be placed on Restatement-like rules is that they attempt to give an accurate statement of the law at a particular moment in time. This is unsatisfactory, however; the problems with deciding whether a rule is a rule of law are deeper than a missing time parameter. A better historical explanation seems to be that in 1923, when the restatement project began, not everyone was aware that a problem even existed. What is now called conceptualism was then the general outlook, and the possibility of change over time was simply not faced up to (see Hart and Sacks 1958, pp. 764–766; Gilmore 1974, pp. 67–69).

Two exceptional people, aware that they were stating only the rules of the day and that future revisions would be necessary, were Corbin (1914, p. 243; 1928, p. 604) and Benjamin Cardozo, then a member of the New York Court of Appeals and vice-president of the American Law Institute. Cardozo said, "Restatement will clear the ground of débris. It will enable us to reckon our gains and losses, strike a balance, and start afresh. This is an important, an almost inestimably important, service. But hereafter, as before, the changing combinations of events will beat upon the walls of ancient categories" (1924, p. 19).

To begin to model the tension between recognized categories and new combinations of events, an AI knowledge base needs to include cases as well as rules. One might look ultimately toward a program that automatically revises the rules to fit the cases. But the notion of fitting rules to cases is not well defined here. Even if it were, automatic rule revision seems not to be a good description of how humans deal with the interaction of old rules and new cases. Revising the rules in the contracts Restatement took almost twenty years.

A little less ambitiously, an AI program would be able to be told about new sources—newly decided cases, for instance, or old cases not included in the initial knowledge base—and to fit these cases into its existing rule structure, perhaps forcibly. The decisions, used as annotations to the rules, could begin to change the rules' status and their meaning. The rules, with previous annotations, would guide the interpretation of new decisions. Working this idea out would indeed let new cases put pressure on old categories. Some suggestions about how it might be done are given in chapter 3.

The idea suggested looks not to continually revised rules but to stable rules with changing meaning. This is roughly Levi's characterization of law as a system of rules that change as the rules are applied (1949, pp. 3–4). The degree of change it can allow for before the old rules break down entirely is limited, but for contract law it may be enough. The first Restatement did last some thirty years.

Levi's (1949) characterization is worth examining more closely. He describes change in the law as a cyclical process: legal concepts are created, they are used for a while, they break down. Throughout there is reasoning by example from the cases, but in the middle period, while the concepts are relatively fixed, the reasoning may seem to be mostly deductive. It seems fair to assume that the law of offer and acceptance is in Levi's middle stage. Levi's description is richly suggestive of elements that legal reasoning programs will need to take into account:

It may be objected that this analysis of legal reasoning places too much emphasis on the comparison of cases and too little on the legal concepts which are created. It is true that similarity is seen in terms of a word, and inability to find a ready word to express similarity or difference may prevent change in the law. The words which have been found in the past are much spoken of, have acquired a dignity of their own, and to a considerable measure control results. As Judge Cardozo suggested in speaking of metaphors, the word starts out to free thought and ends by enslaving it. The movement of concepts into and out of the law makes the point. If the society has begun to see certain significant similarities or differences, the comparison emerges with a word. When the word is finally accepted, it becomes a legal concept. Its meaning continues to change. But the comparison is not only between the instances which have been included under it and the actual case at hand, but also in terms of hypothetical instances which the word by itself suggests. *Thus the connotation of the word for a time has a limiting influence— so much so that the reasoning may even appear to be simply deductive.*

But it is not simply deductive. In the long run a circular motion can be seen. The first stage is the creation of the legal concept which is built up as cases are compared. The period is one in which the court fumbles for a phrase. Several phrases may be tried out; the misuse or misunderstanding of words itself may have an effect. The concept sounds like another, and the jump to the second is made. *The second stage is the period when the concept is more or less fixed, although reasoning by example continues to classify items inside and out of the concept.* The third stage is the breakdown of the concept, as reasoning by example has moved so far ahead as to make it clear that the suggestive influence of the word is no longer desired. (Levi 1949, pp. 8–9; emphasis added; footnote omitted)

2.3.5 The Purposes of Rules

The first Restatement was criticized for not stating reasons for the rules. In rule-based AI programs, reasons are usually omitted too. To Lon Fuller, an opponent of legal positivism, this would be a disastrous omission from a program for legal reasoning.

Positivism emphasizes the pedigrees of legal rules; for case law this means that the support for a rule is to be sought in its relation to the precedents. To Fuller the more important support came from the ends that the rules were intended to serve. Law was not just a set of rules but an activity, namely "the enterprise of subjecting human conduct to the governance of rules" (Fuller 1969, p. 106). Adequate description of the rules could not leave out purpose: "[Y]ou cannot describe what a judge is doing without taking into account what he is trying to do" (Fuller 1946, p. 392). But when we take purposes into account, we are—contrary to positivism—letting the question, Is this a law? overlap with the question, Is this a good law? "In the field of purposive human activity . . . value and being are not two different things, but two aspects of an integral reality" (Fuller 1940, p. 11).

What kinds of purposes, then, do the rules of contract law serve? As the overall goal, Fuller put forth and immediately rejected the simple statement, "Men should perform their agreements." A properly qualified version, he suggested, would turn out more as follows:

If a society wishes to achieve the prosperity and efficiency that comes from a division of functions or labor, and *if* no other means for achieving that division (such as a caste system) is available, then at least *some* agreements will have to be enforced by the law, *provided* it is demonstrated that unorganized moral pressures tending toward contract observance require the reinforcement of the law in order to make them effective. (Fuller 1946, p. 385)

Even if AI knew how to represent such a statement of purpose, its role in reasoning about particular cases would be unclear.

Reasons for individual rules, of course, might be stated more narrowly without trying to relate them to one general goal. Even here legal writing has provided no useful classification of the kinds of reasons that one might wish to state and no ready account of how reasons are to be attributed to case law rules at all. In fact, such an account could not be self-contained; it would involve both the problem of how precedents should be interpreted and used and the problem of justifying decisions that create new rules or modify old ones. The strategy followed in this study, therefore, is to try to do without explicit representations of the purposes of rules. We may still learn something from seeing where the program breaks down for want of knowledge about what the rules might be for.

3 Design II: When the Rules Run Out

Chapter 2 led to several conclusions about the design of a knowledge base for legal reasoning. First, the knowledge base may properly be organized in terms of legal rules, even in a field where the law develops mainly through decisions in individual cases rather than through the enactment of rules as statutes. There were some qualifications on this conclusion. It assumes that the particular legal area to be modeled—here, offer and acceptance in contracts—is relatively well developed and stable. A rule-based model would be less appropriate for tracing the development of a new legal concept through the discontinuities of a historical series of decisions. In addition, a rule-based model of case law must be understood, like any academic legal writing, as a secondary source. The official sources are the decisions. There has never been agreement on what it would mean for rulelike generalizations from decisions to be both accurate and appropriate. Thus, the basis for even uncontroversial rules remains undefined in legal theory.

Second, the rules in the knowledge base need not be entirely consistent. Even in legal areas that lend themselves to rule-based statement, there may be some points at which lawyers need to be aware of several incompatible rules, none so thoroughly established as to eliminate the others as candidates for adoption. Representing such rules does require that the candidate rules have been formulated in advance and identified as competitors.

Third, it was suggested that some degree of change in the rules could be reflected, without rewriting the rules themselves, by using cases as annotations to the rules in the knowledge base. How this would work remains to be explored.

Finally, there was a decision, for the time being, not to try to represent the purposes of rules. Stating reasons for the rules is at least as problematical as stating case law rules themselves.

This chapter now takes up the problem of applying a rule to the stated facts of a case. How far is it possible or appropriate to model the application of rules as straightforward deduction? Is there a dividing line between conclusions that can be reached deductively, without room for expert disagreement, and conclusions that depend on judicial discretion? If so, conclusions in the first class can safely be drawn by a program. Conclusions in the second class would be those that, in Llewellyn's language, require the judge to select the just conclusion, or the wise conclusion, from a set of technically defensible possibilities. For conclusions in the second class, a program can produce at most some arguments relevant to the choice. Programs will not be in a position to make the choice until we are satisfied that we have analyzed fully and encoded correctly the concepts of wisdom and justice. That time will surely never come.

3.1 The Problem of Applying a Rule

Consider the first fact asserted in the sample problem in section 1.2.1: "On July 1 Buyer sent the following telegram to Seller: 'Have customers for salt and need carload immediately. Will you supply carload at $2.40 per cwt?'" Compare the Restatement definition of an offer: "An offer is the manifestation of willingness to enter into a bargain, so made as to justify another person in understanding that his assent to that bargain is invited and will conclude it" (Restatement of Contracts, Second, sec. 24). The problem, clearly, is how the language of rules connects with the language in which facts are stated.

As a beginning we might try to sort out some of the kinds of words and phrases that occur in the rules. The kinds mentioned are intended only to suggest the variations. The classification is neither clear-cut nor exhaustive.

3.1.1 Defined Predicates

Some words may be taken as strictly technical, their meanings being stipulated by further rules. In contract law, *offer*, *acceptance*, and *consideration* are among the words of this kind. In an AI knowledge base, the rules stipulating their meanings would usually be written in an if-then form, with a left-hand side that contains a list of *preconditions* or *antecedents*, and a right-hand side, or *consequent*, that specifies some conclusions to be drawn if all the preconditions are true. A typical consequent would be that an offer exists and that its important roles, such as the offeror, the offeree, and the terms, are filled by specified items.

Legal cases do exist in which even stipulative definitions are unreliable. In tax law, McCarty discusses several cases in which the Supreme Court added new requirements to a statutory definition of tax-free corporate reorganizations (1977, pp. 846–849). In contracts, Corbin discusses a case in which the United States government should have been held to be a person, notwithstanding a statutory definition that stated exactly the contrary (Corbin 1950, vol. 3, sec. 543D, supp. 1971). It was only with the assumptions summarized at the beginning of this chapter that we were able to take case law-based definitions to be reliable. On those assumptions, the serious problems with applying rules begin where the rules run out—that is, where an antecedent uses a predicate not defined by further rules. What kinds of predicates are used only in the antecedents of rules?

3.1.2 Variable Standards

H. L. A. Hart singles out one special class of legal predicates, which he calls *variable standards* (1961, pp. 128–130). These include phrases like *reasonably certain* (of the terms of a possible offer), a *reasonable time* (as the time limit for accepting some offers), and, from tort law, *due care*. The presence of a word like *reasonable, due,* or *fair* suffices to identify a variable standard. The choice of words is an acknowledgment that there is usually room for discretionary judgment in deciding whether the standard has been met. Accordingly, an AI program should usually consider the satisfaction of a variable standard to raise a significant issue. The exceptions, in which a program could be competent to resolve the issue, would be the extreme cases. On an issue where reasonableness is normally a question for the jury, the extremes would correspond to cases where the judge may properly take the question away from the jury, on the basis that a reasonable jury could decide it only one way.

3.1.3 Other Special Phrases

At the other extreme from wholly technical terms and variable standards, legal rules also use as predicates English words so ordinary that, apparently, any native speaker could say with some confidence whether they apply. Some examples, to be discussed below, are *vehicle*, *sleep*, and *cattle*. Between the extremes, there are phrases whose words are ordinary but would not often be combined outside a legal context into just these phrases. Examples discussed in the literature include *inherently dangerous* (Levi 1949) and *manufactured product* (M. Moore 1981). In contract law, phrases like *manifestation of willingness to enter into a bargain* also fit the description, with the added complication of involving expressed intentional states.[1] Some individual words, like *manifestation* and *willingness*, also seem to fit into this group.

These expressions are highly abstract. If taken as ordinary language, the bounds of their applicability are very unclear. But as H. L. A. Hart points out, such expressions cannot be adequately handled by treating them only as ordinary language that needs to be made more precise. Hart states the difficulty in terms of the open texture of language. The last part of the following quotation could have been a warning to AI programmers:

Whichever device, precedent or legislation, is chosen for the communication of standards of behaviour, these, however smoothly they work over the great mass of ordinary cases, will, at some point where their application is in question, prove indeterminate; they will have what has been termed an *open texture*. So far we have presented this, in the case of legislation, as a general feature of human language; uncertainty at the borderline is the price to be paid for the use of general classifying terms in any form of communication concerning matters of fact. Natural languages like English are when so used irreducibly open textured. It is, however, important to appreciate why, apart from this dependence on language as it actually is, with its characteristics of open texture, we should not cherish, even as an ideal, the conception of a rule so detailed that the question whether it applied or not to a particular case was always settled in advance, and never involved, at the point of actual application, a fresh choice between open alternatives. . . . *If the world in which we live were characterized only by a finite number of features, and these together with all the modes in which they could combine were known to us, then provision could be made in advance for every possibility. We could make rules, the application of which to particular cases never called for a further choice. Everything could be known, and for everything, since it could be known, something could be done and specified in advance by rule. This would be a world fit for "mechanical" jurisprudence.* (Hart 1961, pp. 124–125; emphasis added)

The alternative to an exhaustive specification of features, as legal writers see it, involves (at least in part) reasoning from the precedents. Levi, who takes legal reasoning to be primarily reasoning by example, remarked that "the legal process does not work with the rule but on a much lower level" (1949, p. 9). Corbin made a similar comment: "A 'rule of law' has no content divorced from its applications; it is by a series of more or less analogous 'applications' (decisions) that it is stated and revised and restated; and every application to new facts adds to (or subtracts from) its content and, soon or late, compels a new 'Restatement' and a new 'Revision.' This is the evolutionary process by which the growth of law occurs" (Corbin 1961, p. 199). These characterizations are consistent with the idea, commonplace among lawyers, that general terms without examples are largely empty of meaning and that their meaning changes as the examples change. On this view, *inherently dangerous, manufactured product,* and the like come close to being legal idioms. The meaning—given by example, not by definition—may depend on more than the meanings of the component words.

Reasoning from the particular examples in past cases, though, is unlikely to give a definite answer to the question whether a predicate is satisfied in a new case. It seems to follow that undefined legalistic phrases, like variable standards, must almost always be treated as raising significant questions. This means that, whatever a given AI rule base fixes as the space of possible analyses of cases, we have so far found little prospect for generating less than the whole space when any particular case is examined.

3.1.4 Ordinary Words

Remaining to be considered are those legal predicates that look like ordinary, readily understood English words. They are, of course, also subject to the difficulties of open texture. In legal discussions that look for a dividing line between hard cases and routine, clear cases, these ordinary-language predicates are the favorite examples. They are discussed in the next section in connection with the hard case-clear case distinction. A clear case is taken to be one that raises no hard questions—that is, no issues on which experts could genuinely disagree and, therefore, no issues requiring branch points in the program's output graph.

3.2 The Problem of Hard and Easy Questions

3.2.1 Results from Legal Theory

Although hard cases are the ones that get critical attention, most legal writers have assumed that some cases involve only easy questions (Cardozo 1921, p. 164; Cardozo 1924, p. 60; Hart 1958, pp. 606–615; Hart 1961, pp. 121–132; Dworkin 1977b, p. 1248). Recent work, however, has questioned this long-standing assumption (M. Moore 1981), and even Hart agrees that "it is a matter of some difficulty to give any exhaustive account of what makes a 'clear case' clear" (1967, p. 271).

The best-known discussion of the clear case is Hart's (1958). His terminology, distinguishing between the core meaning of a general term and its penumbra of uncertainty, had previously been used by Dickinson (1931) and Williams (1945):

A legal rule forbids you to take a vehicle into the public park. Plainly this forbids an automobile, but what about bicycles, roller skates, toy automobiles? What about airplanes? Are these, as we say, to be called "vehicles" for the purpose of the rule or not? If we are to communicate with each other at all, and if, as in the most elementary form of law, we are to express our intentions that a certain type of behavior be regulated by rules, then the general words we use—like "vehicle" in the case I consider—must have some standard instance in which no doubts are felt about its application. There must be a core of settled meaning, but there will be, as well, a penumbra of debatable cases in which words are neither obviously applicable nor obviously ruled out. These cases will each have some features in common with the standard case; they will lack others or be accompanied by features not present in the standard case. . . .
. . . .
. . . [T]he hard core of settled meaning is law in some centrally important sense and . . . even if there are borderlines, there must first be lines. (Hart 1958, pp. 607, 614)

Moore, having examined the core-penumbra distinction in the light of current semantic theory, interprets the core, for natural-kind words at least, as consistent with Putnam's (1970, 1975) theory of meaning:

Included in the core of any natural kind predicate are both descriptions (Putnam's "core facts" or stereotypes) and weak paradigms. The descriptions are usually fairly good indicators that the predicate is being accurately applied; the paradigms are usually fairly good examples of the type of thing the predicate describes. The core, however, is never a secure bastion within which a formalist can say, "anything with these properties is an F," or "if anything is an F, this is." On no theory of meaning is Hart's core that kind of secure bastion. . . . (M. Moore 1981, p. 291)

The question then becomes: If the descriptions and examples are only "usually fairly good," when is it permissible for a program to jump to the conclusion that on some particular issue they are good enough?

The lawyer's natural inclination is to answer "never." Thus Moore, having shown that the connection between words in rules and words in fact statements is not analytic, concludes, "[T]here are no easy applications of rules to facts, and hence, no easy cases" (1981, p. 292).

The force of this conclusion may become clearer with an example. Hart had said that general words used in rules must have some "core of settled meaning," some "standard instance," that was law. Fuller (1958), replying to Hart, puts the following case:

Let us suppose that in leafing through the statutes, we come upon the following enactment: "It shall be a misdemeanor, punishable by a fine of five dollars, to sleep in any railway station." We have no trouble in perceiving the general nature of the target toward which this statute is aimed. Indeed, we are likely at once to call to mind the picture of a disheveled tramp, spread out in an ungainly fashion on one of the benches of the station, keeping weary passengers on their feet and filling their ears with raucous and alcoholic snores. This vision may fairly be said to represent the "obvious instance" contemplated by the statute, though certainly it is far from being the "standard instance" of the physiological state called "sleep."

. . . Suppose I am a judge, and that two men are brought before me for violating this statute. The first is a passenger who was waiting at 3 A.M. for a delayed train. When he was arrested he was sitting upright in an orderly fashion, but was heard by the arresting officer to be gently snoring. The second is a man who had brought a blanket and pillow to the station and had obviously settled himself down for the night. He was arrested, however, before he had a chance to go to sleep. (Fuller 1958, p. 664)

The assumption is that the first man should not be fined and the second should. Yet the case will appear simpler to a program than the "vehicle" example, for here there is likely to be a direct match or mismatch between "sleep" in the rule and "sleep" or "not sleep" in the input. If a program relies on this simple match, it will fail to recognize the presence of a hard question, and it will omit an arguably just decision from the set of possible decisions that it generates.

Various devices could be used to get the desired nonobvious result. Fuller suggested that *sleep,* as used in the statute, should be taken to mean something like "to spread oneself out on a bench or floor to spend the night, or as if to spend the night" (1958, p. 664). Harris (1979, p. 5), dealing with an example that would be similar to the present one if the statute were worded "No person shall sleep . . . ," proposes that *no* is not really a universal quantifier or, alternatively, that *person* means something like "person who is not a passenger." Even more bizarre constructions of language can be found. Moore (1981, p. 191) mentions a case in which *Indians* was held to include Chinese;[2] and Simpson (1964, pp. 547–548), that *cattle* has been held to include geese. The last example comes from a common law context, not a statutory one: the English action of cattle trespass came to cover many kinds of domestic animals (but not dogs and cats), which were all called "cattle" for the purpose of that action (see generally Williams 1939). (For a survey placing such examples in a broader legal background, see Fuller 1967.)

For an issue to be easy, one would like it to be an issue on which, for some reason, constructions like those above are unacceptable (or, possibly, so well established that within the law their oddity is no longer noticed). In addition, determining that an issue is easy should itself be an easy task; otherwise we will be only relocating issues rather than dismissing them.

But legal theory provides no account of easy issues that meets both requirements. Moore, for example, argues with respect to statutory rules that a literal reading may always "produce results that are contrary to the statute's purpose, are unfair or unjust in some more general way, or are simply contrary to common sense" (1981, p. 278). Therefore every application of a predicate involves an ethical question as well as a question of meaning. To resolve the ethical question, it is insisted by Moore, Fuller, and others that one must consult the purpose of the rule. The conclusion this suggests is that an issue is easy only if the purpose of the rule and the core meaning of its language both give the same answer. On this view, determining that a question is easy becomes a very difficult task. Moore, dealing with statutory purpose, concludes that the judge must construct the purpose of the rule and that its construction requires a "theory of the nature of an ideally good and just society" (1981, p. 293).

3.2.2 The Need for Heuristics

Moore's argument led to the conclusion that no one is justified in dismissing any questions as having answers too obvious for argument. If Moore is right, an AI program should treat every question of the satisfaction of an undefined legal predicate as a hard question. There are no legal issues that it can reliably resolve. The illustrations that led to this conclusion involved ordinary-language predicates, but the arguments apply equally to distinctively legal words and phrases.

Still, humans treat questions as easy all the time. This is illustrated even in the supposed counterexamples discussed earlier. Consider again the rules prohibiting vehicles in the park and sleeping in the railway station. The discussion proceeded as if the cases considered involved only one question: the application of *sleeping* or *vehicle* to the situation. It was taken for granted that we understood, for purposes of the case at hand, that the place was a park or a railway station and that the event occurred in the place. One can readily imagine other cases where these were the predicates raising significant issues. Suppose the defendant was admittedly sleeping by the wall of an admitted railway station, but it was an outside wall so that he was on the station platform rather than inside the building. Would this count as being in the station?

Further, suppose we are given the scenario from the viewpoint of the police, who must decide whom to arrest, rather than from the viewpoint of the judge, who is presented with already identified defendants. If the meaning of *sleeping* is entirely open, how do the police know enough to arrest only the two people described and not others in the station who were walking around, drinking coffee, and conversing?

If a program must treat every question as a hard one, then every antecedent containing an undefined predicate will raise at least one hard question in every case. If the antecedent contains variables not yet bound, it will raise as many hard questions as there are candidate bindings, and apparently there will be as many candidate bindings as there are individual constants and existential variables occurring in the problem statement.

The situation, then, is this: If we leave too little room for hard questions, we are in danger of eliminating analyses that humans find worth considering seriously. If we leave too much room, we will generate a very large number of analyses that humans would find preposterous.

Obviously the situation calls for heuristics, not certain knowledge. Since they are only heuristics, it is necessary to make a further qualification on how the program's output is to be understood. As a mere taker of exam questions, its task is unchanged: if we can find good heuristics for minimizing the number of issues it misses and the number of nonissues it finds, it may still pass the test. But any more serious application, such as a consultation system, will require a further allocation of responsibility between the program and the user. According to the initial allocation, the program was to find the technically defensible analyses and the human to decide among them. One qualification, already made, was that the program would miss good analyses requiring new rule formulations. The further qualification is that the program may sometimes bypass the analysis leading to the fair decision by treating a question of predicate application as easy. Although a human user should always consider second-guessing the program, the program might still be useful if it sometimes suggests good issues that the human would have missed.

3.3 Heuristics for Resolving Easy Questions

So far, we have seen that there is no ready-made dividing line between hard and easy questions that can itself be easily applied. If a heuristic distinction is to be attempted, what should the heuristics be able to do?

1. For variable standards (section 3.1.2), it should be possible to recognize extreme cases when they occur. If the rule calls for something to be done within a time that is reasonable under the circumstances, and the problem states that the relevant action was done immediately, a program should be able to conclude that "immediately" was soon enough.

2. For legal predicates too far removed from everyday usage to have much intuitive meaning (section 3.1.3), there should be knowledge about the kinds of situations these predicates have standardly been used to cover. Suppose A writes to B, "I hereby offer to sell you my car for $1,000." One does not need a full analysis of *manifestation*, *willingness*, and the like to conclude that this is a manifestation of

willingness to enter into a bargain. If B then replies, "I don't want to buy it" or "I'll pay you $850," it again should not take very complex reasoning to conclude that this is not a manifestation of assent to the terms of an offer.

3. For a predicate whose satisfaction or nonsatisfaction seems to be clear—either because, as in point 1, the predicate is a variable standard and the situation presents an extreme case; or because, as in point 2, the predicate has standardly been used to include or exclude situations of the kind presented; or simply because the predicate has a known ordinary usage (section 3.1.4) from which the answer follows—there should be a way of defeating the apparently clear conclusion when the occasion requires it. Usually the program should take the obvious for granted: that someone walking around in a railway station is not sleeping; that someone sleeping in a park is not sleeping in a railway station. The problem is how it can do so and still recognize that cases like Fuller's—the sleeping passenger and the vagrant trying to sleep—raise hard questions.

To begin to meet all three of these requirements, a single mechanism, based on using examples, is proposed. Since it is a single mechanism, there is no need to distinguish sharply among the various kinds of legal predicates. The general idea is, first, to allow every undefined predicate in a legal rule the potential for raising a hard question and, second, to provide means for concluding fairly quickly, in any particular case, that most questions of predicate application are easy. Questions found easy are resolved immediately, and the remainder—the hard questions—are left for further consideration.

3.3.1 Ordinary Language and Legal Language

Above it seemed unnecessary to make sharp distinctions among the types of undefined legal predicates. It is important, though, to distinguish between legal predicates and ordinary-language predicates. Ordinary-language predicates provide the vocabulary for stating the facts of a case—taking "facts" here as specifying roughly the level of concreteness at which witnesses must ordinarily testify. In this sense, "Joe said he wanted to buy Bill's car" could be a fact, but "Joe manifested willingness to enter a bargain" is not. The truth value of the second sentence is immaterial. It states not a fact but a legal conclusion.

Legal predicates are taken to include all the predicates that occur in legal rules.[3] Thus there is no point at which a legal predication follows automatically from assertions of fact. This much leaves room for both believed testimony that the defendant was observed to be sleeping in the railway station (in the ordinary-language sense) and for a conclusion that the defendant was not sleeping (in the relevant legal sense). But it also leaves open how legal conclusions ever connect with assertions of fact.

As the first part of an answer to that question, observe that the ordinary and technical uses of *sleeping* are not entirely distinct. In choosing words in which to formulate a legal rule, one draws on their ordinary meanings. When cases arise after the rule has been formulated, ordinary usage may suggest an answer as to whether the rule applies. Other considerations may suggest a different answer. If these prevail, the technical usage then begins to diverge from ordinary usage. There are not a pair of word senses, or of homonyms, from the beginning.

A first heuristic for deciding whether a question is easy, therefore, begins by assuming tentatively that the legal predicate being tested is used with its ordinary meaning. Whatever knowledge of ordinary usage is available can now be used to try to show tentatively whether the predicate is satisfied. The knowledge need not be very sophisticated to permit tentative conclusions like the following:

Fact	Instantiated antecedent of rule	Conclusion
(sleep A)	(sleep A)	true
(truck A)	(vehicle A)	true
(goose A)	(cow A)	false
(agent Act1 A)	(agent Act1 B)	false
(driving-speed Act1 80)	(and (driving-speed Act1 80) (> 80 55))	true

All that have been used here are a simple generalization hierarchy (a truck is a vehicle), with provision for disjoint subsets (geese are not cattle); a rule that an act has only one agent, together with knowledge that different constants denote different individuals (*A* is not *B*); and procedural knowledge for testing the predicate ">" ("greater than").

The rules actually used in the program will be discussed at greater length in chapter 5. They are meant to reflect general nonlegal knowledge for reasoning in a commonsense way about the world. What they provide, of course, falls infinitely short of general human common sense. To refer to the rules in a way that suggests their purpose but keeps them distinct from general human commonsense knowledge, I will call them *CSK rules.*

The first heuristic then states: If an answer can be derived using such CSK rules and if no objections to using this answer can be found, assume that the question of predicate satisfaction is easy and that its answer is the answer just derived.

3.3.2 Some Roles for Cases

The problem is how to determine that a legal predicate, not defined by further rules, is clearly satisfied (or clearly not satisfied) by the facts of a case being analyzed. The first heuristic called for trying to derive a tentative conclusion, on the assumption that the legal predicate was used with its ordinary or commonsense meaning. This leaves some questions open:

1. What if no answer can be derived from the CSK rules?

2. Assuming that an answer can be derived, from CSK rules or some other knowledge source, what can be recognized as an objection to using this answer? How is an objection to be handled?

The answer to both involves using precedents. The precedents are thought of as giving the legal predicate a partial extensional definition.

Suggesting a Tentative Answer

The reasoning suggested by the table above implies a very shallow level of knowledge in the CSK rules. It is clearly insufficient to derive even tentative answers to questions like: Is this a manifestation? Is it a manifestation of willingness to do something? Is it a manifestation of willingness to enter a bargain? This is a defect, because abstract words also have ordinary meaning, and, as Levi observed, their connotations may suggest an answer.

In some AI work, the tendency at this point would be to try to give a full analysis of the ordinary meaning of the troublesome predicates. This is a very difficult task. According to the dictionary, to *manifest* is to show plainly; compare Allen (1981) for an analysis of the contrasting word *hide*. But such work also seems to look toward stating necessary and sufficient conditions for finding an instance of the concept. This leaves out the fact that in borderline situations, which legal problems often exemplify, human knowledge of ordinary usage often does not yield a single answer anyway. For the purpose of separating easy legal questions from hard ones, it is the central situations that most need to be represented. In terms of the core-penumbra metaphor, one should be able to represent core situations without foreclosing argument about penumbral ones. The idea to be exploited here is that the cases contain a great deal of information about what the central situations are. That is, the cases can be used to help fill in commonsense knowledge that is missing from the CSK rules.

The gist of the second heuristic, then, is the following: If no answer about the satisfaction of a legal predicate can be derived using the CSK rules, then look for cases showing that the facts of the case at hand present an instance of one of the central kinds of situations that the predicate has been used to cover in the past. Or, as an alternative that may sometimes be feasible, look for cases showing that the situation described in the case at hand is a situation from which application of the predicate has standardly been withheld.

Recognizing Objections to a Tentative Answer
Moore (1981) pointed out that a literal reading of a rule might be objectionable because it was unjust, unfair, contrary to the purpose of the rule, or contrary to (human) common sense. First, let the literal reading be equated with the program's reading using CSK rules. How could a program recognize any of the objections to this reading? As a beginning, there is a knowledge source that Moore's discussion left out.

The legal situation to which Fuller and Moore direct their attention involves rules that have been enacted by a legislature and that no previous cases have interpreted. The rules of contract law, however, are largely derived from precedents. They do not look only to the future; they are also a summarization and editing of the past. If there are past cases that are inconsistent with a literal reading of the program's legal rules, knowledge of these cases can be provided to the program. Although the program lacks concepts like fairness or purpose, the cases may provide an indirect representation. The cases reflect indirectly what others have believed to be the proper inter-pretation of the rules, perhaps because of what they believed to be required by fairness, common sense, or the purposes of the rules. Thus, matching the case at hand to a precedent that has already rejected the literal meaning of the rule provides a first, limited possibility for recognizing that an answer is objectionable.

Now consider a slightly broader version of the literal reading of a rule. In this version the CSK rules are supplemented by representations of core situations based on the cases, and a tentative answer about whether a legal predicate is satisfied has been derived using the second heuristic. There still may be other cases casting doubt on this answer. Perhaps the case at hand has special features that courts have already recognized as calling for exceptional treatment. Perhaps the precedents are such that lawyers would find them inconsistent. Again, making use of the precedents can go part of the way toward enabling a program to recognize, when appropriate, that a tentative answer is objectionable.

The third heuristic, then, will work similarly to the second: Whatever tentative answer has been derived, look for cases calling for the opposite answer. What the program should do on finding such a case is discussed in section 3.4.2.

3.4 Representing and Using Cases

3.4.1 A General Representation

The next problem is how past cases should be represented. This section considers a general-purpose representation, and the next discusses how it can be streamlined for the purpose of recognizing and resolving easy questions.

The Facts of Cases
The most important part of a representation for cases is the representation of the facts and the outcome. For contract law, Corbin provides the model:

Corbin counseled not only that we should study all the cases but that we should study them not so much for their doctrinal statements as for what he liked to call their "operative facts." Furthermore, Corbin practiced what he preached, not only in his teaching but in his writings which culminated in his great treatise on contracts. . . . In Corbin we find painstaking factual analyses of all the cases, even those of minor importance which are relegated to the footnotes. Indeed the practice of paying an obsessive regard to the facts of cases, while disregarding their doctrinal content, became after World War I, and has since remained, a characteristic of most American legal scholarship. (Gilmore 1977, pp. 79–80)

The American emphasis on facts may be somewhat different from the English practice:

[I]n England the precise facts of prior cases are not looked to with particularity; what is important in the precedents—the cases which, being in the same general area, are in point—is the process of reasoning by which they were decided, the general principles which they illustrate.

Having been trained as an American lawyer, I find this approach to the use of precedent shocking. I know that a case stands on and for its own precise, particular facts. I tell my students with wearisome iteration: Never mention a case without stating its facts; never quote general language from an opinion, divorced from the factual context in which the language was delivered; take care of the facts and the law will take care of itself. (Gilmore 1961, p. 1042)

It is a matter of interpretation, of course, to say what the facts of a case are. There is a trade-off between literal accuracy (reproducing the court's description of the facts precisely) and providing structure (for instance, by omitting irrelevant details, inferring items not mentioned, and replacing particulars by some more general level of description). The first is the approach of full-text information retrieval systems; in pure form they force the user to guess what words judges would have used in their opinions (see generally Sprowl 1976; Bing and Harvold 1977).[4] The second approach, the traditional one, is always open to the objection of possible misinterpretation; an example is Gilmore's charge that Williston performed major surgery on the reported facts of contracts cases (Gilmore 1974, pp. 22–28).

The second approach nevertheless is the one taken here. Representations of cases thus become a personal construct, just as much as representations of rules.

The Reasoning in Cases

To make previous cases usable for recognizing and deciding easy questions, we need to say what it means for the application of a legal predicate to have been an issue in a previous case. The question here is not how to represent the facts of cases but how to represent the reasons for decision.

One of the first lessons of law study is that, to make sense of the cases, one cannot count very heavily on what the opinions say. That legal scholarship emphasizes facts, not doctrinal statements, is only part of the reason. Another is that the decisions—as represented, for example, in a casebook like Fuller and Eisenberg (1981)—span a long period of time, come from many different jurisdictions, and occasionally are included for the purpose of showing how wrong-headed courts can be. Even if the casebook were limited to decisions of a single court, as are casebooks in constitutional law, the coherence of their doctrinal statements would still be highly dependent on the judges' craftsmanship.

To shape these materials into a coherent picture, one must allow opinions to be freely reinterpreted. Then each opinion can be viewed as using a subset of precisely the rules that are stored in the knowledge base. And if an opinion uses these rules, it can be represented by the same sort of graph structure that the program generates in analyzing a new case. This time the graph can be marked to show how the decision actually went. If the opinion is clear, there will be only one marked path from the root to a terminal node, from the facts to the outcome. If the opinion is unclear, more than one path can be marked. Along a path, issues argued by the parties or discussed by the court will appear as branch points.

There will be other issues that one discovers in trying to analyze the cases in terms of the program's legal rules. Most of these will be issues that were not considered worth mentioning in the opinion; occasionally there will be a serious question that everyone overlooked. For both kinds the graph could record the answer given without a branch point.

This representation still does not say, however, which aspects of the facts were considered relevant to determining the satisfaction of which legal predicate. Often the opinion of the deciding judge is unclear; and in any event later judges, in following the decision or distinguishing it, will reinterpret relevance for themselves. This is one reason why descriptions of legal reasoning as analogical reasoning are persuasive. Here, for example, is Hart's description of the reasoning in cases where judges have discretion:

Faced with the question whether the rule prohibiting the use of vehicles in the park is applicable to some combination of circumstances in which it appears indeterminate, all that the person called upon to answer can do is to consider (as does one who makes use of a precedent) whether the present case resembles the plain case "sufficiently" in "relevant" respects. The discretion thus left to him by language may be very wide; so that if he applies the rule, the conclusion, even though it may not be arbitrary or irrational, is in effect a choice. He chooses to add to a line of cases a new case because of resemblances which can reasonably be defended as both legally relevant and sufficiently close. In the case of legal rules, the criteria of relevance and closeness of resemblance depend on many complex factors running through the legal system and on the aims or purpose which may be attributed to the rule. To characterize these would be to characterize whatever is specific or peculiar in legal reasoning. (Hart 1961, p. 124)

For the purpose of determining heuristically that some questions are easy, that the present case is a plain case, an additional tie needs to be made between legal predicates and the elements of past cases that satisfied them or did not. Making this tie is taken up next.

3.4.2 Abstract Examples for Resolving Easy Questions

Standard Examples

Sources of Standard Examples   One role for cases is to provide knowledge about the central kinds of situations to which a legal predicate has been applied. Typically, though, it is borderline situations that are litigated, not the central ones, and it is borderline cases on which most studies of legal reasoning concentrate. To reconcile any seeming inconsistency here, one need only recall that making out a case for recovery generally involves the application of numerous legal predicates. In any particular lawsuit, relatively few of these will be in serious issue. Standard examples, then, should arise from the cases with respect to points on which there was not disagreement.

In the general representation for cases already discussed, it was anticipated that applying the rules in the knowledge base to the facts of reported cases would yield many such points, which had to be decided to reach a conclusion in the case but were neither argued by the parties nor mentioned in the court's opinion. On such points, where everyone takes the answers for granted, the applicability of a predicate may seem more a matter of common sense than of any technical knowledge. If someone sends a letter, of course the sender has manifested something; if the letter says "I accept your offer to buy my car," of course it manifests willingness to enter an exchange. In an opinion describing such events without discussion, it will be difficult to find any further facts reported that bear directly on the satisfaction of these particular predicates. At least in situations like these, it is fair to say that the question was easy and to pick out a definite subset of the reported facts that made it so.

For any given predicate as used in a particular rule, one may expect to find many cases silently treating the satisfaction of that predicate as an easy question. Some of these cases will have similar subsets of facts relevant to the predicate. Even within the limits of a casebook— which should provide a reasonable amount of case knowledge for a program analyzing examination questions—there may be dozens of cases, litigated on other points, that treat letters, telegrams, and utterances as manifestations. For the purpose of disposing of easy questions quickly, therefore, a case-by-case representation is inappropriate; rather, the case knowledge needs to be abstracted.

The result of this abstraction is a set of fact patterns to be associated with a legal predicate. A pattern may be supported by several cases, and a case that has treated several issues as easy may contribute to several such patterns. In general, a new case in which every question of predicate satisfaction can be answered either by CSK rules or by matching one of these patterns will be a plain case. Plain cases, Hart suggested, are "only the familiar ones, constantly recurring in similar contexts, where there is general agreement in judgments as to the applicability of the classifying terms" (1961, p. 123). Of course, the general agreement may be that the classifying term is not applicable. There may therefore be patterns providing examples of the kinds of things that are not covered by the predicate as well as positive examples.

Patterns may be based on hypothetical cases as well as actual ones. Hypotheticals are a common form for the expression of legal knowledge; they are convenient because they can be designed to illustrate a single point and their fact situations are vastly simplified from the details of real cases. (For some English examples, see the two illustrations included in the Restatement section quoted in section 2.3.1.)

When a hypothetical example is stored in the knowledge base, the assumption is simply that the author has thought about the example and formed an opinion that it would clearly satisfy or clearly not satisfy the appropriate predicate. Thus one could add to the knowledge base, without knowing of any cases on the point, that a message sent by electronic mail would also count as a manifestation.

For variable standards, circumscribing the relevant facts is far more difficult than for predicates like *manifestation*. Suppose some case takes for granted that replying to an offer within two days is replying within a reasonable time. The assumption depends on much more than the length of the time interval. Some of the other considerations mentioned in the Restatement are "the nature of the proposed contract, the purposes of the parties, the course of dealing between them, and any relevant usages of trade" (Restatement of Contracts, Second, sec. 41, comment b). An attempt to state a definite rule requires an escape clause: "*Unless otherwise indicated by the language or the circumstances,* and subject to the rule stated in section 49 [concerning the effect of delay in communication of an offer], an offer sent by mail is seasonably accepted if an acceptance is mailed at any time before midnight on the day on which the offer is received" (ibid., sec. 41(3); emphasis added).

Trying to identify and weigh the aspects of a case relevant to reasonableness is not a task to be undertaken as part of the quick identification and resolution of easy questions. Therefore one should expect to have very few examples of plain cases satisfying (or failing to satisfy) variable standards. Section 3.2.2 suggested that an act said to have been done immediately would be a good example of an act done within a reasonable time. What makes this example appropriate is that *immediately* and *reasonable* share the same context dependence.

Standard Examples versus Rules   The patterns used are universally quantified formulas. For a pattern to justify the conclusion that the associated predicate is clearly satisfied or clearly not satisfied, the formula must be true in the case being analyzed—not just analogous to something that is true in the case. How, then, are these patterns, here called *examples,* any different from rules?

In fact there are several differences. First, there is a conceptual difference: the rules are understood as using only legal predicates, but the examples are expected to be in the representational counterpart of ordinary language. This is the distinction made in section 3.3.1. It is by way of commonsense examples that "legalese" gets its meaning. Second, and most important, the examples—the patterns—are not intended to exhaust the possibilities. They represent only salient possibilities, kinds of situations to which the applicability of some legal predicate has been treated as clear or intuitively seems clear. To try to make them do more would be, as Hart said (1961, p. 125), to try to reduce the world to a finite number of features all known in advance.

Operationally the nonexhaustiveness of examples makes a significant difference. Suppose P is a proposition using a predicate defined by legal rules, and Q a proposition using a predicate whose meaning is known only to the extent of the examples. If the rules all fail to establish P, then the negation of P may be concluded. This corresponds to the fact that a plaintiff who fails to prove the elements of a case simply loses; things that might be true but have not been shown do not help.

Now let Q be one element of plaintiff's case. Some facts relating to its predicate have been established (in practice, this means that bindings have been found for any variables occurring in Q). The facts may or may not be within the predicate's meaning. The meaning of a legal predicate is a question of law, not a matter for proof. If all the examples associated with the predicate (positive and negative) fail to match, the conclusion is that there is a hard question. A corresponding branch point goes into the output graph. On one branch, the negation of Q is asserted, and, assuming there are no rules by which to prove P without proving Q, the negation of P follows. On the other branch, Q is asserted, and the attempt to complete the proof of P can proceed.

A third difference between rules and examples is that it is anticipated that the examples may be inconsistent in ways not recognized in advance. Perhaps one case has treated it as obvious that a predicate is satisfied, while another has treated it in a similarly described situation as obviously not satisfied. Or perhaps the case being analyzed contains an unusual combination of features, some matching a positive example and some matching a negative one. Matching both positive and negative examples also produces a hard question.

A fourth point distinguishes the examples not from legal rules but from the CSK rules proposed in section 3.3.1. The latter are context independent: for simplicity (not accuracy) it is assumed that whatever an ordinary-language predicate means, it always means the same thing.[5] Legal predicates, however, are taken to have local meaning. The point is important as an aid to avoiding mechanical jurisprudence (or, more aptly for present purposes, conceptualism). The ideal of conceptualism, Hart observed, "is reached when a general term is given the same meaning not only in every application of a single rule, but whenever it appears in any rule in the legal system. No effort is then ever required or made to interpret the term in the light of the different issues at stake in its various recurrences" (1961, p. 127).

To avoid this result, each occurrence of a legal predicate in a rule is linked directly to the further legal rules or examples that expand it. Thus it can be taken into account, for example, that it is one question whether a bicycle is a vehicle within a rule prohibiting vehicles in the park, and a quite separate question whether it falls within a requirement that vehicles travel on the right-hand side of the road. To keep the meaning of *vehicle* local is to reflect the fact that different rules do have different purposes, though neither purpose is represented directly.

Using Examples   The program's method for deciding that a question is easy can now be sketched. There are two possibilities. One is the situation where not even a tentative answer to the question of predicate satisfaction can be derived using just the facts stated in the problem and the program's CSK rules. Here the approach is to try to match both positive and negative examples of the predicate. If no match can be found or if there are both positive and negative matches, then the question is treated as a hard question in the manner explained. Otherwise, the question is assumed to be easy, and the answer is recorded according to which kind of example matched.

The algorithm is more complicated than this statement suggests because of the possibility that the formula containing the predicate also contains unbound variables. Different matches may then generate different bindings, and a failure to match any examples will generate none. How this is handled is explained in chapter 6.

The second situation is the one where a tentative CSK answer has already been derived. Here the question is whether there are cases showing that this answer is inappropriate. Again assume for simplicity that the formula contains no unbound variables. Then one may begin by trying to match only positive examples or only negative examples, whichever would give the opposite of the tentative answer. If no match is found, the question is assumed to be easy, and the tentative answer holds.

If there is a match, then the further possibility that there are conflicting cases must be taken into account. Accordingly the next step is to look for examples that would support using the CSK answer. If a match is again found, then the cases point both ways and the question is hard.

Otherwise we are left with a CSK answer that says one thing and a technical answer that says the opposite. In the current program, the assumption is that technical meaning has diverged from ordinary meaning, that the technical meaning should prevail, and therefore that there is no hard question.

Abnormal Examples and Defeasibility

The standard examples discussed are only stereotypes. They presuppose a context in which the situation is otherwise "normal," in much the same way that birds can normally fly (Reiter 1978) and a boat can normally be used to cross a river (McCarthy 1980). But it is part of the concept of open texture that indefinitely many kinds of extra facts, by making the situation "abnormal," can defeat the stereotypical conclusion.

How is this defeasibility of legal conclusions related to the recognition of hard legal questions? Hart (1958) spoke of debatable cases as those that lack some features of the standard case or that are accompanied by features not present in the standard case. The absence of expected features is relatively easy to test for. It is recognizing the relevance of extra features—that the bird has a broken wing, that the boat has no oars—that creates the problem. Fuller (1958, p. 663) puts another case that complements these AI examples: The rule prohibits vehicles in the park. A group of people wants to bring a truck into the park. There is nothing wrong with the truck; it works perfectly. But the group is a patriotic organization, the truck is a relic from World War II, and the group wants to place it on a pedestal as a war memorial. Does the rule prohibit the action? It is not an easy question.

Finding a dividing line between clear cases and hard cases thus involves the general problem of nonmonotonic reasoning (*Artificial Intelligence* 13, nos. 1–2, 1980). In law, only a little writing has attempted to treat the problem in comparable terms (Hart 1949; Baker 1977).

The heuristics presented allow for defeasibility of conclusions to a limited extent. They depend on the existence of precedents to show that an apparently easy question is hard after all (or that, although easy, its answer is different from the obvious one). Precedents may be known that give words like *vehicle*, *sleep*, and *cattle* a surprising interpretation. Their facts might be encoded as positive and negative examples in the same way as for standard examples.

The way the heuristics use examples of nonstandard situations can perhaps be shown best with a familiar AI illustration. Suppose a legal rule calls for showing that something can fly, and that the CSK rules say that something can fly if and only if it is a bird. Then the known exceptions are written as examples, attached to the predicate *fly* in the legal rule. For instance, one might have, as negative examples, *(penguin x)*, *(ostrich x)*, and *(dead x)*. There might also be a positive example saying that all magical things can fly: *(magical x)*. The heuristics can then conclude that

1. Tweety, known only to be a bird, can fly.
2. Henry, a penguin, cannot.
3. Pegasus, a magical horse, can.

On the other hand, if the facts given say that Henry is a magical penguin or that Pegasus is dead, the conclusion is that their flying ability is a hard question.

It is true that these conclusions are reached at some cost. Before accepting conclusion 1, the program must check the negative examples to see that nothing changes the CSK conclusion. For conclusion 2, assuming there is a CSK rule saying that penguins are birds, it is necessary to check the negative examples and then, since one does match, to check the positive examples as well. Inefficiency, however, is not the main problem. In the legal domain, extensive testing seems quite reasonable. If one thinks of the examples as corresponding to decided cases, then it is relevant to observe that human legal research does take longer as the number of decisions on the topic increases.

A greater problem with the current heuristics is that they will sometimes fail to recognize stored examples as relevant. The critical point is the selection of facts to be included in the examples. If an example states the facts as specifically as the opinion does, then most examples will never match a new case, and the heuristics will find them irrelevant. Although partial matching or analogy is an obvious possibility, its use is inconsistent with the goal of resolving easy questions quickly.

The alternative is to generalize the opinion's statement of facts—for instance, by redescribing geese as domestic animals or by omitting the circumstance that it was 3 A.M. when the passenger was found sleeping in the railway station. Here, however, is a problem inherent in the system of precedent: one does not know, at least until the next case is decided, how far the last one can safely be generalized (Llewellyn 1930, pp. 48–49, 54–55, 66–68; Stone 1964, pp. 267–274).

In the development of a knowledge base for offer and acceptance cases in contracts, the surprise has been that the current heuristics are so far good enough. Part of the reason is the narrow scope of the present knowledge base. Another part is that the law has some other means for managing questions that might otherwise have to be treated in terms of defeasibility.

One is the use of variable standards in the law. Rather than setting up a tightly worded rule and letting its conclusion be defeated occasionally, one may use a word like *reasonable* and leave it to the trier of fact (jury or judge) to decide how much weight to give to the various considerations, for and against a finding of reasonableness, that are present in the particular case. In the program, treating most applications of variable standards as hard questions means that there is no tentative conclusion to defeat.

Another factor is the flexibility with which case law rules may be stated. Statutory rules, in contrast, are tied to language that a legislature has adopted and that only the legislature can amend. If circumstances defeat the literal application of the statute, its words may be forced to bear new meanings. But if circumstances defeat the literal application of a case law rule, one is free to rewrite the rule instead. An illustration comes from the cattle trespass example, in which *cattle* was held to include geese. The action for cattle trespass is nonstatutory, but it dates back to a time in English common law when fixed forms of words were far more important than they are now. Modern treatments of the action, in the United States at least, now state the rule more generally—for instance, in terms of "livestock" (Restatement of Torts, Second, sec. 504).

In contracts, the second Restatement was published in 1981. It is not surprising that no seriously outdated wordings have been encountered. There has been uncovered, however, one area in which the present formulation of a legal rule is unsatisfactory and where the appropriate reformulation is not yet clear. This area is discussed in section 7.3.2. Developing the knowledge base to deal with it in more depth will present a first occasion for the nonliteral reading of a rule.

As the knowledge base is extended in the future, two general issues about defeasibility are expected to arise. One is how to give a program enough general knowledge to enable it to go beyond the stored precedents, however they are stated. In the case of the truck that is to be a war memorial in the park, it should always require a closely matching precedent to conclude definitely that the truck is permitted. It should not require a precedent to be able to see, in the face of a seemingly obvious conclusion that the truck is a vehicle and therefore prohibited, that some unanticipated kind of fact is relevant (here, that the truck is to be part of a monument) and makes the conclusion nonobvious after all.

The second issue, a separate one, is what triggers the use of whatever knowledge the program does have. For contract law and many other legal areas, the issue is especially well focused with respect to defenses (Hart 1949). Some examples of defenses to contract actions are fraud or duress in obtaining the agreement and illegality of the actions agreed to. Roughly, a defense is an established category of facts that, if instantiated, will prevent formation or enforcement of a contract, but whose absence need not be shown as part of a plaintiff's case for recovery on the contract.

If the program's knowledge base were extended to cover all of contract law, should it check for every known defense in every case? Even within the topic of offer and acceptance, it is not clear that every known type of defect should always be tested for. For instance, the findings of offer and acceptance may be defeated if "all the parties to what would otherwise be a bargain manifest an intention that the transaction is not to be taken seriously" (Restatement of Contracts, Second, sec. 18, comment c, "Sham or jest"). In the current knowledge base, this last ground for defeat is simply omitted. It should be treated in a future version in conjunction with the general problem of reasoning about cases involving misunderstanding between the parties.

The appropriate eventual treatment of defenses and similar defects is likely to depend on how a legal reasoning program is to be used. If the objective were a psychological model of a lawyer analyzing a case or a student answering an examination question, then the trigger for considering particular defenses might well be based on a theory of reminding (Schank 1982). The theory would need to account not only for how significant issues come to be noticed but also for how they may be overlooked. An expert consultation system, on the other hand, is likely to be useful just to the extent it is better than humans at noticing significant issues. In such a system, used perhaps to help identify all the arguments that a lawyer (or his opponent) might make, a user option for exhaustive consideration of defenses could prove worthwhile. The problem would then be how efficiently the program could reject most or all of them as clearly inapplicable.

3.5 Approaches to Hard Questions

The previous section concerned a program's ability to distinguish hard questions from easy ones. It was proposed that a program ought to be able to resolve at least some questions on its own; others, the hard questions, would have to be left to human judgment. There was a proposal for using precedents to aid in the heuristic recognition of hard questions. Some shortcomings of the heuristics were discussed—primarily, the fact that no amount of knowledge of precedents will be a full substitute for the general knowledge needed to recognize, in an arbitrary fact situation, the relevance of new features or new combinations of features that may convert a seemingly easy question into a hard one. Finally the section considered some reasons why, despite these shortcomings, the present heuristics have worked adequately so far. Some of the reasons concerned the law's own resources for dealing with defeasibility. Others simply reflected the narrow coverage of the present knowledge base.

In this section, the assumption is that the program has succeeded in identifying some set of questions raised by a new case as hard questions. By hypothesis these are the questions requiring human judgment. Still, the program might do more. The final stage of the reasoning process, which remains for future development, would be to produce arguments on both sides of the hard questions. The arguments would be attached, as annotations, to branch points in the output graph. If the relative merits of the arguments could be evaluated, the result would be a set of recommendations as to how to prune the graph. With enough pruning recommendations to leave only one path through the graph (or several paths leading to equivalent results), the annotations would correspond to one possible decision in the case.

What kinds of arguments might be used? Both Hart and Levi, among many others, speak of comparing cases. For Levi, the appropriate comparisons depend on whether "the society has begun to see certain significant similarities or differences" (section 2.3.4 above). For Hart, comparing cases involves finding "resemblances which can reasonably be defended as both legally relevant and sufficiently close," where "the criteria of relevance and closeness of resemblance depend on many complex factors running through the legal system and on the aims or purpose which may be attributed to the rule" (section 3.4.1 above). Clearly, enabling a program to make useful comparisons will require much development beyond present AI techniques for reasoning by analogy. (For a brief review of AI work on analogy and related topics, see Mostow 1983.)

Of course there are other AI methods besides analogy for reasoning about questions to which no certain answer can be found. The next section considers why some of these methods are inappropriate to the present research. Then, to provide some perspective on all computational approaches to hard legal questions, the chapter concludes by summarizing the corresponding views of one well-known legal writer, Ronald Dworkin.

3.5.1 Some Inapplicable AI Approaches

Asking the User
Many expert systems, in reasoning about a problem, encounter subproblems whose answers they are unable to derive. The most straightforward technique is for the system to ask the user to supply the answer.

For a legal reasoning program, asking the user has only limited applicability. If the examination-taking situation were taken seriously, asking the user would correspond to a student's asking the teacher for help with the test. In a potentially useful application, such as a consultation system, there is a different objection.

The present research assumes that all relevant matters of fact have already been stated. The assumption is not typical for consultation systems generally, but it does apply to other legal situations besides taking examinations. A judge does not ask the parties to supply more facts, but decides the case on the evidence given. For someone studying a case already decided, the only available facts are those presented in the opinion.

The questions the program might ask, then, do not involve simple facts that a user can readily supply. To decide whether a particular predicate is satisfied is to draw a legal conclusion calling for informed judgment. It might be just this judgment that the user of a consultation system lacks. Furthermore, because many legal predicates look identical to ordinary-language predicates, a naive user might not realize that professional knowledge was called for at all.

When the program identifies a question as hard, it could ask whether the user wishes to assume a particular answer. It must still be prepared to cope with the user's declining to do so. There is no point making the user run the program again and again on the same problem in order to test the consequences of different assumptions, or in stopping the analysis short for want of an assumption. In the most general case, the user would refuse to assume conclusions on any hard questions at all.

The research here focuses on the general case. If the program can manage the multiplicity of analyses that may result from identifying all the hard questions before any are resolved, it will in fact be demonstrating one of the skills that lawyers need.

Probabilistic Reasoning

Another common AI approach, when the conclusion to be drawn from the data is uncertain, is to use probabilistic reasoning. Examples are provided by several medical diagnosis programs (see generally Szolovits and Pauker 1978). Standard probability theory, though, has been extremely difficult to apply to expert systems. The MYCIN program (Shortliffe 1976), for example, links data to conclusions with numerical qualifiers called *certainty factors*. Originally certainty factors were understood as an approximation to conditional probabilities (ibid., p. 160); now they are called a "somewhat groping attempt to cope with the limitations of probability theory" (Buchanan and Shortliffe 1984, p. 215). Even in such variations, however, the relationship between data and conclusions is generally empirical, and a large part of the task is to try to determine the "true state of the world" (Szolovits and Pauker 1978, p. 119).

For the hard legal questions examined in this study, the assumption is that we already know the "true state of the world." There is no hidden reality to be discovered or, remaining undiscovered, to be "covered for"; the question is how to characterize the reality that is known. Accordingly, probability theory is not just limited but inapplicable. A good statement of the point comes from John Wisdom:

In courts of law it sometimes happens that opposing counsel are agreed as to the facts and are not trying to settle a question of further fact, are not trying to settle whether the man who admittedly had quarrelled with the deceased did or did not murder him, but are concerned with whether Mr. A who admittedly handed his long-trusted clerk signed blank cheques did or did not exercise reasonable care, whether a ledger is or is not a document, whether a certain body was or was not a public authority.

In such cases we notice that the process of argument is not a *chain* of demonstrative reasoning. It is a presenting and representing of those features of the case which *severally cooperate* in favour of the conclusion, in favour of saying what the reasoner wishes said, in favour of calling the situation by the name by which he wishes to call it. The reasons are like the legs of a chair, not the links of a chain. . . . [T]he process of deciding the issue becomes a matter of weighing the cumulative effect of one group of severally inconclusive items against the cumulative effect of another group of severally inconclusive items, and thus lends itself to description in terms of conflicting "probabilities". This encourages the feeling that the issue is one of fact—that it is a matter of guessing from the premises at a further fact, at what is to come. But this is a muddle. . . . The logic of the dispute is not . . . a matter of collecting from several inconclusive items of information an expectation as to something further, as when a doctor from a patient's symptoms guesses at what is wrong, or a detective from many clues guesses the criminal. It has its own sort of logic and its own sort of end—the solution of the question at issue is a decision, a ruling by the judge. But it is not an arbitrary decision . . . ; and though the decision manifests itself in the application of a name it is no more merely the application of a name than is the pinning on of a medal merely the pinning on of a bit of metal. . . . Whether Mr. So-and-So of whose conduct we have so complete a record did or did not exercise reasonable care is not merely a matter of the application of a name or, if we choose to say it is, then we must remember that with this name a game is lost and won and a game with very heavy stakes. With the judges' choice of a name for the facts goes an attitude, and the declaration, the ruling, is an exclamation evincing that attitude. But *it is an exclamation which not only has a purpose but also has a logic*, a logic surprisingly like that of "futile", "deplorable", "graceful", "grand", "divine". (Wisdom 1945, pp. 193–195; footnote omitted)

Fuzzy Sets
The legal questions we are considering are hard not because of doubt about the state of the world but because of doubt about whether to apply the relevant legal words. This comment suggests the relevance of another body of work, fuzzy set theory (Zadeh 1965; Gaines 1976; Gaines and Kohout 1977). The theory is described as a "tool for reasoning with the *inherently imprecise concepts* of systems engineering," which is "based upon, and expected to model, *human linguistic reasoning* with such concepts" (Gaines and Kohout 1977, p. 2).

The basic idea is that whether an entity is a member of a set (or an instance of a concept) need no longer be a simple yes-no decision. Instead one may represent grades of membership, on a scale from 0 to 1. For the rule prohibiting vehicles in the park, we might say that a truck is a vehicle to degree 1; a bicycle, to degree 0.7; a tricycle, to degree 0.3; and a baby carriage, perhaps, to degree 0.001.

There are some difficulties here. One is that the law in most situations does not provide for degrees of membership or degrees of truth. A criminal defendant is found guilty or not; a civil defendant is found liable or not; and for the purpose of a particular rule an object is a vehicle or not. However hard the question of membership may be, there must finally be a decision that rules the object in or out.

Second, fuzzy set theory does not address the question of how the initial assignment of grades of membership is to be made. To assign a grade is to draw a significant conclusion. Legal arguments about how a decision should go—about what factors are relevant and how much they should count for—could perhaps be recast as arguments about grades of membership; but it is doubtful that anything would be gained in translation. As work on legal argument proceeds in the future, the first major step will be to identify the classes of arguments that a program should be able to make about hard questions and the kinds of knowledge needed to support such arguments. Both the argument types and the knowledge sources are likely to be far too disparate to be usefully reduced to a single mathematical formalism.

3.5.2 Ronald Dworkin: An Idealized Legal Approach

Ronald Dworkin is a critic of legal positivism who disputes the idea that judges have discretion in any significant number of cases. He argues that even hard cases have right answers, and he provides a description as elaborate as any in the literature of how right answers could be found. If this description could be made computational, it would tell how an AI program should proceed when the rules run out. A distinction between hard questions and easy questions would become unnecessary, because the same process could resolve them all. Dworkin says, though (and properly, as will become clear), it is no part of his theory "that any mechanical procedure exists" (1977a, pp. xiv, 81). The theory is nevertheless worth presenting as a measure for comparison with AI programs' present and future capabilities.

For Dworkin, as for Fuller, law is not simply a set of properly pedigreed rules (Dworkin 1977a, p. 44; 1977b, pp. 1202, 1256). The alternative he explores is stated mainly in terms of how judges should decide hard cases. Dworkin's particular quarrel is with the positivists' idea that, when it is not clear what the rules require, the judge makes new law retroactively and may justify the decision on any reasonable grounds at all (Dworkin 1977a, pp. 32–34, 101–105).

The starting point of the argument is that rules exist, and create rights, within an institutional framework. When the rules (and surrounding conventions) fail to answer a question, they fail in a particular way: "They are not incomplete, like a book whose last page is missing, but abstract, so that their full force can be captured in a concept that admits of different conceptions; that is, in a *contested* concept" (Dworkin 1977a, p. 103; see also Gallie 1956). The official charged with deciding a hard case (whether a judge or a referee in chess) must construct the concept; and constructing it requires alternating between two kinds of questions: (1) Why, in the case of this institution, do the rules create or destroy any rights at all? That is, what justifies the institution's existence, and what version of the concept does that justification best support? (2) What version of the concept is best supported by the features of the existing institution? (Dworkin 1977a, pp. 103–104). When the institution is a court of law and the concept is one like contract or property, the first question leads the judge to political philosophy, and the second, to the precedents.

But the doctrine of precedent is itself a contested concept. Dworkin locates its justification in the "fairness of treating like cases alike" (1977a, p. 113) and its institutional features in the way that the doctrine is actually used and discussed.

Dworkin constructs an account of precedent based on the "concept of principles that 'underlie' or are 'embedded in' the positive rules of law" (1977a, pp. 105, 115). There are several differences between rules and principles (ibid., pp. 22–28). A typical rule is "A will is invalid unless signed by three witnesses"; a typical principle, "No man may profit from his own wrong." Rules are applicable in all-or-none fashion: if the preconditions are satisfied, the conclusion follows. A complete and accurate statement of a rule will list all exceptions in the statement of preconditions. If two rules are in conflict, one of them must be invalid. Principles, on the other hand, are general considerations that supply reasons for a decision without automatically requiring that decision. If principles can be said to have exceptions, the exceptions are not enumerable. Valid principles may conflict; unlike rules, they have a dimension of weight or importance by which conflicts can be resolved. A final feature of principles distinguishes them not from rules but from policies (Dworkin 1977a, pp. 82–84; 1977b, pp. 1204–1211): arguments of principle are directed toward showing that people have rights, whereas arguments of policy try to show that a decision will advance some collective goal of the political community. For example, an argument for subsidizing aircraft manufacturers on the ground that it will protect national defense is an argument of policy, not principle. Both kinds of argument are appropriate in support of legislation, but only arguments from rules and principles, according to Dworkin, should be used in adjudication.

Given the distinction between rules and principles, a hard case becomes a case whose decision does not follow from the rules alone (on easy cases, see Dworkin 1977b, p. 1248). For the judge faced with a hard common law case, the question becomes, "What set of principles best justifies the precedents?" and this question "builds a bridge between the general justification of the practice of precedent, which is fairness, and his own decision about what that general justification requires in some particular hard case" (Dworkin 1977a, p. 116). An imaginary judge named Hercules, whom Dworkin endows with "superhuman skill, learning, patience and acumen" (ibid., p. 105), will try to answer the question by constructing "a scheme of abstract and concrete principles that provides a coherent justification for all common law precedents and, so far as these are to be justified on principle, constitutional and statutory provisions as well"; for "he does not satisfy his duty to show that his decision is consistent with established principles, and therefore fair, if the principles he cites as established are themselves inconsistent with other decisions that his court also proposes to uphold" (ibid., pp. 116–117). But total consistency is too much to require; justification of the entire institutional history may be attainable only by adopting arbitrary distinctions and unappealing principles (ibid., p. 119). It is better to allow for the possibility that some past decisions were mistakes (ibid., p. 121).

With this background it becomes possible to state Dworkin's test for the correctness of a legal conclusion. It is assumed that there is some body of uncontroversial rules (Dworkin 1977a, p. 105):

A proposition of law, like the proposition that Tom's contract is valid, is true if the best justification that can be provided for the body of propositions of law taken to be settled provides a better case for that proposition than for the contrary proposition that Tom's contract is not valid, but is false if that justification provides a better case for that contrary proposition. (Dworkin 1978, pp. 28–29)

A similar test holds for whether a general principle—not yet applied to a specific case—"is 'embedded in' or 'implicit in' or may be 'inferred by analogy' from a set of earlier decisions. . . . [A] principle bears that relationship to earlier decisions, or other legal material, if the principle figures in . . . the best justification of that material" (Dworkin 1977b, p. 1252).

The quality of a justification is to be measured in two dimensions: the dimension of fit, which asks how much of the existing legal material must be taken as mistakes, and the dimension of political morality, which asks about the soundness of the political or moral theory on which the justification is based (Dworkin 1977b, p. 1252; 1978, pp. 30–31). Because people who hold different moral theories will assess the second dimension differently, decisions in hard cases will remain controversial. But if moral skepticism is wrong—that is, if it is not the case that all moral theories are equally good—then even hard cases will usually have right answers, and Dworkin thinks he will have explained the recalcitrance of the so-called myth that there is one right answer in a hard case (1977a, p. 290; 1978, p. 31).

4   Related Work

The last two chapters have provided some background for viewing legal reasoning programs in the context of related work in jurisprudence. This chapter considers legal reasoning programs themselves, both actually implemented and merely proposed. Section 4.1 begins by surveying some other contexts in which legal reasoning programs have been placed. For some writers, for instance, computerization has been not a way to extend jurisprudence but to abolish it, putting a supposedly scientific method in its place. For others, AI methods in law may be only a way to improve on conventional data processing. Despite the different emphases in such writing, it is not immune from criticism from a jurisprudential viewpoint. Sections 4.2 through 4.4 examine the previous programs from such a viewpoint. Section 4.2 considers programs whose knowledge base consists only of rules; section 4.3, those whose knowledge base is limited to cases; and section 4.4, the two previous AI programs that have tried to incorporate a more realistic model of the sources of legal knowledge. Finally, section 4.5 comments on some proposed uses of legal reasoning programs.

4.1 Legal Theory and Computer Programs

Since the earliest days of computing, law has been seen as a prospective domain for AI. The American legal realist Jerome Frank reacted to Wiener's *Cybernetics* (1948) by sketching a program and its limits:

It is conceivable that an "ultra-rapid" legal-logic machine could promptly answer questions like these: (1) Given a specific state of facts, F, what possible alternative legal rules, R's, will logically lead to a desired decision, D? (2) Given a legal rule, R, and a desired decision, D, what possible alternative states of fact, F's, will logically yield that decision? (3) Given a specific legal rule, R, and a specific state of facts, F, what is the logically correct decision, D?

Anyone who believes such a machine can supplant the human process of judging is hoping to revert, in a scientific way, to the "mechanical" method of the ordeals. I, who have done my fair share of jeering at "mechanical jurisprudence," have no such hope. Yet I think there is much merit in the idea of such a machine. . . . [I]t seems to me that judges and lawyers would benefit from having relatively simple problems—type (3)—speedily and correctly answered, and from having put before them promptly all possible alternative solutions of more complicated problems, i.e., type (1) and (2) problems.

. . . .

Such a machine would not reduce, but would increase, the need for legal intelligence: great skill would be necessary in formulating the questions put to the machine. Semantic difficulties would, too, in many instances, prove a stumbling block.

Moreover, even were such a machine to disclose all possible available alternative legal rules, the judges (except when bound by statute or precedents) would still have to exercise "the sovereign prerogative of choice" between the rules, on the basis of the judges' conscious or unconscious notions of policy. The machine might give judges the benefit of offering the alternatives clearly. But it would not realize the hope of Leibniz who thought that, if there were such a machine, then "If controversies were to arise, there would be no more need of disputation between two philosophers [or lawyers, we may interpolate] than between two accountants. For it would suffice [for them] . . . to say to each . . . : Let us calculate." Mr. Justice Douglas had in mind the judges' "sovereign prerogative of choice" when, in effect answering Leibniz, he said, "The law is not a series of calculating machines where . . . answers come tumbling out when the right levers are pushed." (Frank 1949, pp. 206–208; footnotes omitted)

The machine that Frank proposed would have been an AI program, conceptually based in traditional jurisprudence. The work reported in this study is in much the same spirit as Frank's proposal.

Early work on computers and law did not take the direction Frank suggested. What happened instead was the founding of a field that called itself *jurimetrics* (Loevinger 1949, 1961, 1963). Traditional jurisprudence, it was said, was sterile; its questions were meaningless and its methods futile (Loevinger 1949, p. 467). Computers would never be able to simulate judicial reasoning because "[l]egal terms are almost all vague verbalizations which have only a ritualistic significance. . . . [B]y present methods, the determination of every genuine legal issue is made at the sub-verbal (and usually subconscious) level, where formal 'logic' can neither exist nor exert influence" (ibid., pp. 471–472). Jurisprudence was to be replaced by jurimetrics, defined as the "scientific investigation of legal problems" (ibid., p. 483). And the way to be scientific was to study behavior, not verbiage, to quantify, and to make predictions (see Loevinger 1961). The question to ask about judges was not how they reason or should reason but "what statistical measures will most conveniently summarize the behavior of individual judges in various categories of cases" (Loevinger 1949, p. 486). In short it was behaviorism, not cognitive science, that shaped much early work on computer approaches to legal reasoning.

The concerns of jurimetrics were soon sketched out as including three main fields: behavioral analysis (and prediction) of judicial decisions, legal information retrieval, and the uses of symbolic logic in law. (For an overview, see Jones 1962, Baade 1963, and the early volumes of the *Jurimetrics Journal*, which began publication in 1959 as *M.U.L.L. (Modern Uses of Logic in Law)*.)

The attitudes Loevinger and his colleagues expressed were never adopted by the legal profession generally. (Two good critiques of the behavioral analysis projects are Fuller 1966 and Stone 1966; see also Tapper 1973.) As a movement within the legal profession, jurimetrics has not been much heard from since the early 1970s. At about the same time, AI began to reach a stage where it seemed likely to have something to contribute to the study of legal reasoning (B. Buchanan and Headrick 1970; Slayton 1974).

Whether or not one likes the theory, jurimetrics certainly was marked by a theoretical bent. It was also marked by a fascination with new tools, including statistics and formal logic, as well as computers. There has been another line of approach that may share the interest in tools but that has no theoretical pretensions. A very early example is Kelso (1946), who saw legal information retrieval as mostly mechanical drudgery that computers could readily perform (pp. 385, 392).

More recent work displays a similar spectrum from theoretical to practical concerns. Interest in the theoretical side of legal reasoning is particularly marked in McCarty (McCarty 1977, pp. 837–841; McCarty, Sridharan and Sangster 1979, pp. 9–17; see also Slayton 1974). Some other projects seek only to create practical computer-based tools—tools that lawyers will find helpful or that will reduce the cost of legal services or improve judicial administration. Sprowl (1979), who describes a system for drafting legal documents, sees "automating the legal reasoning process" as part of "a revolution in law office management" (p. 4). A predecessor system, used to interview clients and draft divorce complaints, was motivated in terms of providing legal assistance to the poor (McCoy and Chatterton 1968; McCoy 1976; Sprowl 1979, p. 6, n. 4).

Even nontheoretical projects, though, may take an implicit stance on theoretical issues of legal reasoning. For the purpose of comparing previous work to that reported here, two such issues are of particular interest. First, what is the nature of the knowledge base? Does it consist only of rules, only of cases, or some combination of the two? Is it seen as a full representation of the law? Second, is the legal knowledge used in a way that leaves room for hard questions, and, if so, how are they handled? Sections 4.2 through 4.4 are organized around the first question, considering rule-based programs, example-based programs, and finally two projects that look toward a more comprehensive representation of legal knowledge.

The appropriate answers to the questions depend to some degree on the program's particular task. Most AI work in law, like the present study, deals with tasks of legal analysis, and the following sections therefore concentrate on those. Other legal tasks to which AI techniques have been applied experimentally include drafting, estate planning (Michaelson 1982, 1984), information retrieval (Hafner 1981; Walker 1981; Karlgren and Walker 1983; deBessonet and Cross 1985), and court management (J. Buchanan and Fennell 1977; J. Buchanan 1981). There has also been interest in the psychological side of lawyers' performance, for instance as a subject for protocol analysis (Johnson, Johnson, and Little 1984; Stratman 1984).

4.2 Rule-based Programs

Most legal analysis programs have worked with a knowledge base consisting only of rules. To the extent that the knowledge base rules are equated with rules of law and are expected to produce definite conclusions about particular cases, such programs are in danger of implementing the same conceptualist model of law that lawyers have rejected since the realist criticisms of the 1930s.

Several programs illustrate the problem. The earliest is that of Maggs and deBessonet (1972), who looked toward developing "a generalized formal language approach to the analysis of systems of legal rules" (p. 159), which would permit "questions of an extremely specific nature" to be answered (p. 160). Maggs and deBessonet used a set of rules based on statutes and expressed in a normalized propositional calculus. The main element of the program was a theorem prover, implemented in Lisp and using a British Museum algorithm (Newell, Shaw, and Simon 1957). Suggested applications of the program included determining whether the rules were consistent and nonredundant, answering questions about liability, and generating questions to be asked in a client interview.

Popp and Schlink's (1975) program, JUDITH, was an interactive consultation system closely patterned on MYCIN (Shortliffe 1976). Its rule base, which apparently dealt mostly with the law of negligence, was drawn from the German Civil Code. The program's dialogue with the user proceeded top-down, asking yes-no questions in an attempt to establish a basis for liability. A user response meaning "I don't know" was permitted; its effect was to invoke the next lower level of rules. The authors suggested that, if the rules bottomed out and the response was still "I don't know," the program should refer the user to an information retrieval system.

Popp and Schlink acknowledged that German law had had a "case law revolution," but they placed their program in an earlier tradition:

The historically minded reader will easily recognize a notion of German Pandectist tradition in which it was common to think of the law as a pyramid of legal categories, and to think of norm atoms, norm molecules, norm elements and their amalgamations in an almost chemical sense. . . .

. . . JUDITH in a sense leans on this heritage. It lives in what is called dogmatics, and the concocted deductive style of legal reasoning that has its methodological as well as its sociological aspect. The methodological aspect creates an urge for total systemization of statutory rules, court decisions, and academic research into a consistent body of legal information. (Popp and Schlink 1975, p. 313)

Next came McCarty's (1977) program, TAXMAN I, to be described in section 4.4.2. McCarty now characterizes TAXMAN I as "an excellent model of a 'deductive' or 'mechanical' jurisprudence" (McCarty, Sridharan, and Sangster 1979, p. 13).

More recently Sprowl (1979) has developed a system that can draft legal documents like wills and divorce complaints and can fill in forms like tax returns. The text produced can include both standard passages, or boilerplate, and the results of computations based on client-specific data. The theory behind the system is that

it should be possible for a specialist in an area of law to create within a central computer an image of the law in his or her area of specialization. . . .

When . . . displayed or printed, the law should appear just as it does in a book of statutes—it should be written in English, and it should be fully understandable to anyone trained in the law. Whenever the law changes, it should be possible for the specialist to revise this image of the law using conventional computer-based text-revision techniques. The specialist should be able to maintain within the computer a set of statute-like statements that completely define the law as it relates to his or her specialty. (Sprowl 1979, p. 5)

The English-like appearance of this image is achieved by using whole phrases as variable names (such as "the name of the testator") and whole sentences as names for unanalyzed propositions (such as "the estate may be probated without court appearance"). Statute-like statements can then be written as if-then-otherwise expressions, whose operands are Boolean combinations of these propositions. Sprowl characterizes the system as a direct successor to Popp and Schlink's project (Sprowl 1979, p. 12, n. 20).

An intellectual source common to Sprowl and to Maggs and de-Bessonet is the work of Layman Allen (1957, 1963, 1980; Allen and Engholm 1978). Allen's main concern has been poor legal draftsman-ship, particularly inadvertent syntactic ambiguity. The cure he advocates is the writing (or rewriting) of statutes and other legal instruments in a normalized form that disambiguates the meaning and scope of connectives—that is, in a version of the propositional calculus. Numerous applications of the normalization idea have been suggested, including automatic deduction of the legal consequences of a set of propositions (Allen 1963). But in avoiding a conceptualist position—that deduction from unambiguous rules is all that is required to reach legal decisions—Allen encounters another difficulty: "[W]hen a law has already been enacted, any form of the statute other than the original enactment represents an interpretation. It is important that any representation which purports to correspond to a statute say neither more nor less than the statute itself does" (Allen and Engholm 1978, p. 396). Unfortunately, normalizing an existing statute so as to remove ambiguity necessarily means that the official and unofficial versions no longer say the same thing. One cannot have it both ways.

Representing the law as a body of clear rules might suffice for some limited purposes. Sprowl compares his system's capabilities not to those of a human lawyer but only a magnetic card typewriter (1979, p. 74). Yet in a later paper (Sprowl and Staudt 1981), it is reported that the system is still being used to draft wills for clients of a law school teaching clinic, although the estate-planning expert who created the relevant knowledge base has left the project (p. 726). Since the remaining attorneys are not estate-planning specialists (p. 729), one wonders how future needs for knowledge base revision will come to their attention. Another drafting program (Boyd and Saxon 1981), inspired by Sprowl's, faces up to the potential problem by trying to keep the attorney-user more actively involved in the drafting process and to provide help and warnings wherever the law is unclear.

A few recent AI programs represent the law as a body of rules. Waterman and Peterson (1980, 1981, 1984), working with product liability cases in tort law, deal with a special kind of task: given the facts of a case, not to determine whether liability exists but to model the behavior of lawyers and claims adjusters in reaching a settlement out of court. The content of legal doctrine is only one factor affecting a settlement decision, and the actors may use the doctrine in a simplified form. Even so, the authors have run up against a need to use cases in reasoning about predicates like "reasonable and proper" and "foreseeable" (1981, pp. 18, 26) and to incorporate methods for dealing with the actors' "uncertainties about proving factual issues and applicable legal doctrine" (1981, p. 26).

Hustler (1982) is concerned with the aptness of the PROLOG language for legal reasoning. Primary attention is given to representing legal rules as PROLOG clauses, and a small implementation is presented with one very simple example from the law of battery. Although the discussion recognizes several of the problems—representing the facts, linking the facts with the rules, and identifying significant questions—the implementation does not have much to say about any of these. Given a statement of facts, the program tries to find a proof of liability; if an element of the proof is missing, it asks the user. The program recognizes only positive responses, however; answers of "no" and "I don't know" would be treated identically. In Hustler's PROLOG model, therefore, a plaintiff has either a clear case for recovery or none at all.

In a series of recent papers, Marek Sergot has also considered the use of logic programs to represent rules of law (Sergot et al. 1986; Sergot 1985; Bench-Capon and Sergot 1985). The main example is an encoding of rules for British citizenship, based on the British Nationality Act of 1981. One reason for this choice of domain was that the act was new and so not yet encumbered by a body of cases interpreting the rules. Nevertheless the project has converged on many of the same concerns as the present study, such as the need to allow for conflicting rules, open texture, and defeasible conclusions. How far such needs can be accommodated within an extended PROLOG is under investigation.

4.3 Example-based Programs

Within AI, only one current project concentrates entirely on the use of cases in law. This is the work of Edwina Rissland, whose special interest is the use of examples in reasoning (Rissland 1982, 1983, 1985; Rissland, Valcarce, and Ashley 1984; see also Ashley 1985). Originally concerned with the elements of mathematical knowledge, in which examples figured prominently (Rissland 1978), she has turned to law as another domain where cases have an important role. The current work deals largely with hypothetical cases, especially as they may be used in law teaching and in developing arguments in preparation for litigation. The principal domain is the law of trade secrets, as applied to the protection of software. Each case, hypothetical or actual, is represented in a frame-based format, where the slots are chosen to correspond to classes of facts, called *dimensions*, that have been identified as legally significant in the secondary literature. Unlike most other projects, which take the description of the case at hand as fixed, Rissland's HYPO program treats the description as a hypothetical situation that is to be modified, along specified dimensions, to produce a new hypothetical case that is stronger for a specified party. The modifications are guided by comparison with cases stored in the knowledge base; they are to be used for purposes such as developing an argument from the precedents, assessing the strength of one's case, and coping with uncertainty about what will be proved at trial. Another aspect of the project involves the classification of detailed moves in argumentation, particularly the various purposes that can be served by introducing new facts or deleting facts from one's description of a situation.

Another group of programs uses decisions in past cases as the knowledge base for analyzing others. Examples are Kort (1963), Lawlor (1963a, 1963b, 1972, 1980), Mackaay and Robillard (1974), and Haar, Sawyer, and Cummings (1977); related work includes Bing (1980), Borchgrevink and Hansen (1980), and Tyree (1981). These are not AI programs; the earliest ones are part of the behaviorally oriented jurimetrics movement. The programs are concerned with predicting judicial decisions, or more generally with analyzing judicial behavior, from a data base in which legal rules have no role. Traditional modes of reasoning are replaced by mathematical methods—for instance, Boolean algebra or regression analysis.

In these programs, the data concern the fact patterns in a large number of somewhat similar cases.[1] The universe of possible fact patterns is defined by a predetermined set of propositions, some subset of which (or their negations) is taken to represent the facts of any particular case. Types of cases represented in this way have included Supreme Court cases on the right to counsel under the Fourteenth Amendment (Lawlor 1963a, 1963b), Canadian cases on whether profits are ordinary income or capital gain (Mackaay and Robillard 1974), and Connecticut cases on amendments to local zoning regulations (Haar, Sawyer, and Cummings 1977). Although there has been rather little discussion of the adequacy of this method of representation, a few writers have seen problems in separating findings of fact from legal conclusions (Fuller 1966, pp. 1613–1616; Tapper 1973, pp. 250–251), and Lawlor has mentioned difficulties in determining what the judges believed the facts of the case to be (1963a, pp. 103–104), in categorizing facts appropriately (1972), and in deciding what aspects of the facts should be included (compare the dispute between Wiener, 1962, and Lawlor, 1963b, over whether "the case arose in Alabama" states a relevant fact in a Supreme Court case concerning the right to counsel).

Whatever the problems in representing the cases, the outcome of each case is viewed as a mathematical function of its encoded facts. The general task is to determine a good function, which may then be used to predict the results in other cases. Usually these other cases are also past decisions, which have been purposely excluded from the training set. The most publicized exception was Lawlor's successful prediction (1963b) that the Supreme Court would overrule its decision in *Betts v. Brady*,[2] a right-to-counsel case, and uphold the petitioner's claim in then-pending *Gideon v. Wainwright*.[3] The key to the prediction was the use of separate functions for each individual justice, coupled with personnel changes on the Court since the earlier cases. Some equally publicized criticism of the approach appears in Wiener (1962).

The significance—intended or actual—of much prediction research has been unclear. The paper by Haar, Sawyer, and Cummings (1977) is an exception. By reflecting on their statistical results in the light of a traditional legal analysis of the same cases, the authors are able to provide recommendations for attorneys and litigants in zoning cases and to raise questions about zoning law for the attention of both court and legislature (pp. 742–750).

Some other papers, particularly early ones, are open to a very different reading. If computers could predict decisions accurately, why not let them make the decisions in the first place? Computers have been talked of as potential replacements for judges for much longer than AI has had the concept of consultation systems to assist, not replace, the human professional. Prediction programs have usually provided the context for such proposals, but the resulting arguments are equally applicable to AI programs. We will return to such arguments in section 4.5.

4.4 More General Programs

4.4.1 Meldman's Dissertation

Meldman's dissertation (1975) was a design for a program to analyze problems involving assault and battery. It was the earliest AI work to represent more than one source of legal knowledge. As such it was an important first step toward developing more comprehensive models of legal reasoning.

Like offer and acceptance, assault and battery is a case law area in which the knowledge is commonly expressed in terms of general rules. For Meldman the dichotomy between specific cases and general rules was in part a distinction between primary and secondary authority (1975, p. 23). The most general rules in the knowledge base were attributed to secondary authority, specifically to a fictitious encyclopedia called Corpus Juris Mechanicum (p. 107). To justify the use of rules that obviously lacked authoritative status as law, Meldman adopted the expedient of assuming that the courts had held Corpus Juris Mechanicum to state the rules correctly (p. 135). The rules are seen as stating generalized fact situations, and the analysis of an input problem as a matter of "matching the specific facts being analyzed to the more general facts contained in the doctrines" (p. 9).

In contrast to the secondary nature of general rules in Meldman's work, the cases stand as primary legal authority (p. 23). The question then arises, as it always does in studies of legal reasoning, how a case can be authority for anything beyond its own particular facts. Meldman manages the answer in a very simple way: the case is itself represented as a rule. The content of the rule differs from the rules of secondary authority only in that it is "often more specific" (p. 132); the form differs in that it is attributed to a particular decision, whose specific facts are also stored but not used in the reasoning process (pp. 132–133).

With this legal knowledge base, Meldman's system accepts a set of facts and attempts, as its top-level goal, to establish the presence of one or more intentional torts (p. 171). Subgoals can be established in several ways: by type, by element, by example, and if all else fails by asking the user (pp. 160–166). The first three methods have counterparts in the present program. They correspond, respectively, to applying a set of rules that give alternate ways of reaching the same conclusion (for instance, assault and battery are types of intentional torts), to testing the antecedents of a single rule (for instance, the elements of battery would be a list of antecedents), and to testing an antecedent by example. In Meldman's model, examples may match either exactly, with the help of an abstraction hierarchy; or by analogy (pp. 155–157).

The version of analogy used is far too simple, as Meldman recognized (p. 157). In effect it simply permits the rule of a case to be temporarily generalized by replacing all its predicates by their parents in the abstraction hierarchy. For example, given the case-derived rule that the contact element of battery is satisfied when "one person strikes an article of clothing on another person" (p. 143), together with the input fact that Howard Hood grabbed an umbrella held by Gordon Good, analogical matching succeeds on the following basis: (1) in the abstraction hierarchy, an umbrella is a personal accessory, which is analogous to an article of clothing since both are movable objects; (2) "grab" and "strike" are analogues since they have the common parent "contact event"; and (3) similarly "on" and "held by" have the common parent "contact relation" (pp. 197–199). In fact Meldman's presentation bears a noticeable resemblance to Austin's discussion of analogy (1885 ed., pp. 638–641), with which Austin himself was never satisfied (see ibid., p. 989; Stone 1964, pp. 312–316).

The most troublesome point about Meldman's model of legal reasoning, however, arises even in using cases for exact (nonanalogical)
matching. The model relies heavily on the idea of the rule of a case,
also called its *holding* or its *ratio decidendi*. The concept of a holding
is utterly standard; one characterization is as "a general rule without
which the case must have been decided otherwise" (Wambaugh 1894,
p. 18). No one has ever succeeded, however, in getting from this
rough commonsense description to a satisfactory explanation of how
there can be a unique such rule. Further, cases are used in many
ways other than for their (putative) holdings; Llewellyn (1960, pp.
75–92) identified sixty different and legitimate uses, illustrating each
from recent decisions. By allowing each case to be used only for its
holding, treating ascertainment of the holding as unproblematical,
and assuming that the set of holdings will add up to a consistent
whole, Meldman portrays legal reasoning as much simpler than it
really is.

4.4.2 McCarty's TAXMAN

A continuing AI project with goals similar to those of the present
research is Thorne McCarty's TAXMAN system (McCarty 1977;
McCarty, Sridharan and Sangster 1979; McCarty and Sridharan 1980,
1982). Both projects look toward giving a computational description
of legal reasoning that is rich enough to allow for the phenomena
that legal theorists find interesting—as opposed, say, to describing
only phenomena that can be handled by existing AI methods.

McCarty's first program, TAXMAN I (1977), used an entirely rule-
based model. All concepts, legal and factual, were either primitive
or fully defined in terms of primitives. Needing a legal area whose
concepts could be treated in this way with some plausibility, McCarty
chose the taxation of corporate reorganizations. The top-level concepts were certain types of reorganizations defined by the Internal
Revenue Code. The gist of the code provisions is that, if what would
otherwise be taxable income arises out of one of these reorganizations, no tax will be imposed.

The input to TAXMAN I was a representation of the facts in a
corporate reorganization case. Typical facts were statements like
"Phellis owns 250 shares of the common stock of the Delaware corporation" and "the Delaware corporation transferred its assets to the
New Jersey corporation" (1979, p. 7). The program was written in

Microplanner (Sussman, Winograd, and Charniak 1971), which McCarty modified so as to attach time variables to assertions and thereby to represent the state of the world at various times within a single database (1977, p. 865). Using the modified Microplanner procedures, the program determined whether, according to its definitions, any of three different types of tax-free corporate reorganizations had taken place.

McCarty had two important reasons for choosing corporate reorganizations as the topic in TAXMAN I. One was the prospect of being able to span the domain with a small set of primitives. The second was the interestingness of what the program could not do. There are three cases, all decided by the Supreme Court during the 1930s, in which the literal statutory requirements for a tax-free reorganization were met, but the income in question was held to be taxable nevertheless. In each case the Court introduced a new requirement for nontaxability and found that this additional requirement was not met (see McCarty 1977, pp. 846–850). The concepts the Court used, which go under the names of "continuity of interest," "business purpose," and "step transactions," became McCarty's prime examples of *amorphous concepts*, which TAXMAN I was unable to represent (McCarty, Sridharan, and Sangster 1979, p. 3).

Understanding the nature and use of amorphous concepts is the major goal of TAXMAN II. In that work, now using the representation language AIMDS (Sridharan 1978), two styles of conceptual representation are provided. The simpler, which provides the capabilities of TAXMAN I, is called a *logical template* representation (McCarty and Sridharan 1980); it corresponds in the present research to reasoning from rules. With respect to logical templates, the main extension beyond TAXMAN I is that the formerly primitive terms *stock* and *bond* are now to be broken down and expressed as bundles of rights in the earnings, assets, and control of a corporation (1979, pp. 56–59; see McCarty 1983).

More interesting is the representation for concepts treated as amorphous, which correspond approximately to the open-textured predicates of this study. The representation is called a *prototype-and-deformation* model of conceptual structure. It is described as having three elements:

1. There is an *invariant* component to provide necessary, but not sufficient, conditions for the existence of the abstraction. Even this component would be optional, however.

2. There is a set of *exemplars,* each of which matches some but not all of the instances of the concept. It is important, however, that this component be something more than an unordered, unstructured set, for that would give us only a disjunctive specification of the concept. Therefore:

3. There is also a set of *transformations* in the definitional expansion which express the *relationships between the exemplars,* i.e. which state that one exemplar can be *mapped* into another exemplar in a certain way. (McCarty and Sridharan 1982, p. 7)

Algorithms for using the prototype-and-deformation structures are still under development (see ibid., pp. 21–22, 27; Nagel 1983).

The exemplars of the prototype-and-deformation model correspond to the representations of cases in the present research. The TAXMAN work goes beyond that reported here by making it possible to say not only that certain situations present instances of a legal concept but also, by means of the transformations, to give one kind of account of why they are instances. In addition, McCarty and Sridharan want their program not just to use static prototype-and-deformation structures in reasoning about a new case but, modeling the process of legal argument, to construct new ones dynamically.

There are other respects in which the present research goes beyond the TAXMAN work. TAXMAN I analyzed a corporate reorganization case in the logical template style of reasoning, treating the concept of a tax-free reorganization and all subsidiary concepts as having clear-cut answers that the program could determine. Descriptions of TAXMAN II have so far focused on a different set of cases. In these cases the question is what constitutes income, within the meaning of the 1913 constitutional amendment authorizing a federal income tax. The work assumes that the meaning to be given to *income* is the only significant issue in the case to be analyzed and that both the issue and the potentially relevant precedents have already been identified when the program's analysis begins. The work on prototypes and deformations, then, is concerned with ways of arguing a hard question. It has not yet said how rule-based reasoning and prototype-based reasoning are to be combined. That is, in terms of the four levels of processing proposed in section 1.3.2, the TAXMAN II model appears to skip from level 2 (applying rules) to level 4 (arguing hard questions). It does not address the problem of deciding which questions are worthwhile prospects for invoking the computationally expensive process of partial matching to a prototype.

A second major difference between the TAXMAN work and this study is the choice of a legal subdomain. In selecting corporate tax problems, McCarty has emphasized that the relevant factual situations "can be described fairly completely using a manageable set of primitive terms" (McCarty, Sridharan, and Sangster 1979, p. 6). This is so, the authors argue, because the corporate tax domain is for the most part a "tidy world of formal financial rights and obligations"; it is "itself an artificial domain, a formal construct" (ibid., p. 7). In contrast, McCarty has repeatedly challenged the possibility of adequately representing the facts of a contracts case. For example:

It is inconceivable . . . that [current] formalisms would be rich enough, in their present state of development, to represent the relevant facts of a garden-variety contract or tort case, or a securities fraud case, or, in the extreme, a first amendment case. In these areas, . . . even though the present approaches to the representation of human actions, beliefs, intentions, motivations, etc., might conceivably be adequate, *in principle*, they would clearly be inadequate in practice. (Ibid., pp. 8–9; see also McCarty 1980a, p. 29; McCarty 1980b, p. 299.)

Perhaps so. But if we are ever to have general legal reasoning programs, we must investigate the actual representation requirements in some detail. Chapter 5 presents a first attempt in this direction.

4.5 A Misuse of Programs

Within AI, expert systems are often described as systems to assist professionals, not to take their place. Chapter 8 will comment on some of the kinds of assistance that a legal analysis program might provide, after the details of the present program have been examined. The question of AI programs as replacements for human judgment, however, calls for earlier consideration. The *Wall Street Journal* has run a story with the lead sentence, "Could a computer ever pass a bar examination . . . ?"[4] The *San Francisco Examiner* has asked, "Would you accept a computer as your attorney?"[5] Articles like these make it important to be clear about the fact that legal reasoning programs are not substitutes for people. The point was debated twenty years ago in an even stronger form.

The earliest suggestions were that computers could serve as judges. Not all the proposals were serious. The first one came from Harold Lasswell, a political scientist and Yale law professor, who considered the idea of replacing the Supreme Court by a "bench of judicial robots." Why one robot was not enough was not discussed;

the idea may have been that hard cases would be decided by a vote of the random number generators the robots were to incorporate (Lasswell 1955, pp. 398–399). Glendon Schubert, reading Lasswell's paper as tongue-in-cheek but deciding to take it literally, said that the decision-making procedure could readily be generalized to replace all the United States courts of appeals as well as the Supreme Court and that the main problem would be the introduction of more certainty into the law than we are prepared to tolerate (Schubert 1968, pp. 61–63). With somewhat more restraint, Lawlor suggested that computers could decide routine cases (1963a, pp. 108–109). Anthony D'Amato, in a 1977 paper called "Can/Should Computers Replace Judges?" argued that a replacement could save much time and money and that the way to decide whether to institute such a change is by a cost-benefit analysis. Tyree (1980) offered a comment on the mathematics of prediction programs under the title "Can a 'Deterministic' Computer Judge Overrule Himself?"

Other writers have taken the prospect of computer judges very gravely indeed, with the danger perceived as coming from programs that are claimed to predict judicial decisions accurately. A good example is Julius Stone's 1966 lecture, "Man and Machine in the Search for Justice, or Why Appellate Judges Should Stay Human" (in Stone 1966; for references to other examples, see ibid., pp. 51–54, nn. 2–9).

Stone distinguishes two universes of thought. One is that of the outside observer, within which prediction programs operate. The other is the universe of the appellate judge, confronting "the duty of making *his* authoritative decision" (Stone 1966, p. 74). The act of judgment is a creative act, which the judge should perform "with integrity on the basis of such experience, insight, and emotion as it has been given him to acquire *up to the very moment of performance*" (ibid.). The ingredients of this judgment include not only intellectual operations but also "unanalyzed and even unintellectualized experience": "In due course, no doubt, the present act of doing justice will, in its turn, be reduced to intellectualized forms which can be processed independently of nonintellectual elements. But not so with the *present* act of judgment or (we should rather say) with the judgment *still to be made here in the present*" (ibid., p. 80).

Stone's evaluation of prediction programs is similar to Weizenbaum's better-known discussion of AI programs:

The very asking of the question, "What does a judge (or a psychiatrist) know that we cannot tell a computer?" is a monstrous obscenity. . . .
Computers can make judicial decisions, computers can make psychiatric judgments. . . . The point is that they *ought* not be given such tasks. They may even be able to arrive at "correct" decisions in some cases—but always and necessarily on bases no human being should be willing to accept.
. . . [T]he relevant issues are . . . ethical. They cannot be settled by asking questions beginning with "can." The limits of the applicability of computers are ultimately statable only in terms of oughts. What emerges as the most elementary insight is that, since we do not now have any ways of making computers wise, we ought not now to give computers tasks that demand wisdom. (Weizenbaum 1976, pp. 226–227)

Weizenbaum's point extends beyond the judicial function. There have also been proposals to replace lawyers by computers in interviewing and advising clients, much as some thought Weizenbaum's ELIZA might replace expensive human psychotherapists. Colin Tapper writes, "[M]any of the currently unassisted poor might well prefer a classless, impartial and knowledgeable machine to their conception of the average legal adviser" (1973, p. 208).

Some suggestions for computerized legal advice would remove even the safeguard of a supervisory law office setting. McCoy, whose drafting system was used for wills as well as divorce complaints, speculated about the possibility of a "'will vending machine' (next to airport insurance desks, perhaps)" (McCoy 1976, p. 148; see also ibid., pp. 231–233). Another paper (Thomas 1979) discusses laymen's possible use of legal analysis programs, specifically TAXMAN (McCarty 1977) or a reasoning program based on statutory normalization (cf. Allen 1963). The question considered is whether use directly by laymen would amount to unauthorized practice of law. For programs using normalized statutes, the author concludes not, because "nothing is lost in translation" and the programs "only use logical analysis" (Thomas 1979, pp. 50, 51).

If such proposals are taken seriously, the problems of legal theory become practical ones: why should we believe that any advice the program gives is good advice or that anything the program says is true? To the extent that the legal theory is made explicit, such a program can more readily be criticized either for implementing the theory inadequately or for embodying a theory that is wrong. If a program fails at this level, it can be rejected as a substitute for human lawyers without even reaching the issues Stone and Weizenbaum raise. And as the previous sections have shown, existing legal analysis programs are not based on a satisfying account of what it might mean for a judgment to be legally correct.

Someone may object that human lawyers also lack a tenable theory of what they do. The difference is that, in people, bad theory can be tempered by unarticulated knowledge. John Dewey's story is worth remembering: "There is the old story of the layman who was appointed to a position in India where he would have to pass in his official capacity on various matters in controversy between natives. Upon consulting a legal friend, he was told to use his common-sense and announce his decisions firmly; in the majority of cases his natural decision as to what was fair and reasonable would suffice. But, his friend added: 'Never try to give reasons, for they will usually be wrong'" (Dewey 1924, p. 17). A sense of what is fair and reasonable is just what programs lack.

5.1 Representation Issues

This chapter examines the requirements for representing the facts of offer and acceptance cases, and it describes the particular representation used in the existing program. The sample problem quoted in section 1.2.1 provides the main example.

The encoding of even a single problem raises a wide range of representation issues. The sample problem involves actions and states, discrete physical objects and physical substances, time, speech acts, and reported dialogue with multisentence turns. Any of these alone could be the subject of a major study. (See Schank 1975, actions and states; Lehnert 1978, objects; Hayes 1979b, substances; Allen 1983a, time; Joshi, Webber, and Sag 1981, discourse; and Brady and Berwick 1983, discourse.) Clearly the emphasis will have to be on breadth, not depth, and on finding a way to integrate the treatment of representation problems rather than considering them in isolation. (A comparable range of representation issues is discussed by R. Moore 1981.)

The variety of representation issues points up a significant difference between law and other domains for expert systems. The task of analyzing a legal problem can be viewed as parallel to tasks like chemical analysis, as in DENDRAL (Lindsay et al. 1980), speech understanding, as in HEARSAY-II (Erman et al. 1980), or medical diagnosis, as in MYCIN (Shortliffe 1976; Buchanan and Shortliffe 1984). In each case the task is to reason from given data to a higher-level interpretation of the data. For other systems, however, the range of allowable data is strictly limited—at the extreme, to descriptions of instrument readings. In legal problems the potential data are not limited in this way. The facts are descriptions of human activity, and it seems impossible to set a priori bounds on the kinds of facts that may need to be represented because they are relevant to the analysis of a particular problem. Accordingly, a good language for representing legal problems should look toward extensibility, not closure.

The representation issues critical for legal problems will vary with the particular legal area studied. In corporate tax law, for instance, McCarty has found it important to study in depth the deontic concepts of permission and obligation (see McCarty 1983). In offer and acceptance problems, the central issue is representing what people have said to one another, for the sake of reasoning about the legal consequences of what they said. The representation must be able, among other things, to distinguish between what sentences were produced and what speech acts were performed, and between speech acts (possibly indirect, possibly unsuccessful) and the legal acts they may accomplish. It is also necessary to provide for distinguishing what is presupposed from what is stated; for talk about things whose identity cannot be determined; and for some degree of coherence in the sentences of a single utterance. Section 5.4 explains how these requirements have been handled. As a basis for section 5.4, the underlying representation is described in sections 5.2 and 5.3.

There are some noteworthy omissions from the list of representation topics. One is the goals and plans of the actors in the problem, their motivations and intentions. The sample problem itself says very little about such matters; this is typical for contracts problems, which tend to say what happened but not why.

In much current work on natural language, it is considered central to be able to reconstruct an actor's intentions or motivations from what the actor said. The reconstruction may be either at a very detailed level—for example, that A asked a question of B because A wanted to make a (polite) request of B (Allen 1983b)—or at a very general level—for example, that A wrote to B because A wanted to hire B as a lawyer (Lehnert et al. 1983). If this approach were taken to narratives that state contracts problems, it would lead to an emphasis on being able to answer questions like these:

• Why did Buyer ask whether Seller would supply a carload of salt? (Because he wanted Seller to supply a carload of salt.)

• Why did Buyer want a carload of salt? (Because he had customers for salt.)

• Why did Buyer tell Seller to ignore the purchase order? (Because he had received a better offer.)

The last two of these questions, however, are not the most pertinent ones for deciding whether Buyer contracted to buy a carload of salt. While it would be desirable to give the program enough knowledge to be able to answer general nonlegal questions about the input, the initial emphasis has been on trying to see what knowledge is central to the legal analysis.

The first question, on the other hand, is important as a basis for legal analysis. The inference it calls for—from a literal question to an indirect request—could appropriately be made at read time, before any legal knowledge is brought into play. But to process the problem from the original English, many other kinds of read-time inferences would also be required: resolving pronoun references, filling out ellipses, resolving certain syntactic ambiguities, and so on. The focus of this work is on defining the target representation that might result from such an initial processing and on applying legal knowledge to this result. Therefore the results of many read-time inferences have simply been supplied by hand. The most general guideline in supplying such inferences has been to avoid introducing conclusions that might prejudice the legal interpretation of the facts. That is, legal issues should not be decided by the parser.

If the parties' intentions are omitted from the representation, can we possibly have an adequate base for reasoning about the legal consequences of their actions? In fact the significance of intentions varies with the particular legal area. In criminal law they are very important. In assault and battery, which are intentional torts, Meldman's program had to be told that the requisite purpose or belief was present. In contract law, there was once a theory that a contract could not be formed without a "meeting of the minds." Later the theory was largely discarded in favor of an "objective theory" of contracts. Williston writes, "In some branches of the law, especially in the criminal law, a person's secret intent is important. In the formation of contracts it was long ago settled that secret intent was immaterial, only overt acts being considered in the determination of such mutual assent as that branch of the law requires" (Williston, 1957 ed., sec. 22; footnotes omitted). Admittedly the status of subjective intention is not so clear as Williston makes it; Fuller and Eisenberg (1981, chap. 8) provide an excellent overview of the difficulties. Nevertheless Williston's simplification is good enough to get us started.

Closely related to the omission of an explicit representation of intentions is the omission of an explicit representation for the parties' knowledge and beliefs. In fact some of the most interesting cases in contract law arise because the parties had conflicting or mistaken beliefs—sometimes about the state of the world, sometimes about the interpretation of the language they have used.[1] Such cases, for which the current representation is not adequate, provide the main counterexamples to Williston's generalization about not considering subjective states of mind. They are excluded in part because the legal analysis of these cases has often been so unsatisfactory.[2] Extending the program to deal with them is a challenge for future research. An even broader area for future research would be the investigation of patterns of reasoning about intention in the law. Almost certainly a concept like criminal intent, or even intention so far as it is relevant in contract situations, will require more subtleties of representation than AI work has so far captured.

5.2 Basic Elements of the Representation

5.2.1 Choice of Language

Two basic ideas have guided the attempt to work out a suitable representation for legal problems. One was that frame-based languages (Bobrow and Winograd 1977; Brachman 1978; Sridharan 1978), reinterpreted as ways of encoding statements that could also be made in standard logic (Hayes 1979a; Nilsson 1980, chap. 9), provide a useful discipline for thinking about what kinds of entities and relations should be present in the domain. The other was that the representation should be shaped primarily by what the problems require and not by the features that happen to be available or unavailable in any particular representation language. The latter point seems obvious, but it is easily lost sight of—either in the present atmosphere, where there are many competing systems for expert system development (Friedland 1985), or in the atmosphere when this work was undertaken. There had been a strong call for a general-purpose AI representation language (Bobrow and Winograd 1977); the language envisioned had failed to materialize; and numerous languages, all locally developed and with some claim to generality,

were in various stages of implementation, documentation, and de-
bugging (Nii and Aiello 1979; Stefik 1979; Genesereth, Greiner, and
Smith 1980; Greiner and Lenat 1980; Van Melle et al. 1981). Furthermore, given the exploratory nature of current research in legal reasoning, a major part of the task is to discover what language features
are important for stating and reasoning about legal problems. Despite
some attempts to compare languages (Hayes-Roth, Waterman, and
Lenat 1983), a good fit between task domain and representation
language remains hard to identify in advance.

The work on the representation thus proceeded in two steps: deciding what to say and then finding a suitable language in which to
say it. The first part used an informal notation whose syntax was
along the lines of KRL (Bobrow and Winograd 1977). As an example,
the English sentence "Buyer sent Seller a telegram" became, at this
stage, something like the following:

Send1: a Send with
        Agent = Buyer
        Beneficiary = Seller
        Object = (Telegram1: a Telegram)

In this same stage, there was an effort to specify just what kinds of
inferences based on the representation would be required.

The language chosen for the second stage was MRS (Genesereth,
Greiner, and Smith 1980). Since the input syntax of MRS is based on
the predicate calculus, the language provides great flexibility as to
what may be said and at least the prospect of a clear semantics. After
a straightforward (manual) translation from the intermediate notation, the MRS version of the previous sentence becomes:

(send Send1)
(agent Send1 Buyer)
(ben Send1 Seller)
(obj Send1 Telegram1)
(telegram Telegram1)

Below, unary predicates will often be referred to as the names of
classes, binary predicates as slots, and the second argument to a
binary predicate as a filler. The classes currently used, and their
arrangement into a generalization hierarchy, are shown in figures 5.1
and 5.2.

- Event
  - Simple-event
    - Act
      - Ordinary-act
        - Transfer
          - Begin-transfer
            - Send
              - Mail
            - Ship
          - End-transfer
            - Receive
            - Deliver
          - Supply
        - Utter
      - Speech-act
        - Assertion
        - Yes-no-question
        - Request
        - Declaration
      - Legal-act
        - Offer
          - Counteroffer
          - Offer-to-modify
          - Modification-of-offer
        - Acceptance
        - Rejection
        - Revocation
    - Other-simple-event
      - Die
  - Complex-event
    - Exchange
      - Sale

Figure 5.1
Elements of the abstraction hierarchy: part 1

- State

    - Have
    - Need
    - Want

- Symbolic-object

    - Sentence
    - Proposition

- Physical-thing

    - Physical-object
        - Animate-object
            - Human
        - Inanimate-object
            - Document
                - Telegram
                - Letter
                - Form-document
            - Building
                - House
    - Physical-substance
        - Salt
        - Seed
        - Money
        - Land

- Measure

    - Volume
        - Carloads
        - Barrels
        - Bushels
    - Weight
        - Pounds
        - Cwt
    - Value
        - Dollars

- Time

    - Time-point
    - Time-line
    - Time-interval

Figure 5.2
Elements of the abstraction hierarchy: part 2

Since MRS is not a frame-based language, it does not have built-in concepts such as generalization hierarchies, slots, and fillers. Whatever inferences are to be made must be supported by explicit rules, stated either declaratively or as attached procedures. The rules used are described in section 5.3. They do include some default reasoning, which MRS makes possible by providing a *thnot* operator (Winograd 1980b) in addition to standard logical negation.

5.2.2 Problem Structure and Time

Since MRS uses a predicate-calculus syntax, the facts of a problem are stated as a set of logical formulas. An offer and acceptance problem, however, describes a sequence of events, and the processing strategy is to analyze them one by one. Accordingly it is convenient to partition the formulas into subsets. These are labeled *Event1, Event2, . . . , Event-n.*

The partitioning generally follows the division of English text into sentences and paragraphs. In the sample problem of section 1.2.1, Event1 is the sending of Buyer's first telegram to Seller. The formula (*telegram Telegram1*) is placed in Event1; it is not repeated in Event2, which says that Telegram1 was received. To achieve the partitioning, only one clause of the English text required rearrangement: "which Buyer received the same day" occurs in the description of the sending of the second telegram (Event3), but it is moved to become a separate event, Event4.

The MRS language provides a context mechanism that is convenient for implementing the partitioning and for several other purposes. An MRS data base may be segmented into any number of contexts, called *theories* or, sometimes, *worlds.* One theory is always designated as the current theory; it is into this theory that any newly asserted propositions will be entered. Any number of additional theories may be designated as active; propositions in all active theories as well as the current theory are available for retrieval. Finally, it may be asserted (globally) that one theory includes another. The propositions in all theories reachable, by inclusion relations, from the current theory or an active theory are also available for retrieval.

Each label *Event-i,* then, becomes the name of an MRS theory, in which just the formulas describing the corresponding event are asserted, and which can be activated alone or in combination with other theories.

Not every statement in a problem can be conveniently associated with a particular event. There may be quasi-universal generalizations: "The course of post between city A and city B is three days." There may be statements that something did not happen: "Buyer never replied to this letter." And assertions about the time lapse between events are easier to use if a time line is stored separately from the events themselves. The representation therefore allows for an additional MRS theory, which might be called *Event-independent-facts*. In the sample problem, *Event-independent-facts* contains only the following time line:

(time-line TL1)
(points TL1 (seq Start-July1 T1 T2 End-July-1
                Start-July12 T3 T4
                Start-July13 T5 T6 T7 T8
                Start-July14 T9 End-July14))
(value Start-July1 701)
(value End-July1 702)
(value Start-July12 712)
(value Start-July13 713)
(value Start-July14 714)
(value End-July14 715)

Here TL1 is a time line, and *seq* is a function symbol, understood to map its arguments to a sequence. T1 through T9 are the symbolic names assigned to the times of events 1 through 9. Each time point is taken to have a numeric value, usually unknown but within known bounds. Since offer and acceptance problems most often measure time in days, a day is taken to be the unit interval.[3] The scheme for assigning numbers to days, or the algorithms for using the numbers, would require generalization for events in more than one month.

For the problems considered so far, the sequencing of events and the explicit time line provide almost as much as need be said about time. Two other constructs that have been used are *time-intervals*, defined by start and end points, and the relation *follows* between two points. The latter provides an alternative to setting up additional time lines in representing tensed sentences in dialogue. Often, however, the representation of tense has been omitted where it is not significant in the legal analysis.

5.2.3 Ordinary Acts and Physical Objects

Of the nine events in the sample problem, eight are events of sending or receiving a telegram or other document. Since these are the simplest aspects of the problem to represent, we will begin with them.

The representation of acts, like sending and receiving, is quite standard. Generic types of acts become unary predicates, and instances of acts become individual constants: hence *(send Send1)* (see Davidson 1967; Charniak and McDermott 1985, chap. 1). A unary predicate may have an associated set of slots, or cases (see Winograd 1983, sec. 6.5), for stating relationships between an instance of the predicate and other entities in the domain. For acts, the slots include an *agent;* a *time,* which should be an instance of the class *time-point;* if appropriate, an *object;* and also if appropriate, a *beneficiary* corresponding to a syntactic indirect object. The representation for the first clause of the sample problem, "On July 1 Buyer sent the following telegram to Seller," is thus as shown in section 5.2.1, with the addition of the clause *(time Send1 T1)* and with the time line shown in section 5.2.2. Similarly the second event, "Seller received the telegram the same day," becomes

(receive Receive2)
(agent Receive2 Seller)
(time Receive2 T2)
(obj Receive2 Telegram1)
(ben Receive2 Buyer)

Here the *beneficiary* slot, for symmetry, is used for the person from whom the object was received.

Objects are represented similarly to acts but with less generally applicable sets of slots. For the sending and receiving events in the problem, the only physical objects needed are *Buyer* and *Seller* (presumably instances of class *human,* although they might be organizations), three instances of *telegram,* and the purchase order (taken to be an instance of *form-document*). In addition, there is an instance of *time-point* for each event.

A question that arises immediately is how large the lexicon for acts and objects should be. Sending and receiving, for example, have a common element of transferring. Looking ahead to the content of the telegrams, so do events of shipment, delivery, and supplying.

Should these all be reduced to a single predicate, say *transfer*? (Compare Schank 1975; Wilks 1977.) The answer given here is no. Instead the several English verbs are retained as unary predicates; the classes so established are all asserted to be subclasses of *transfer*, and a presumption that differently named classes are disjoint is carefully avoided. The general objective of this approach is to permit distinctions fine enough to suit the problems, without requiring excessive detail. Several considerations seem to support its appropriateness.

Law problems, unlike the problems analyzed by most expert systems, are not stated at a uniform level of concreteness or detail. In fact there is no level of detail that can always be regarded as ultimate (Anscombe 1958). A good first indicator of the appropriate level of detail is the words used in the problem statement itself. If the problem speaks of supplying something, it may be unnecessary to ask what further facts—perhaps about shipment and delivery—constitute this supplying. If the problem speaks of sending and receiving, it may be unnecessary to construct an explicit scenario showing how these are or might be connected. Providing predicates at various levels of abstraction, then, seems to make for a relatively economical, relatively natural initial problem representation.

Besides the overlap between more general and more specific predicates, the retention of English words as predicates also produces overlaps within a general level of abstraction. For example, the same event in the world may often be describable as both a *send* and a *ship* or as both a *receive* and a *deliver*. The troublesome situations, however, are likely to be the ones in which nearly coextensive predicates are not both applicable. A package can be delivered to you, by being placed on your doorstep, but can still be stolen before you receive it. By keeping nearly coextensive predicates in the lexicon, we can make room for distinctions that are sometimes critical without having to state explicitly the ways things like receipt and delivery usually work and the ways things can go wrong. If *send, receive,* and *deliver* were all represented only as *transfer*, either the distinctions among them would be lost, or it would be necessary to represent the transmission of a letter as a long sequence of transfers, some of which would involve the internal workings of the post office. Yet that is beyond the detailed knowledge of most people, so it should surely also be beyond the knowledge base requirements for the program.

With respect to physical objects, using English words as predicates may lead to less overlap rather than more. Wilks (1977, p. 11.) pointed out that no representation by a small set of primitives can be expected to distinguish among a hammer, a mallet, and an axe. Still, someone who enters a contract to buy a hammer can justifiably complain if he gets a mallet or an axe instead. The distinction is simply made by marking *hammer*, *mallet*, and *axe* as disjoint sets; similarly *elm* and *beech*. As Putnam (1975) observes of these last two words, it is quite possible to use the symbols properly without formal definitions and without being able to tell the trees apart in practice.

5.2.4 States, Events, Substances

To be able to represent the contents of the documents exchanged, we need to be able to talk about several more kinds of entities than have been introduced so far. Consider Buyer's first telegram to Seller, sent at time *T1*: "Have customers for salt and need carload immediately. Will you supply carload at $2.40 per cwt?"

Have and Need
Have and *need* are evidently states, not acts. States are given slots for a *subject* rather than an agent and a *time* that is an interval rather than a point. *Need* is constrained to take a propositional object. With some additional filling in, "need carload immediately" is initially translated as:

Buyer needs, during a time interval *I1* that contains *T1*:
that Buyer have a carload of salt during an interval *I2*.

To say that *I2* should start "immediately" relative to *T1*, the best approach may well be to make a place for the English word itself in the internal representation. This has not been implemented, however.

There is no attempt here to identify the predicate *have* with a particular sense of the word *have*. An unabridged dictionary lists seventeen senses for *have* as a transitive verb, most of them with several subsenses. Again the general maxim being followed is: Do not make more distinctions than the problems require. In "Have customers for salt" it is sufficient for the present to represent Buyer as saying that he stands in some unspecified relation to customers for salt—provided we can represent "customers for salt." If finer distinctions become necessary for future problems, at least some of the different kinds of having could be introduced as subclasses of *have*.

Exchanges and Other Events

The second sentence of the telegram, "Will you supply carload at $2.40 per cwt.?" is initially expanded to a yes-no question, with the propositional content "Seller will supply a carload of salt at $2.40 per cwt." Supplying is an act, but what is it to supply something at a price? To make a place for the prepositional phrase, we can introduce the concept of an *exchange* consisting of two acts (arbitrarily called *event1* and *event2*). A further rewriting gives, as the propositional content of the sentence:

There is an exchange, in which

event1 is a future supplying, by Seller to Buyer, of a carload of salt, and

event2 is a future transfer of $2.40 per cwt. of the salt.

An exchange is understood to be a kind of *complex-event*; a *sale* is one kind of exchange. Also available is a class called *simple-event*, which is a superclass of *act*. A kind of *simple-event* that is not also an act is *die*; this is relevant in contracts problems because the death of either the offeror or the offeree is often said to terminate the power to accept an offer.

With the introduction of the class *sale*, a fairly reasonable representation of "customers for salt" becomes possible. The convention is adopted that *event2* of a sale should be filled by a transfer of money.[4] Then *customer* can be defined as a composition of slot names: x is a *customer* from a sale y, if z is the *event2* of y and x is the *agent* of z. Similarly the *goods* in a sale y become the *object* of *event1* of y.

Salt, Money, and Their Measurement

The next problem is the representation of the things to be exchanged: a carload of salt and some money. For the present purpose, it is not necessary to provide much knowledge about the properties of salt as a substance or of *salt* as a mass noun. In the problems looked at so far, physical substances can be treated similarly to physical objects in that reference is always to a chunk of the substance. Offering to buy some salt is thus like offering to buy a car. In neither case need the particular object or chunk have been identified at the time the offer is made. (For instance, the car may have to be manufactured.) Similarly, money can be treated as a substance, with dollars as the usual unit of measurement. For the time being, land is classified as a substance as well, as in "A offered to sell B a parcel of land."

To provide for units of measurement, a new class called *measure* is introduced. Subclasses include measures of *volume, weight,* and *value*; subsubclasses include *carloads, cwt,* and *dollars.* Each of these lowest-level measure predicates has a single slot, *number.* Thus, "one carload" could be written

(carloads C1)
(number C1 1) .

Finally, *substance* predicates are given a slot for *quantity,* to be filled by a *measure.* "One carload of salt" then becomes

(salt Salt1)
(quantity Salt1 C1)

with *C1* as above. Obviously the *quantity* relation is one to many, since the same chunk of a substance may be measured by volume, by weight, or even in dollars' worth. Different measures of the same type might also be used, as in the following:

(salt Salt1)
(quantity Salt1 Weight1)
(cwt Weight1)
(number Weight1 3)
(quantity Salt1 Weight2)
(pounds Weight2)
(number Weight2 300)

To summarize, a particular sale of a carload of salt, by Seller to Buyer, at $2.40 per hundredweight, can be represented as in figure 5.3. In the last line of the figure, "*" is a function symbol for multiplication.

5.3 Knowledge about Domain Entities

Section 5.2 introduced several kinds of objects and relations among them. What knowledge about such objects and relations does the program actually have? What there is is embodied in rules expressed

```
(sale Sale1)
    (event1 Sale1 Trans11)
    (transfer Trans11)
        (agent Trans11 Seller)
        (ben Trans11 Buyer)
        (time Trans11 T11)
        (obj Trans11 Salt1)
            (salt Salt1)
            (quantity Salt1 Vol1)
                (carloads Vol1)
                (number Vol1 1)
            (quantity Salt1 Weight1)
                (cwt Weight1)
                (number Weight1 N1)
    (event2 Sale1 Trans12)
    (transfer Trans12)
        (agent Trans12 Buyer)
        (ben Trans12 Seller)
        (time Trans12 T12)
        (obj Trans12 Money1)
        (money Money1)
        (quantity Money1 Dol1)
            (dollars Dol1)
            (number Dol1 (* 2.40 N1))
```

Figure 5.3
Representing a particular sale of a carload of salt

in MRS's logic-like notation. These are the CSK rules referred to in sections 1.3.1 and 3.3.1. The rules permit several kinds of inferences, mostly standard ones. The types of rules used are summarized below. Some of the examples refer to classes not yet mentioned; these will be discussed in section 5.4.

5.3.1 A Generalization Hierarchy

The first group of rules implements a generalization hierarchy. The current contents of the hierarchy were shown in figures 5.1 and 5.2.
    The rules implementing the hierarchy are of the following kinds:

• Rules stating subset-superset relations. For example, simple events and complex events are kinds of events:

IF   (or (simple-event $x) (complex-event $x))
THEN   (event $x)

The notation used here is a slight modification, for readability, of the form used for input to MRS. Symbols beginning with "$" are understood to be universally quantified variables.

• Rules stating that certain subsets are mutually exclusive and exhaustive of the parent set. For example, simple events and complex events are the only kinds of events:

IF   (event $x)
THEN   (xor (simple-event $x) (complex-event $x))

• Rules stating that certain subsets are mutually exclusive (but not necessarily exhaustive). The currently used categories of speech acts provide an example. If something is any of the known kinds of speech acts, it is exactly one such kind:

IF   (or (assertion $x)
           (yes-no-question $x)
           (request $x)
           (declaration $x))
THEN   (xor (assertion $x)
           (yes-no-question $x)
           (request $x)
           (declaration $x))

The occasion has not arisen for rules stating that certain subsets q exhaust a parent set p, even though they may not be mutually exclusive. But such rules could be provided in the form

IF   (p $x)
THEN   (or (q1 $x) (q2 $x)) .

Classes may also be stated to be coextensive. Thus *purchase* is equivalent to *sale:*

IFF (sale $x)
   (purchase $x) .

The rules shown are stated in an abbreviated input form. Internally most of them are expanded. For example, MRS automatically rewrites *(IFF P Q)* as two statements, *(IF P Q)* and *(IF Q P)*. The exclusive-or operator, *XOR*, is an extension to the MRS vocabulary. Internally, the mutual exclusivity of the four kinds of speech acts is expressed by twelve rules, each of the form *(IF P_i (NOT P_j))*. The internal representation of the hierarchy uses about one hundred rules.

A few kinds of entities are used that are not shown in figures 5.1 and 5.2. These include numbers, strings (which function only as comments), and sequences of entities.

5.3.2 Slots and Fillers

The second group of rules concerns the slots provided for expressing relations among domain individuals. These rules are of the following kinds:

• Rules specifying what slots always have fillers. For example, every exchange has an *event1* and an *event2*:
IF   (exchange $x)
THEN   (and (exist y (event1 $x y))
                (exist z (event2 $x z)))

• Rules specifying for what slots the filler is unique. For example, an act has at most one agent:
IF   (and (agent $act $x)
                (not (= $x $y)))
THEN   (not (agent $act $y))

• Rules specifying what can be inferred about an entity by virtue of its filling a particular slot. For example, the *time* slot of a simple-event is filled by a time-point:
IF   (and (time $x $t) (simple-event $x))
THEN   (time-point $t)

• Rules specifying that if only one filler is known, it can be assumed to be unique. For example, an utterance or speech act might be addressed to more than one person, but if only one addressee ("beneficiary") is mentioned, a single addressee will be assumed. By combining standard and nonstandard forms of negation, the rule gives an example of default reasoning:
IF   (and (ben $act $x)
                (not (= $x $y))
                (thnot (ben $act $y)))
THEN   (not (ben $act $y))

Further predicates may be introduced as specializations or compositions of slot names. For example:

• Specialization of slot names
In an exchange that happens to be a sale, the *event2* slot may be referred to as the *payment* slot:
IF   (and (sale $x) (event2 $x $y))
THEN   (payment $x $y)

In an act that happens to be an offer, *offeror* and *offeree* are special names for the agent and beneficiary:

IF   (offer $o)
THEN   (IFF (offeror $o $a) (agent $o $a))

IF   (offer $o)
THEN   (IFF (offeree $o $b) (ben $o $b))

• Composition of slot names
The person who makes the payment in a sale is called the *customer*:

IF   (and (sale $x) (event2 $x $y))
THEN   (IFF (customer $x $z) (agent $y $z))

Many of the rules about the existence, uniqueness, and value of fillers exist only in comments. Existence rules have been used sparingly, because MRS does not handle existential quantifiers in a general enough way. In fact the current version of MRS (Genesereth et al. 1984; Russell 1985) has dropped them entirely. For the other kinds of rules, the limitations arise from the present program implementation. All rules about classes and slots are placed in a single MRS theory (overoptimistically named *Commonsense*). Without more knowledge about what rules should be tried when, the presence of very many rules would be computationally overwhelming. Making the implementation efficient in this respect has been given a low priority, however. The greater concern has been for expressive adequacy and for the interaction of these commonsense rules with legal knowledge.

5.3.3 Other Relations

The representation includes a few relation symbols that are not well viewed as expressing slot-filler relationships. Most of these are tested procedurally. They include the relation *follows*, which may hold between two time points; *member*, of a sequence and an object that may occur in it; *null*, of a sequence; and equality (written as "=") between two objects. For arithmetic, MRS provides the relations ">" (greater than) and "<" (less than), as well as function symbols such as "+" (plus) and "*" (times). In the version of MRS used, equality was also assumed to be a relation between numbers; this was generalized for the present program.

Finally, the program uses some declarative rules (also in the theory *Commonsense*) for reasoning symbolically about numbers it cannot evaluate. For example, if two symbols can be shown to designate the same time point, then the symbols for their values designate the same number:

```
IF        (and (time-point $t1) (value $t1 $n1)
              (time-point $t2) (value $t2 $n2)
              (= $t1 $t2))
THEN    (= $n1 $n2) .
```

Arithmetic may also have to be done symbolically:

```
IF        (and (> $z 0) (= $x $y))
THEN    (< $x (+ $y $z)).
```

5.4 Representing Reported Speech

5.4.1 New Kinds of Entities

The generalization hierarchy of figures 5.1 and 5.2 contains three kinds of objects that have not yet been discussed: speech acts, legal acts, and symbolic objects. This section discusses the representation of what has been said in terms of these kinds of entities.

Symbolic Objects and Speech Acts
A document is a physical object; representing what it says (or what the author of the document said) requires introducing symbolic objects. The initial link is made by way of the *content* slot of a document, which takes a sequence of sentences as filler.

A *sentence*, then, is the first kind of symbolic object. Sentences have several slots, the first of which is a *text* string serving only for the convenience of the human reader. More significant is the slot *prop-content*, which takes another kind of symbolic object, the *proposition* that the sentence literally expresses. *Proposition* is here used in Searle's sense (1969, pp. 22, 29), according to which the following sentences all have the same propositional content:

Sam smokes habitually.

Does Sam smoke habitually?

Sam, smoke habitually!

Accordingly, the propositional content of a sentence says less than needs to be said about it. Another slot, called *literal-force*, gives the illocutionary force that attaches literally to the sentence. The filler of the literal-force slot, in turn, is a new kind of act, a *speech-act*. The kinds of speech acts currently used in the program are assertions, yes-no-questions, requests, and declarations. The list is clearly incomplete, but it can be extended as needed. Assertions correspond roughly to the class Searle calls *representatives* or *assertives* and requests to Searle's *directives* (Searle 1975b). Questions could have been a subset of requests. Declarations are discussed in the next section.

To illustrate, suppose that on July 5 Buyer had wired Seller, "Did you receive my telegram?" The July 5 wire could then be represented (omitting tense) as follows:

(telegram Telegram2)
(content Telegram2 (seq S2))
(sentence S2)
(prop-content S2 (prop exist R (and (receive R)
                                (agent R Seller)
                                (obj R Telegram1)
                                (ben R Buyer))))

(literal-force S2 Q2)
(yes-no-question Q2)

Here *prop* is a function symbol that is taken to convert a logical formula to a term. The prop function also has other uses, apart from sentences and speech acts; one is to provide the object of a *need*, as mentioned earlier. For convenience in referring to propositions without repeating the entire embedded formula, often rather long, a proposition may also be given an atomic name, which is asserted to be equal to the function expression. The fourth formula above could thus have been written:

(prop-content S2 Prop2)
(= Prop2 (prop exist R (and (receive R)
                        (agent R Seller)
                        (obj R Telegram1)
                        (ben R Buyer))))

As a variation on the example of representing the contents of a document, suppose that Buyer had asked Seller, in conversation, "Did you receive my telegram?" The two lines above that refer to Telegram2 (together with the representation of the sending of the telegram) would then be replaced by the following:

(utter U2)
(agent U2 Buyer)
(ben U2 Seller)
(obj U2 (seq S2))

Thus the event gives rise to both an *utter*, which is considered an *ordinary-act*, and to at least one speech act for each sentence uttered. The distinction between utterances and speech acts corresponds approximately to Searle's distinction between utterance acts and illocutionary acts (1969, pp. 23–24).

However a sentence is produced, it may give rise to more than one speech act. The literal-force slot allows for one speech act, usually determined by syntactic mood. To provide for indirect speech acts, sentences also have a slot called *effective-force*. In the sample problem, the quoted sentence "Will you supply . . . ?" can then be represented as expressing both a question and, indirectly, a request:

(sentence S13)
(text S13 "Will you supply carload at $2.40 per cwt?")
(prop-content S13 Prop13)
(literal-force S13 Q13)
(yes-no-question Q13)
(effective-force S13 R13)
(request R13)

A fully detailed representation would show in addition that the agent and beneficiary of each speech act are the same as the agent and beneficiary of the underlying sending or uttering event. The object of each speech act is a proposition. For the speech act in the literal-force slot, this is the same as the propositional content of the sentence:

(obj Q13 Prop13)

For a speech act in the effective-force slot, the object is normally this same proposition but could be a different one.

Finally, the effective-force relation is one-to-many. It may turn out that "Will you supply carload at $2.40 per cwt?" has the effect not only of a request but also of an offer. The representation of a speech act resulting in an offer is discussed in the next section.

Speech Acts and Legal Acts

It would be convenient if all the assertions in a problem were statements of fact, from which statements of legal conclusions could be kept neatly separated. This is not the case. Besides the factual assertions about sending and receiving, the sample problem contains one assertion that in effect stipulates a legal conclusion, without stating the underlying facts on which the conclusion is based. This is Event6, which states: "Later on July 13 another party offered to sell Buyer a carload of salt for $2.30 per cwt."

Accordingly we introduce a new class of acts, called *legal-acts*, with subclasses that include offers, acceptances, and the like. Legal acts have the same slots as acts generally and may have others besides. Some slots are given specialized names; for instance, the agent and beneficiary of an offer can also be called the offeror and offeree. The object of an offer is always a proposition, in particular a proposition for an exchange. An offer also has terms, represented by another proposition that spells out the details of the proposed exchange. Event6 can then be represented (except for the details of its terms) as follows:

(offer O6)
(offeror O6 3rd-Party)
(offeree O6 Buyer)
(time O6 T6)
(obj O6 (prop exist Sell6 (exchange Sell6)))
(terms O6 Prop6)

Additional slots for an offer—not needed for the sentence quoted above—include its *embodiment* (for instance, a telegram) and an *act* by means of which the offer was made (for instance, sending the telegram). The distinction between an instrumental act, like sending or uttering, and a legal act, like offering or accepting, makes it easy to maintain the necessary distinction between the time the instrumental act is done and the time when it takes legal effect. To emphasize the distinction, the time slot of a legal-act may also be called the *effective-time*.

The classes legal-act, speech-act, and ordinary-act are understood to be disjoint. Since the central kinds of legal acts are offer and acceptance, this treatment may be surprising. For one thing, the speech act literature often mentions offering and accepting as speech acts. For another, the legal literature has often analyzed an offer as a conditional promise, with a return promise as one way of accepting.[5] And promising is a prototypical speech act (Searle 1969). Why not treat offers and acceptances simply as speech acts, then?

First, the legal literature is not based on a speech-act analysis. For example, what the law counts as offering, accepting, or promising can be performed nonlinguistically:

A, on passing a market, where he has an account, sees a box of apples marked "25 cts. each." A picks up an apple, holds it up so that a clerk of the establishment sees the act. The clerk nods, and A passes on. A has promised to pay twenty-five cents for the apple. (Restatement of Contracts, Second, sec. 4, illustration 2)

A, who is about to leave on a month's vacation, tells B that A will pay B $50 if B will paint A's porch while A is away. B says he may not have time, and A says B may decide after A leaves. If B begins the painting, there is an acceptance by performance which operates as a promise to complete the job. (Ibid., sec. 50, illustration 1)

Second, the speech act literature generally uses *offer* and *accept* in a nonlegal sense. Searle, for instance (1975a, p. 79), gives as examples of offering "Could I be of assistance?" and "Would you like some more wine?" Neither of these would be an offer in the legal sense because neither looks toward an exchange; the hearer is not expected to do anything in return for the assistance or the wine. Closer to the legal usage of *offer* is what Searle calls a *proposal*, with the example "Let's go to the movies tonight" (ibid., p. 61).[6] The relevant responses to a proposal are described as including "acceptance, rejection, counterproposal, further discussion, etc. (theory of speech acts)" (ibid., p. 63). Not discussed, however, is whether proposals are to be classified as commissives or directives or as belonging to some other category. In fact there are elements of both the commissive and the directive. Thus it seems likely that *propose*, as in "I propose we go to the movies tonight," would have to be recognized as one of the "some few verbs mark[ing] more than one illocutionary point" (Searle 1975b, p. 368). There is a similar difficulty in classifying *offer*, in the legal sense, as either a commissive or a directive.

The question remains how to represent a sentence that contains an explicit legal performative. The sample problem, for instance, might have said not "Another party offered to sell Buyer a carload of salt" but "Another party said to Buyer, 'I offer to sell you a carload of salt.'" Suppose that the embedded sentence were represented as a speech act of offering, with the propositional content that the third person will sell Buyer a carload of salt. The trouble here is that the speech act may fail; it may be, in Austin's phrase, an "act purported but void" (1962, p. 18). But with a representation that uses a speech act of offering, an inference from "there is an unsuccessful offer" to "there is an offer" would wrongly seem legitimate.

To prevent such inferences, the propositional content of the embedded sentence "I offer to sell you a carload of salt" (call it S6') is taken to be that an offer exists:

(sentence S6')
(text S6' "I offer to sell you a carload of salt")
(prop-content S6' Prop6')
(= Prop6'
    (prop exist O6 (and (offer O6)
                        (agent O6 3d-Person)
                        (ben O6 Buyer)
                        (obj O6 (prop exist Sell6 (exchange Sell6)))
                        (terms O6 Prop6))))

The literal force of the sentence is then taken to be a declaration:

(literal-force S6' Dec6)
(declaration Dec6)

This use of *declaration* as a kind of speech act is based on Searle (1975b). As Searle describes them, declarations are illocutionary acts in which

the state of affairs represented in the proposition expressed is realized or brought into existence by the illocutionary-force indicating device, cases where one brings a state of affairs into existence by declaring it to exist, cases where, so to speak, "saying makes it so." . . .
. . . It is the defining characteristic of this class that the successful performance of one of its members brings about the correspondence between the propositional content and reality; successful performance guarantees that the propositional content corresponds to the world: if I successfully perform the act of appointing you chairman, then you are chairman; if I successfully perform the act of nominating you as candidate, then you are a candidate; if I successfully perform the act of declaring a state of war, then war is on; if I successfully perform the act of marrying you, then you are married.
. . . .
Declarations bring about some alteration in the status or condition of the referred to object or objects solely in virtue of the fact that the declaration has been successfully performed. This feature of declarations distinguishes them from the other categories. (Searle 1975b, pp. 358–359)

The fit between Searle's description and sentences like "I offer
. . ." or "I accept . . ." depends on what is taken to be the propositional content of the sentence. If the propositional content of an offer
is that the speaker will do an action A1 and the hearer will do an
action A2, then "I offer . . ." is not a declaration. The actions do not
happen just by virtue of the offer. A successful offer does nonetheless
change the status of the people referred to. It gives the offeree a
power to accept and thereby to bind the offeror to a contract. Con-
struing the propositional content to reflect this fact, the definition of
declarations fits nicely. Accordingly, an utterance of the form "I offer
to do A1 if you will do A2" is given the following speech act representation: "I declare: there (hereby) exists an offer, by me to you,
according to which I will do A1 and you will do A2."

This representation also leaves room for separating the theory of
speech acts from the legal doctrine about what counts as a successful
act of offering or accepting. Searle observes that, in general, declarations involve "an extra-linguistic institution, a system of constitutive rules in addition to the constitutive rules of language, in order
that the declaration may be successfully performed. . . . It is only
given such institutions as the church, the law, private property, the
state, and a special position of the speaker and hearer within these
institutions that one can excommunicate, appoint, give and bequeath
one's possessions, or declare war" (Searle 1975b, p. 359). Here, of
course, the institution is the law and the extralinguistic rules are the
rules of contracts.

An interesting consequence of the representation is that it allows
declarations, like other speech acts, to be made indirectly. Consider
"I accept your offer," said after the deadline for acceptance, as stated
in the offer, has passed. The declaration is unsuccessful, but according to the legal rules it may still have effect as another offer. If the
program finds that it does have this effect, it creates an instance of
the legal act of offering. It could be asserted, at the same time, that
the sentence has the *effective-force* of a declaration that an offer
exists.

5.4.2 Other Issues

Paraphrasing Reported Sentences
The discussion so far leaves several questions open about how to
represent what the actors in a problem have said to one another.
First, the sentence-by-sentence representation of a document or an

utterance assumes that what was said consists of complete sentences. In the sample problem, this is not the case. Figure 5.4 compares the content of the documents exchanged, as stated or described in the English problem statement, with the initial paraphrase into separate sentences or sentence fragments.

In the second telegram (shown in the figure), there is an ambiguity in the phrases "immediate shipment" and "cash on delivery." They may be, like "carload of salt," a description of the offer, or they may be a description of the exchange the speaker contemplates. Legally the choice should be immaterial, and the second reading has been adopted.

In the purchase order considerable simplification has been made. The relationship between what is said and its placement, on the face or reverse of the form, has been omitted. As a partial substitute, the purchase order is represented as a kind of form-document, and a form-document is given slots for a fixed-part and an individualized-part. The title of the form, "Purchase Order," is assigned to the fixed part and is represented simply as a request that a purchase exist. Also in the fixed part is the simplified statement about when payment is due. There is no representation for the concept of filling in blanks on a form; instead a whole sentence is constructed as part of the individualized part.

Some of the parties' quoted words have also been omitted from the representation. As already noted, "immediately" is not represented. It could be translated as "within an interval of size <n>," but the appropriate size is too context dependent, and too uncertain even within a fixed context, to be specified in any useful way. "Payment shall not be due" is treated as if it said "payment shall not be made" (for the complications in representing "due," compare McCarty 1983). In the last telegram, the sentence "Ignore purchase order mailed earlier today" is omitted entirely (except as a string in a text slot), for want of a good analysis of "ignore." Morphologically the sentence seems to request someone not to know something. Even writers whose main focus is on knowledge and belief have not considered how that can be rendered sensibly.

Existential Expressions
Much of the content of the documents concerns future events and entities (some salt, some money) that have not been individuated. A consequence is that the propositional content of a sentence is usually

THE JULY 1 TELEGRAM, BUYER TO SELLER

Direct quotation of contents:
> "Have customers for salt and need carload immediately. Will you supply carload at $2.40 per cwt?"

Text slots: (text S11 "Have customers for salt")
(text S12 "Need carload immediately")
(text S13 "Will you supply carload at $2.40 per cwt.?")

THE JULY 12 TELEGRAM, SELLER TO BUYER

Direct quotation of contents:
> "Accept your offer carload of salt, immediate shipment, terms cash on delivery."

Text slots: (text S21 "Accept your offer carload of salt")
(text S22 "immediate shipment, terms cash on delivery")

THE JULY 13 PURCHASE ORDER, BUYER TO SELLER

Description of contents:
> ... Buyer sent ... its standard form "Purchase Order" to Seller. On the face of the form Buyer had written that it accepted "Seller's offer of July 12" and had written "One carload" and "$2.40 per cwt." in the appropriate spaces for quantity and price. Among numerous printed provisions on the reverse of the form was the following: "Unless otherwise stated on the face hereof, payment on all purchase orders shall not be due until 30 days following delivery." There was no statement on the face of the form regarding time of payment.

Text slots: (text S31 "Purchase Order")
(text S32 "[Buyer accepts] Seller's offer of July 12")
(text S33 "[On the face of the form Buyer had written 'One carload' and '$2.40 per cwt.' in the appropriate spaces for quantity and price.]")
(text S34 "[simplified] Payment on this purchase order shall not be due until 30 days following delivery.")

THE JULY 14 TELEGRAM, BUYER TO SELLER

Direct quotation of contents:
> "Ignore purchase order mailed earlier today; your offer of July 12 rejected."

Text slots: (text S41 "Ignore purchase order mailed earlier today")
(text S42 "Your offer of July 12 rejected")

Figure 5.4
Initial paraphrases

an existential proposition with several variables. As an example, consider the representation for a particular sale of a carload of salt, shown in figure 5.3. To convert this to a representation of the propositional content of a sentence like "Will you sell me a carload of salt at $2.40 per cwt?" we conjoin the formulas, prefix the existential quantifier and the appropriate variables, and convert the whole to a term with the function symbol *prop*. Figure 5.5 shows the result. The proposition representing the terms of an offer has this same form.

Referring Expressions
In figure 5.5 the only individual constants used were *Buyer*, *Seller*, and the numbers 1 and 2.40. In general, however, definite descriptions cannot be replaced by constants without seriously prejudicing the legal analysis. For instance, the second telegram says, "Accept your offer carload of salt." Since it is for the program to determine

```
(prop exist Sale1 Trans11 T11 Salt1 Vol1 Weight1 N1
             Trans12 T12 Money1 Dol1
             (and (sale Sale1)
                     (event1 Sale1 Trans11)
                     (transfer Trans11)
                         (agent Trans11 Seller)
                         (ben Trans11 Buyer)
                         (time Trans11 T11)
                         (obj Trans11 Salt1)
                             (salt Salt1)
                             (quantity Salt1 Vol1)
                                 (carloads Vol1)
                                 (number Vol1 1)
                             (quantity Salt1 Weight1)
                                 (cwt Weight1)
                                 (number Weight1 N1)
                     (event2 Sale1 Trans12)
                     (transfer Trans12)
                         (agent Trans12 Buyer)
                         (ben Trans12 Seller)
                         (time Trans12 T12)
                         (obj Trans12 Money1)
                             (money Money1)
                             (quantity Money1 Dol1)
                                 (dollars Dol1)
                                 (number Dol1 (* 2.40 N1)) ))
```

Figure 5.5
Representing the propositional content of a sentence proposing a sale of a carload of salt

whether such an offer exists, introducing a constant to stand for the offer would be inappropriate. Either the definite description "your offer carload of salt" or something corresponding to this description must be retained. The method used here is again to bring in an existential variable: "There is an offer, O, made by you for a carload of salt, and I accept O." For simplicity, nothing is said about the uniqueness of the offer. In the cases examined so far, any doubt concerns whether there is even one such object, not whether there may be several.

A complication now arises from the presence of speech acts other than assertions. Had the paraphrase above appeared literally in the telegram, the first clause would have been represented as an assertion and the second as a declaration. If the declaration succeeds, it brings an acceptance into existence but not an offer as well. To reflect the distinction, sentences are given a new slot, for a presupposition. The slot is filled by another proposition. Thus "Accept your offer carload of salt" is represented as shown in figure 5.6.

A convention adopted here is that the proposition expressed by a sentence may use as arguments unproblematical constants, such as *Buyer* and *Seller*; locally quantified variables; and free variables, provided these occur in (or are embedded in) a presupposition of the sentence and are there existentially quantified. A consequence of this treatment is that, since different speakers do not share variables, there is usually no direct test for whether they are talking about the same thing. One can only ask whether the match between the descriptions they use is good enough. For contract law problems, at least, this is exactly as it should be.

Coherence

A document or utterance is not just a collection of unrelated sentences. Connections between the sentences need to be expressed. Two devices for representing the connections have been used. Both are illustrated by the second telegram, whose first sentence ("Accept your offer carload of salt") the previous section discussed in detail. The second (incomplete) sentence is "immediate shipment, terms cash on delivery." Its representation is shown in figure 5.7.

The first connection between sentences is made at a very general level: one sentence tries to accept an offer for an exchange, and the next asserts something about this exchange. The problem is the scope of quantifiers, which are attached at the sentence level. The solution

```
(sentence S21)
(text S21 "Accept your offer carload of salt")
(presupposition S21 Prop2)          ; Presupposition: There is a offer,
                                    ; made by Buyer to Seller, for an
                                    ; exchange, Event1 of which is a
                                    ; transfer of a carload of salt.

(= Prop2 (prop exist Off2
              (and (offer Off2)
                   (agent Off2 Buyer)
                   (ben Off2 Seller)
                   (obj Off2 (prop exist Exch2 (exchange Exch2)))
                   (terms Off2 Prop2a))))

              (= Prop2a (prop exist Exch2 Trans21 Salt2 Vol2
                             (and (exchange Exch2)
                                  (event1 Exch2 Trans21)
                                  (transfer Trans21)
                                  (obj Trans21 Salt2)
                                  (salt Salt2)
                                  (quantity Salt2 Vol2)
                                  (carloads Vol2)
                                  (number Vol2 1)))))

(prop-content S21 Prop21)           ; Propositional content: There is
                                    ; an acceptance by Seller of the
                                    ; offer.

(= Prop21 (prop exist Acc21
               (and (acceptance Acc21)
                    (agent Acc21 Seller)
                    (obj Acc21 Off2))))

(literal-force S21 Dec21)
(declaration Dec21)
```

Figure 5.6
Representing "Accept your offer carload of salt"

```
(sentence S22)
(text S22 "immediate shipment, terms cash on delivery")

(presupposition S22 Prop2)    ; See Figure 5.6

(prop-content S22 Prop22)

(= Prop22 (prop exist Ship22 Imm22 Del22 Tdel22 Trans22 Mon22 T22
             (and
                (initiation Trans21 Ship22)
                  (ship Ship22)
                  (time Ship22 Imm22)
                (completion Trans21 Del22)
                  (deliver Del22)
                  (time Del22 Tdel22)

                (event2 Exch2 Trans22)
                  (transfer Trans22)
                  (obj Trans22 Mon22)
                  (money Mon22)
                  (time Trans22 T22)

                (= T22 Tdel22))))
(literal-force S22 A22)
(assertion A22)
```

Figure 5.7
Representing "immediate shipment, terms cash on delivery"

is a small extension in the use of presuppositions. Two sentences of a document may share a presupposition: here, the presupposition that an offer for an exchange exists. Similarly, although not necessary for the current example, one sentence may presuppose the propositional content of one or more preceding sentences. For the use of presuppositions in this way, the previous section has already made the needed exception to normal quantifier scoping, by allowing variables from a presupposition to occur free in the propositional content.

The second device for expressing coherence operates at a much more detailed level. Assuming that there is to be an exchange, *event1* of which is a transfer of salt, what do references to "shipment" and "delivery" have to do with it? To state the connection, two new slot names are used: a transfer may have an *initiation* and a *completion*, which are themselves transfers. A shipping event then fills the initiation slot; a delivery event the completion slot; and the time of payment is asserted to equal the time of delivery.

Indirect Discourse

In the sample problem, everything Buyer and Seller said was represented as a direct quotation. At the opposite extreme, the problem stated that "another party offered . . ." but left just what this third person said completely unknown. Of course there are intermediate cases. Some additional problems analyzed by the program (from Eisenberg 1982, p. 148) will illustrate:

1. A offers to sell B a parcel of land for $5,000. . . . Assume that B mailed a rejection to A, but later the same day B changed her mind and telegraphed an acceptance to A. The acceptance was in fact received by A prior to the rejection. Is there a contract?

2. On March 1, A wrote to B offering to sell her house for $40,000. The letter stated that the offer would remain in effect for only five days. . . . Assume B received the letter on March 3, and sent an acceptance letter on March 7. Has a contract been formed?

The question is how to represent assertions like "B mailed a rejection" (example 1) and "A wrote to B offering . . ." (example 2). In the first example, it is obvious that mailing a rejection cannot be reduced to performance of the legal act of rejecting; if it were, the question of whether the rejection took effect would not be askable. On the other hand, there is no indication that B said literally, "I reject your offer." In the present formalism, this leaves only one choice for "B mailed a rejection": B mailed a document containing some sentence whose effective-force was a declaration of rejection. The result is shown in figure 5.8.

A peculiar consequence of this representation is that a declaration can succeed as a speech act and still not effect the corresponding

```
(mail M2)
(obj M2 Doc2)
  (document Doc2)
  (content Doc2 C2)       ; C2 is a sequence of sentences,
  (member S2 C2)          ; whose texts are unknown. Some
  (effective-force S2 Dec2) ; sentence S2 in C2 amounts to a
  (declaration Dec2)      ; declaration of rejection of A's
  (obj Dec2 Prop2)        ; offer O1

  (= Prop2 (prop exist R2
              (and (rejection R2)
              (agent R2 B)
              (ben R2 A)
              (obj R2 O1)))))
```

Figure 5.8
Representing "B mailed a rejection"

```
(text S12 "[paraphrase] This offer will remain in effect for only 5
 days")

(presupposition S12 Prop121)     ; Presupposition: O1 has an effective
                                 ; time TO1 with value N1

(prop-content S12 Prop122)       ; Propositional content: O1 has an
                                 ; expiration time TO2, with value =
                                 ; N1 + 5.

(= Prop121 (prop exist TO1 N1
              (and (effective-time O1 TO1)
                   (value TO1 N1))))

(= Prop122 (prop exist TO2
              (and (expiration-time O1 TO2)
                   (value TO2 (+ N1 5)))))
```

Figure 5.9
Representing "This offer will remain in effect for only 5 days"

legal act. An alternative would be to provide a more refined set of relationships between sentences and speech acts than just literal-force and effective-force.

In example 2, "A wrote to B offering . . ." could be represented similarly to example 1. In the context of the whole problem, however, it seems preferable to interpret the sentence as stipulating that a legally effective offer was made. The word *wrote* and the second sentence, "The letter stated that . . . ," present some extra facts about this offer—for example, that its embodiment was a letter. One sentence of the letter can then be asserted to have, as its effective force, an assertion that the offer would remain in effect only five days.

The final difficulty is to represent the content of this assertion without building in an answer to the legal issue: when the five days start to run. This has been done as is shown in figure 5.9.

6 Representing and Using Legal Knowledge

Chapters 2 and 3 were concerned with some general problems about the nature of legal knowledge. Is it reasonable to express legal knowledge in the form of rules? How can rules be applicable to a case but not determinative of its outcome? How can the application of rules in past cases make a difference in their effect on a present case? How, if the rules do not dictate the outcome, can there be any run-of-the-mill cases in which, if the facts are undisputed, there is nothing left to argue about? This chapter describes a knowledge base, and a program that uses it, that try to capture these aspects of legal knowledge.

The program is divided into four levels of processing, each with its own knowledge source or sources. The top three levels have been implemented. The fourth, the argument of questions that lawyers could reasonably disagree on, will require a great deal of further research.

The first three levels of the program are devoted to identifying the hard questions. From an opposite viewpoint, the first three levels try to identify the easy questions and resolve them. In AI terms, the knowledge base fixes a priori some space of possible analyses of a case, and disposing of easy questions amounts to pruning this space as far as possible without eliminating any analyses that competent lawyers might find reasonable. Translating back to legal terms, in the particular context of law examination questions, the task corresponds closely to the kind of issue spotting that law students are expected to perform.

The distinction among different levels of the program is based on the kind of knowledge that each uses. There are three main kinds:

1. Knowledge of the basic legal categories available and the ways that elements of these categories may be ordered. This knowledge is

represented in an augmented transition network, the arcs of which are labeled "offer," "acceptance," and the like.

2. Knowledge of the definitions of the major concepts. The definitions are expressed as if-then rules.

3. Knowledge about undefined predicates used in the *if* parts of rules. This knowledge includes both the CSK rules described in section 5.3 and examples of situations that do or do not satisfy the predicate. Examples are stated in the same language used for representing problems, with some extensions.

After an introductory section on the legal scope of the knowledge base, this chapter takes up these kinds of knowledge in the order listed. Section 6.2 describes the transition network, a simplified version of which was shown in section 1.3.1. Included here are some additions to common network formalisms. One is the attachment of a logical formula to each network arc; the formula serves to coordinate the use of a network with the use of declarative rules. Another addition is the concept of a pending state transition, which allows for a kind of wait-and-see policy in deciding what arc should be followed.

Sections 6.3 and 6.4 concern the representation and use of legal rules. In section 6.3 the focus is on relationships among the rules. Discussed here are competing rules, which reflect disagreement among lawyers about which of several rules is better and also knowledge on the part of any one lawyer that such disagreements exist. Also discussed in section 6.3 is the question, when several (noncompeting) rules are available, of how to decide which ones are worth trying and which not.

In section 6.4 the focus shifts to the individual rule and, in particular, its list of antecedents. There is more to an antecedent than a logical formula. Its other main element, called a *predicate expansion,* is described. This section also discusses some additions to the usual syntax of a logical formula. The central part of the section considers at some length the problem of translating English statements of legal rules into a reasonable formalism at all.

The key element of a predicate expansion is its place for attaching, not a procedure for testing the predicate, but some examples of situations satisfying and not satisfying the predicate. Section 6.5 is devoted to examples: what they mean, how they are stated, and how they are used.

6.1 Scope of the Knowledge Base

The main legal concepts to be represented are the concepts of offer and acceptance. Also needed are closely related concepts such as counteroffer, revocation, and rejection of an offer. For an initial, nontechnical description of the kinds of situations to be dealt with, a good source is Corbin:

An offer is an expression by one party of his assent to certain definite terms, provided that the other party involved in the bargaining transaction will likewise express his assent to the identically same terms. An offer looks forward to an agreement—to mutual expressions of assent.
. . . .
. . . [W]hat change in legal relations is brought about by the making of an offer? It is believed that the best short description of this change is that an offer creates a power of acceptance in the offeree. It will not be disputed by any one that, after an offer is made, a voluntary expression of assent by the offeree is all that is necessary to create what we call contract. (Corbin 1963, sec. 11; footnote omitted)

There are more kinds of offers and acceptances, though, than one might suspect from this quotation. The present knowledge base does not cover all of them. Two of the more significant limitations are the following:

1. Currently only offers made to a particular individual are covered. Omitted, for example, are offers made by an advertisement to the general public, such as an offer of a reward.[1]

2. Currently only acceptances given verbally are covered. These are an important subclass of acceptances, but they are only a subclass. Adapting the traditional terminology, we might call this subclass *acceptance-by-verbal-promise*. Its place in a fuller taxonomy would be as shown here:[2]

- Acceptance
  - Acceptance-by-promise
    - Acceptance-by-verbal-promise
    - Acceptance-by-nonverbal-promise
  - Acceptance-by-performance
  - Acceptance-by-silence

Readers should also be aware of the place of offer and acceptance rules within the law concerning formation of contracts. According to the Restatement, the formation of a contract ordinarily requires a bargain in which there is a "manifestation of mutual assent" to an exchange; and such a manifestation "ordinarily takes the form of an offer or proposal by one party followed by an acceptance by the other party or parties" (Restatement of Contracts, Second, secs. 17, 22).

Although offer and acceptance are thus the typical route to a contract, there are other ways of showing that a contract exists. The offer and acceptance method looks to the formation of a bargain between the parties. There are also contracts without bargains (see Restatement of Contracts, Second, sec. 17), but the present knowledge base does not deal with them.

Similarly, finding an offer and an acceptance is not sufficient to establish that a contract exists. The most important further requirement is consideration. The concepts of consideration and bargain both involve an exchange between the parties, but a bargain without consideration is possible. An example is a situation in which the parties agree that one will pay for the other's doing something that the latter already has a clear legal duty to do. (See Restatement of Contracts, Second, sec. 73.)

Various other doctrines may prevent the formation of a contract or its enforcement. The topics they cover include some kinds of mistakes and misunderstandings, the legal capacity of the parties, the requirement that some contracts must be evidenced by a writing, and defenses such as fraud, duress, and illegality.

In restricting the coverage of the program to the law of offer and acceptance, we focus on the topic that has traditionally been treated first in the study of contract law. But it should be borne in mind that inferring a contract from an offer and an acceptance depends on the assumption that none of the other doctrines would interfere with that conclusion.

Finally, the law concerning formation of contracts has been modified in some respects by state-by-state enactment of a Uniform Commercial Code. Article 2 of the UCC deals with contracts for the sale of goods; contracts of other kinds are still left to case law and sources like the Restatement. The knowledge base contains no representation of the statutory rules as such. The gist of many UCC rules, however, has also been incorporated in the second Restatement of Contracts, and there is an attempt to reflect them to this extent.

6.2 A Transition Network for the Sequence of Legal Events

To give a program some knowledge of law, a first step is to provide it with some legal vocabulary. This first step says nothing about the meanings of vocabulary items. It is at the level of saying that there are such categories as offer and acceptance, or assault and battery, or murder and manslaughter—not at the level of defining them.

For the law concerning formation of contracts, there is a further step short of definition. Because words like *offer* and *acceptance* look to the description of events over time, it is possible to give a grammar for how such events can be ordered. The formalism used for specifying the grammar is a transition network, to which some extra features have been added. The latter make the network comparable to an *augmented transition network* (ATN), as used in parsing English sentences (Winograd 1983, chap. 5). An initial, simplified version of the network was shown in figure 1.2. The actual network is described in this section.

In the development of the network, a question arises almost immediately concerning the relationship between the events of an input problem and paths through the network. A problem describes a sequence of events in the world; a path through the network describes a sequence of legal events. Is there to be an event-for-event correspondence between the two sequences? It is the need to create an appropriate correspondence that accounts for most of the added arcs in the actual network, as shown in figures 6.1 and 6.2, beyond the version of figure 1.2.

6.2.1 States and Arcs

The states of the network are elements of a space of possible legal relations, and its arcs are possible ways of moving among them. Currently the states are as follows:

State 0: No relevant legal relations exist.

State 1: One or more offers are pending; the offeree has the power to accept.

State 2: A contract exists.

State 12: A contract exists, and a proposal to modify it is pending.

The formalism could be extended to a broader class of contracts problems by adding states such as the following:

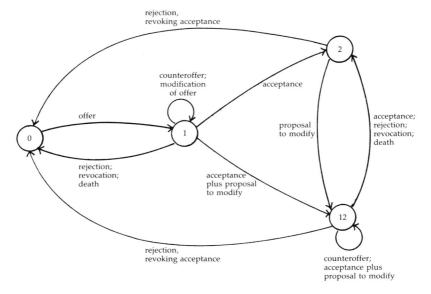

Figure 6.1
Transition network for offer and acceptance problems

State 3:   The contract is discharged (for instance, by having been fully executed).

State 4:   A breach of the contract has occurred.

All states of the network are in effect final states. That is, a sequence of events may or may not lead to the formation of a contract; either outcome is equally "grammatical," and in either case the legal characterizations of the events are to be given.

The arcs of the network correspond to events that can change the legal relations between the parties. The basic arcs, shown in figure 1.2, are labeled "offer," "acceptance," "counteroffer," "rejection," "revocation," and "death." The last four of these arcs are based on section 36(1) of the Restatement:

An offeree's power of acceptance may be terminated by
(a) rejection or counter-offer by the offeree, or
(b) lapse of time, or
(c) revocation by the offeror, or
(d) death or incapacity of the offeror or offeree. (Restatement of Contracts, Second, sec. 36(1))

There is no arc for lapse of time; the passage of time is not an event and is handled separately. Neither is there an arc for deprivation of

FROM STATE 0 (no relevant legal relations):

New state
1	Offer
0	Ineffective event

FROM STATE 1 (offer pending):

New state
2	Acceptance (by offeree)
12	Acceptance plus proposal to modify (i.e., the offeree accepts and proposes to modify the contract so formed)
1	Counteroffer (by offeree)
0	Rejection (by offeree)
0	Revocation (by offeror)
1	Modification of offer (by offeror)
0	Death (of either party)
1	Ineffective event

FROM STATE 2 (contract exists):

New state
12	Proposal to modify (either party proposes to modify the existing contract)
0	Rejection, revoking acceptance (i.e., the previous offeree revokes his acceptance, rejecting the offer instead)
2	Ineffective event

FROM STATE 12 (contract exists and proposal to modify it is pending):

New state
2	Acceptance (of proposal to modify)
12	Acceptance plus proposal to modify (i.e., acceptance of the pending proposal to modify, with a further proposal to modify)
12	Counteroffer (to the proposal to modify)
2	Rejection (of proposal to modify)
0	Rejection, revoking acceptance (i.e., the previous offeree revokes the acceptance that formed the contract, rejects the previously pending offer instead, and by implication revokes or rejects the proposal to modify)
2	Revocation (of proposal to modify)
2	Death (of either party)
12	Ineffective event

Figure 6.2
Arcs of the transition network

legal capacity to enter a contract, because this topic raises a number of issues that are complicated but tangential and unlikely to arise in many problems.

The actual network has more than twenty arcs. Several facts account for the additions.

Ineffective events First, some events described in a problem may have no legal effect at all. Accordingly every state also has an arc labeled "ineffective event," which loops to the same state. (For readability, these are omitted from figure 6.1.) If all other arcs fail, the ineffective-event arc is taken by default. With this addition, each event of an input sequence corresponds to at least one event in the output sequence.

Proposals to modify an existing contract The list of arcs suggested so far is legally incomplete. After a contract has been formed, one of the parties may propose to modify it, and this proposal can itself be an offer. Thus there are a new arc labeled "proposal to modify"; a new combination state, state 12, in which a contract exists and a proposal to modify it is pending; and a new subclass of offers, called *offer-to-modify*, as shown in figure 5.1.

Acceptance proposing to modify the resulting contract It is also possible for a proposal to modify a contract to be made by the same act that creates the contract itself.[3] One possibility would be to let such an act cause two arcs to be followed: first the "acceptance" arc from state 1 to state 2, and then the "proposal-to-modify" arc from state 2 to state 12. The decision here, however, was to add a new arc, "acceptance plus proposal to modify," that goes directly from state 1 to state 12. This approach means that in general one input event is mapped to at most one output event.[4]

Responses to a proposal to modify In state 12, the possible responses to an offer to modify the contract are the same as responses to an initial offer. This fact accounts for much of the complexity of the network. Most of the added arcs, however, represent unlikely situations and are included only for completeness.

Modification of offer Another addition to the list of arcs concerns the possible actions of an offeror in state 1, before a contract has been formed. So far, only revoking the offer has been allowed for; but of course the offeror can also modify the offer. This accounts for the arc labeled "modification of offer" and for another subclass of offers, *modification-of-offer*, as shown in figure 5.1. Again a corresponding arc could be added in state 12—this time to allow for modification of an offer for modification of a contract. Completeness has not been carried to this extreme.

Revoking acceptance of offer   Finally, there is a question whether acceptance of an offer can ever be undone. Typically an acceptance sent by mail is effective on dispatch; on finding such an acceptance, it is appropriate to make an immediate transition to state 2. Suppose, however, that before the acceptance reaches the offeror, the offeree changes his mind and tries, say by telephone, to reject the offer. According to the Restatement an acceptance, once effective, can never be revoked;[5] but there is some case authority that can be read to the contrary.[6] To leave room for this possibility (without saying which rule will be followed), the network is given arcs, from state 2 or state 12 to state 0, labeled "rejection, revoking acceptance."

6.2.2 Additions to the Network

Registers
To keep track of what has been found so far, the transition network uses two registers, *Pending-offers* and *Current-bargain*. The first register is nonempty in state 1; the second, in state 2; and both are nonempty in state 12. Although several offers are permitted to be pending at the same time, this situation is comparatively rare,[7] and full handling of concurrent offers has not been provided.

The content of a register is just a symbol or a list of symbols. For example, *Pending-offers* might contain a list like *(O0041)*. Other facts about the offer *O0041* are retrieved by lookup in the data base. The name *Current-bargain*, rather than *Current-contract*, is used as a reminder that not all the requirements for a contract are covered in the present knowledge base. A *bargain* is taken to have only two slots, an *offer-part* and an *acceptance-part*, which are filled by an *offer* and an *acceptance*, respectively.

The registers record the only statements about a problem whose truth value is time dependent. If a problem said, for example, that

Buyer needed a carload of salt, the translation would be (in part and subject to the choice of names for constants) that *Need1* is an instance of *need* and that the *time* of *Need1* is *Time-interval-1*. These assertions are true before, during, and after the interval.

Arc Predicates, Conditions, and Actions
In the usual formulation of augmented transition networks, an arc has a label to be matched in the input, some conditions to be tested if a match is found, and some actions to be taken if the conditions are satisfied and the arc is therefore followed.

In the present application, arc labels, such as "offer," are used only as identifiers. For direct matching of the arc to the input, there is an arc predicate, such as *(offer $o)*.[8] The predicate is an MRS expression and is tested using the lookup and inference procedures that are part of that language. In general the match will succeed only if the problem stipulates that there is an instance of the corresponding legal concept.

The conditions and actions of an arc are implemented as Lisp procedures. The arc conditions are designed primarily for testing registers, for the purpose of ensuring appropriate bindings of the variables in the arc predicate. The arc actions may test and set registers, look up formulas in the data base, and assert new formulas.

Pending Transitions
If a problem consisted entirely of stipulations—for example, that A made an offer to B, B made a counteroffer, and A accepted the counteroffer—it would be processed using only the mechanisms already described. But such problems are trivial. The next stage of reasoning is to apply the legal rules defining the concepts of offer, counteroffer, acceptance, and the like. These rules have one aspect, however, that requires another addition to the network.

Most offer and acceptance problems do not involve face-to-face conversation. Instead communication is usually by mail or by telegram. Favorite problems involve situations like these:

• A makes B an offer. B sends a letter saying he accepts. The letter is lost in the mail. Is there a contract?

• A makes B an offer. B sends a letter saying he accepts, and at about the same time A sends a letter saying he revokes the offer. Is there a contract?

• A makes B an offer. B sends a letter saying he rejects the offer but then changes his mind and sends a letter of acceptance. Is there a contract?

The test problem of section 1.2.1 is like the third situation but with the order of rejection and acceptance reversed.

Analyzing such problems requires knowing both the defaults for when the various kinds of communications take effect and the kinds of circumstances that can override the defaults. The defaults are that an acceptance is effective when sent and the others when received.[9] Similarly an offer must be communicated to be acted upon. Consequently it often cannot be known at the time of sending whether an explicit performative like "I revoke" succeeds. It may be necessary to look at more than one event to decide whether a particular arc of the network can be followed.

This much is normal in the use of an ATN. In parsing, one must also look at more than one element of the input sequence to decide whether an arc like NP (noun phrase) can be followed. The solution is to create a subnetwork for parsing noun phrases, within which the words of the input can again be taken one by one. But subnetworks are not useful for the legal task. The words of a noun phrase are expected to be contiguous. The events of sending a document and receiving it need not be. Any number of other events may intervene, and how these other events are characterized may affect the characterization of an eventual receipt. A comparable problem in parsing seems to be the handling of discontinuous constituents (see Winograd 1983, pp. 135–136), where the grammar permits not only "He *called up* his mother" and "He *called* his mother *up*" but also, with an entirely different structure (here recall the movie *Up the Down Staircase*), "He *called* the down staircase up." A further complication, in the legal transition network, is that if a false choice is made at some point in the processing, there is no ready way of recognizing the error later. In standard transition networks, the need to backtrack is signaled by an inability to finish processing the input or by finishing in a nonfinal state. In the legal network, since all states are final and have "ineffective event" loops, the signal is not available. Accordingly one would like to avoid the need for backup altogether.

To take care of the difficulty, the idea of a *pending transition* is introduced. If an act is found to qualify as creating an instance of some legal category in all respects except that the communication has not been completed, a pending transition can be recorded. Subsequent events may (1) cause additional pending transitions to be recorded, (2) cause an immediate transition that defeats those pending, or (3) confirm one pending transition, defeating any others. A simple example is given in the next section.

6.2.3 Using the ATN

The top-level loop of the program takes as input a data structure called a *context*, which is a node of the upper-level output graph (see figure 1.1). The context contains a list of events still to be accounted for and a representation of the current configuration of the ATN. Accessible from the context are the program's findings about any events that have already been processed; these findings have led to the current state of the ATN. The task is now to characterize the next event. The program begins by accessing the ATN configuration.

Checking for Confirmation of Any Pending Transitions
The first question is whether any transitions are pending. A pending transition can have been entered, and can later be confirmed, only as a result of applying a legal rule. The details of the rules are deferred to the next section.

By the time any pending transitions have been dealt with, the program has begun to construct the detailed tree representing its analysis of the current event. Typically the detailed tree now contains only a root node; branching is possible, however, as in the case of a hard question about whether a pending transition is confirmed. Different branches may also have led to essentially the same conclusion about whether a transition was confirmed. For this reason, the tree may be pruned before going on to step two.

At the beginning of step two, each leaf of the detailed tree gives the current ATN configuration. If there were no pending transitions or if none was confirmed along the path to a particular leaf, the configuration there is the same as in the surrounding context. Figure 6.3 shows a simplified version of the data structures at this point. The situation illustrated is the very beginning of a problem, where necessarily no transitions were pending.

Root of upper-level tree (context tree):

```
ID:                   C0002
Conclusions so far: NIL
ATN:
     State: 0
     Regs: empty
     Pending transitions: NIL
Unprocessed events: (*EVENT1* *EVENT2* *EVENT3*)
Tree:                 T0004
```

Detailed tree for Event 1 in context C0002:

```
ID:           T0004
New findings: NIL
New-atn-record:
     State: 0
     Regs: empty
     Pending transitions: NIL
Children:     NIL
```

Figure 6.3
Data structures initialized to test what new state transition best characterizes the current event

Checking for Possible New Transitions

The second step is to ask what new transition best accounts for the current event. In the problems considered so far, there are no examples of events that both confirm a pending transition and cause a nontrivial new transition, but constructing an example is not difficult. Consider the following event sequence:

1. Joe wrote to Bill as follows: . . .

2. Bill received Joe's letter.

3. Bill replied to Joe's letter as follows: . . .

Here the first event might cause a pending transition to be recorded; the second might confirm the transition; and the third might cause some new transition (or the entry of another pending transition). The problem statement might, however, have omitted mention of the receiving event, leaving it to be inferred from "Bill replied . . ." It is to allow room for such inferences that the program considers each event with respect to both pending transitions and new ones.

To decide what new transition is appropriate, the program first retrieves the outgoing arcs from the current ATN state. The arcs appear in a fixed order, with the ineffective-event arc always last. Next the program checks whether the event being analyzed is stipulated to be a legal event of an appropriate type—that is, for any available arc (other than "ineffective event"), whether the arc predicate can be directly matched in the input. If so, the arc conditions are tested. These check, for example, on finding a stipulated acceptance, that the object is a pending offer; on finding a death, they check that the subject is either the offeror or offeree of the pending offer. If the conditions also succeed, the state transition is made, and the analysis of the current event is considered complete. Branching in the analysis tree as the result of a stipulation is possible but extremely unlikely.

Usually the event being analyzed does not stipulate a legal characterization, and the first cycle through the available arcs therefore fails. At this stage a second cycle begins, this time using any legal rules saying how an arc predicate can be shown to be satisfied. During the application of rules, the analysis tree is likely to branch. Returned to the ATN level are a list of its leaves, each showing the analysis along one path and indicating one of the following results:

1. Success: Some nontrivial arc is to be taken immediately, provided the arc conditions succeed.

2. Failure: The ineffective-event arc is to be taken.

3. Provisional success: A pending transition is to be recorded. The arc will be taken if the transition is ever confirmed and the arc conditions then succeed.

6.3 Legal Rules: Organization and Structure

The arcs and states of the ATN represent one kind of legal rules: those setting up the basic legal categories and saying how their instances may be ordered. A second class of rules, described in this section, deals with how to recognize instances of these categories. These rules in general are declarative and definitional.

In the present knowledge base, there are rules for each category used as an arc label, except for the labels "death" and "ineffective event." Thus there are one or more rules for how to find each of the following:

Offer
Acceptance
Acceptance plus proposal to modify
Counteroffer
Rejection
Revocation
Modification of offer
Proposal to modify
Rejection, revoking acceptance

In addition, concepts used in the definitions may themselves be defined by further rules. The present knowledge base contains about twenty rules.

These rules are much larger and more complex objects than the rules usually used in expert systems. Most of them correspond to broad legal concepts. Stating just one or a few rules per concept is a common legal way of chunking knowledge. The knowledge itself involves intricacies and subtleties that are typically presented as commentary on the rules. The point can be seen from the Restatement of Contracts, which tries to state systematically and explain all of the concepts of general contract law. In the Restatement, the definitions of offer and acceptance take one sentence each. Explaining what the definitions mean (and what they do not mean), however, requires a whole Restatement chapter of over a hundred pages.

6.3.1 Competing and Complementary Rule Sets

When more than one rule leads to the same conclusion, the relationship among the rules needs to be precisely specified. Two different relationships may hold: the rules are either *complementary*, in that they provide alternate ways of reaching the conclusion, or they are *competing*, reflecting an unsettled state of the law where rules have been formulated but there is disagreement about what the rule should be. The choice between competing rules, if it affects the legal characterization of an event, is always considered to raise a hard legal question. If any rules in the set are tried, all must be. Complementary rules, on the other hand, are tried until one succeeds completely (that is, without raising any hard questions) or the set has been exhausted.

To implement these distinctions, rules are organized into *rule sets*, which are marked as complementary or competing. The present knowledge base contains two pairs of competing rules and three pairs of complementary rules (the other sets are singletons). The competing rule sets concern the concepts of (1) a rejection of an offer that revokes one's previous acceptance and (2) a simultaneous acceptance and proposal to modify the contract. With respect to the first, the disagreement was mentioned in section 6.2.1. Here one rule, labeled the Restatement rule, says in effect that there is no such thing as a rejection revoking an acceptance. The other, labeled as the rule of *Dick v. United States*, permits such a rejection provided, most importantly, that communication of the acceptance has not been completed.

With respect to an acceptance plus proposal to modify, the question again is whether such an event is possible. The old rule, which is not so old that one can ignore it entirely, said no. Either the offeree agreed to exactly what the offeror proposed, or there was no acceptance at all.[10] The newer rule allows for some discrepancies between offer and acceptance, with the changes to be taken as proposals to modify the contract.[11]

In both cases of competing rules, it thus turns out that the disagreement is not over how to define the concept but whether the concept should be available at all—that is, about whether the ATN should contain the corresponding arcs. Although this kind of disagreement was not expected to be the main use of competing rules, the formalism is able to accommodate it. For each pair of competing rules, the rule that says "there's no such thing" is simply given a single antecedent, *Nil*, which always fails.

Of the complementary rule sets in the knowledge base, one deals with alternate ways of showing that a counteroffer exists. The first rule describes a situation in which the offeree proposes different terms for the contemplated exchange; the second, a situation in which the offeree tries to accept the original offer but his acceptance is in some way defective—for instance, by being late.[12] The other complementary rules concern alternate ways of deciding whether an acceptance is timely and alternate ways of deciding when the time period for acceptance begins to run.

6.3.2 Rule Format

The rules in the knowledge base have more structure than simple if-then statements. In fact four data structures are used: the *rule set,* the *rule,* the *antecedent,* and the *predicate-expansion.* The last two will be described in section 6.4.1.

The important fields of a rule set include a list of member rules, the complementary-competing indicator, and the common conclusion, or *consequent,* of the member rules. Usually the conclusion is an existential statement: if certain conditions are true, then (for example) an offer exists. As implemented, the consequent of a rule set is a Lisp function that takes a list of bindings, generates new symbols as needed for any objects (such as an offer) just found to exist, enters assertions about such objects in the data base, and returns the (possibly) augmented binding list.

The rules in a set do not have to have identical consequents. To provide for this, each rule also has its own consequent function, which invokes the common one but may do more. The two counter-offer rules provide an example. The general consequent, which the rules have in common, is that a counteroffer exists and that certain of its slots, such as the *offeror* and *offeree,* are filled in the way determined during application of the rule. But the *terms* of the counteroffer depend on which rule succeeded. For a defective acceptance, they are the same as the terms of the original offer. For the change-of-terms situation, they are like those of the original offer but with changed terms substituted and new terms added.

For an individual rule, then, the parts include a list of *antecedents,* which must all be true for the rule to succeed, and a consequent function (referred to as the *when-tested* field of the rule) to be called if the rule does succeed.

A rule may also have some nonstandard fields. One is a list of *secondary antecedents;* each such antecedent is tested before the consequent is executed, and the result is recorded, but it cannot cause the rule to fail. A secondary antecedent, like any other, may raise a hard question causing the analysis tree to branch, with alternate results recorded at the leaves. Its function is to anticipate hard questions that might otherwise arise later, in a place where they would be more awkward to deal with. Thus the consequent of a rule can contain conditional actions guaranteed to be testable using only data-base lookup. As an example, the most common secondary antecedent calls for deciding whether the means of transmitting a message qualifies as "instantaneous communication."[13] An utterance does qualify; sending a letter does not; and for many other possibilities (including electronic mail) the answer is unknown, so that the tree would branch with opposite assumptions at the new nodes. In a rule that matches the predicate of an ATN arc, the *when-tested* function can now use the recorded result in deciding whether to report that the rule has succeeded provisionally (meaning that a pending transition will be entered) or completely (meaning that the transition can be made immediately, provided the arc conditions also succeed).

If a rule succeeds only provisionally, then some future event is needed to confirm its success. Accordingly rules may contain another field, called *to-confirm*. This is again a list of antecedents, these to be tested in deciding whether a pending transition based on the rules is confirmed. A typical antecedent here checks whether communication of the relevant message counts as completed by the current event—for instance, by the appropriate person's receiving the appropriate document. Finally, a rule with a *to-confirm* field also has a field *when-confirmed*. This last is again a function that invokes the general consequent of the rule set.

6.3.3 Deciding What Rules to Try

Consider the situation in which the program is ready to use legal rules in order to select a new state transition. At this point it is focused on an event, in the context of a particular interpretation of any previous events. The effect of the event on any pending transitions has been determined, with the result that a detailed analysis tree for the event has been started. The program's focus also includes a leaf of this analysis tree, which shows the current configuration of the ATN. (See figure 6.3.) The outgoing arcs from the current ATN state have been retrieved. Finally, it has been found that none of those arcs can be taken on the basis that the event contains a legal stipulation matching the arc predicate. A second cycle through the arcs now begins. Each arc may have an attached set of legal rules. In what order should the arcs be tried?

If the ATN happens to be in state 0, arc ordering is not a problem because there are only two arcs to choose from: if there is no offer, the event is ineffective. From the other states, however, the prospect of blind search through the arcs is unappealing, and not only on computational grounds. If arcs (and therefore rule sets) can be tried in arbitrary order, it appears that the rules must be written in a way lawyers would find most unnatural. Consider, for example, the following sentence from the Restatement: "A purported acceptance conditional on a change of terms commonly has the effect of a counter-offer" (Restatement of Contracts, Second, sec. 70, comment a). Clearly there is some control knowledge here: that the counter-offer rules should not be tried unless the acceptance rules have already been tried and have failed in a particular way.

Two steps are taken to make this kind of knowledge available. First, each leaf node of a detailed analysis tree is given a field called *untried-arcs*. Initially it is set to the entire list of outgoing arcs from the current state of the ATN. Whenever an arc fails, the next arc to try will be selected from this list, which is local to a particular path through the analysis tree and is carried downward as the tree grows. Second, each antecedent of a rule is provided with two fields that can hold lists of arc labels; these are called *eliminate-on-failure* and *eliminate-on-success*. With this information available, testing an antecedent of a rule can result in pruning the list of arcs remaining to be tried in the event that the current arc eventually fails.

The result is to superimpose on the rules a discrimination-net-like structure. As an example, suppose the ATN is in state 1 so that the initial list of arcs to be tried is as follows:

Acceptance
Acceptance plus proposal to modify
Counteroffer
Rejection
Revocation
Modification of offer
Death
Ineffective event

In the course of trying the acceptance rule, this list will be pruned substantially. Assuming, for simplicity, that only one offer is pending, the first antecedents of the rule identify it. The next antecedents require finding in the current event a report of an act that produces a manifestation with some symbolic content. If the acceptance rule fails at this stage, then all the remaining arcs except "death" and "ineffective event" will fail too; if it so far succeeds, it seems safe to conclude that the current event is not a death. Next the rule checks whether the agent of the act is the offeree. If not, the arcs for an acceptance plus proposal to modify, a counteroffer, and a rejection will fail for the same reason. If the act is done by the offeree, one can conclude immediately that it will not turn out to be a revocation or modification of the offer. Further opportunities for pruning occur later in the acceptance rule and in connection with several other rules as well.

The presence of pruning opportunities reflects the fact that similar antecedents may occur in several different rules. For example, the rules for acceptance and acceptance plus proposal to modify are identical in their first ten antecedents. This commonality permits another kind of saving. If the acceptance rule failed at any of these antecedents, the acceptance-plus-proposal-to-modify arc would be eliminated. Therefore if the second arc is actually tried, these antecedents must have succeeded already. So they need not be tried again at all. As one moves further down the list of arcs to try, the number of common elements decreases, but the same technique is still available. This measure, like the ability to eliminate whole arcs from consideration, is extremely helpful in avoiding duplicate computations and producing more natural-looking results than one would get otherwise.

6.4 Legal Rules: Antecedents

The Restatement definitions of offer and acceptance are as follows:

Section 24. Offer Defined.
An offer is the manifestation of willingness to enter into a bargain, so made as to justify another person in understanding that his assent to that bargain is invited and will conclude it.

Section 50. Acceptance of Offer Defined. . . .
(1) Acceptance of an offer is a manifestation of assent to the terms thereof made by the offeree in a manner invited or required by the offer. (Restatement of Contracts, Second, 1981)

This section considers the problem of translating such rules into a testable form—that is, into a suitable list of antecedents.

6.4.1 Elements of an Antecedent

The central element of the data structure for an antecedent is the logical *formula* to be tested, given in a syntax acceptable to MRS. There may also be a list of arcs to eliminate if the test fails and another to eliminate if it succeeds. Finally, there may be a *predicate expansion* for each predicate occurring in the formula. A formula can contain more than one predicate since the logical connectives *and*, *or*, and *if* (as well as *not*) are permitted.

The idea of a predicate expansion is the following. First, any predicate occurring in the formula is taken to be a technical term. This treatment permits, but does not require, the usage of the predicate in a legal rule to differ from any nontechnical usage known to the program (as represented in the CSK rules). Further, the technical meaning of a predicate may be different in different rules. The purpose is to avoid an error of mechanical jurisprudence that AI programs are likely to repeat: the error of assuming that legal predicates correspond to single concepts and mean the same thing wherever in the rules they occur. The predicate expansion gets around the assumption by permitting information about meaning to be local rather than global.

A predicate expansion may identify a rule set by which the predicate is to be tested; it may contain examples of things satisfying the predicate, or negative examples, or both; or it may be empty. Examples and their use will be discussed in section 6.5. Currently it is assumed that rules and examples will not both be present in the same predicate expansion, but a further developed program would undoubtedly need to allow for both.

A predicate expansion might be empty for any of several reasons. First, some predicates are tested procedurally, rather than by the application of declarative rules or by matching to declaratively stated examples. The distinctively legal predicates of this sort mostly deal with descriptions of a proposed exchange. For example, given one description in an offer and another description in a potential acceptance, it is easier to write a matching procedure than to state declaratively when the match would succeed. Such procedures are invoked by way of the general procedural attachment facility in MRS. As a result the corresponding predicates currently have global definitions. It would be easy to attach procedures locally instead by way of the predicate expansion, but so far this has not been necessary.

An empty predicate expansion also may be used where database lookup and possibly deduction using the CSK rules are sufficient to test the formula. For example, if a rule calls for finding an act and the program has no knowledge about any special legal meaning of *act*, the formula will be tested using just the abstraction hierarchy. Or when, in the course of looking for an acceptance, the rule calls for identifying the offeror and offeree of the pending offer, empty expansions for *offeror* and *offeree* have the effect that the program only retrieves assertions made when the consequent of the offer rule was executed.

Finally, an empty predicate expansion may simply represent a situation where more knowledge needs to be filled in. This is not to say that a nonempty expansion means the knowledge is all there.

The testing of any formula is reduced to the testing of one or more atomic formulas, each with its own predicate expansion. The first step is to invoke MRS's proof procedures on the atomic formula. If no special procedure is attached, the proof attempt consists of database lookup and backward chaining of simple if-then rules, such as the CSK rules of section 5.3. A similar attempt to have MRS establish the negation of the formula also may be made. In the case of an empty predicate expansion, this is all that can be done.

If, on the basis of whatever knowledge the program does have, it cannot establish either an atomic formula or its negation, two kinds of action are possible. Which is taken depends on whether the formula contains free variables. If there are no free variables, the conclusion is that there is a hard question, resulting in the addition of new nodes to the analysis tree. This can occur, for example, when the program tries to test whether a particular act, which may turn out to be an act of accepting a particular offer, was done within a reasonable time. In the second case, the atomic formula does contain a free variable, that is, a variable whose scope is the entire rule and for which no binding has been found. Here the conclusion, reached by default, is that the formula is false. Thus, if a rule calls for finding that an act was done and the event under examination says nothing but "it rained," the existence of an act will not be deemed a hard question. There is much room here for empirical study of when default conclusions should be made, and when not, for a program to give a reasonable simulation of human reasoning in law.

During the testing of an atomic formula, one other situation causes branching of the analysis tree. This arises when the formula contains free variables and more than one set of bindings can be found. In this case a new node is created for each binding list. For example, it is often necessary to test whether a particular sequence of sentences (such as the content of a document) says something about an exchange. The document might discuss several exchanges. If so, the

analysis tree will branch, and testing of the rule containing the antecedent will continue separately at each new node.

Because of these possibilities for branching, the procedure that
tests an antecedent takes as input a leaf of the analysis tree being
constructed and returns a list of leaves, the fringe of a subtree rooted
at the input node. If the antecedent has not caused branching, the
list will contain just the input node itself.

6.4.2 Decomposing English Rules

Given the general structure of antecedents, the next question is how
English definitions of legal concepts and other legal rules can be
rewritten as a list of antecedents. This section will review one rule
in some detail to indicate the approach used. The treatment is informal, emphasizing what needs to be said rather than exactly how to
say it. The following section will give the grammar of the formulas
used in the antecedents.

The Offer Rule

The rule that most closely follows the Restatement's version is the
definition of an offer. The corresponding rule in the program has
nine antecedents, one of which invokes another rule, and two secondary antecedents. Figure 6.4 gives an English statement of what
the antecedents should test for and includes the Restatement version
for comparison. In the figure, underlined words correspond to variables that will be bound if the antecedent succeeds. The following
paragraphs comment on the antecedents.

Antecedents 1-3   In the Restatement rule, "an offer is the manifestation . . ." presents the common ambiguity between the act or process
of manifesting something and the object that results. The program's
rule uses the second reading, looking separately for the requisite act
and its agent. The kinds of acts expected to be covered include
sending a document and uttering something. The symbolic content
will be a sequence of sentences.

Antecedent 4   The Restatement's definition of *bargain* is circular; *exchange* is the undefined word in the circle. (See section 2.3.2 above.)
The serious question concerning the antecedent is what it means to
say that the sentences of the manifestation are about an exchange.

RESTATEMENT OF CONTRACTS, SECOND, SECTION 24:

An offer is the manifestation of willingness to enter into a bargain, so made as to justify another person in understanding that his assent to that bargain is invited and will conclude it.

ANTECEDENTS OF THE OFFER RULE:

1. There is an <u>act</u>,

2. which produces a <u>manifestation</u> with some symbolic <u>content</u>, and

3. which is done by some agent, the prospective <u>offeror</u>.

4. The content of the manifestation is, in some appropriate sense, about an <u>exchange</u>.

5. Whatever description of the exchange is given will constitute its <u>terms</u>.

6. The prospective offeror would be a party to the described exchange.

7. By means of the content of the manifestation, the prospective offeror has performed some <u>speech act</u> indicating that he may be willing to enter the described exchange.

8. The terms of the exchange are specified with reasonable certainty.

9. In light of the content of the manifestation, the prospective offeror invites acceptance, by a prospective <u>offeree</u>, of a proposal for the exchange.

   a. The manifestation is addressed to a prospective <u>offeree</u>, and

   b. this person is invited to furnish consideration in the exchange.

   c. The prospective offeror is apparently ready to be bound to a contract for the exchange, without doing anything more.

   Secondary antecedents:

10. Is this a situation involving essentially instantaneous communication of the offer?

11. Does the offer specify any particular form of acceptance? If so, call its provisions about the form the <u>acceptance-terms</u>.

Figure 6.4
Definitions of an offer

Certainly *about* does not mean *denotes:* if the offer rule is to succeed, the exchange should be a future event, which has not yet been individuated. Neither is it necessary that the word *exchange* be used: "I'll sell you my car" should obviously turn out to be about an exchange. The sense of *about* used here is the following. Suppose that every proposition that is part of the symbolic content is true, including presupposed propositions and embedded propositions. In such a world, is there an entity that can be found to be an exchange? If so, the antecedent will succeed, and the variable standing for the exchange will be bound to whatever name the exchange is called by in that hypothetical world. For instance, if the current event states (in effect)

(Joe said *(exist Sale1 (sale Sale1))*),

the hypothetical world will contain

(sale Sale1).

Here the existential variable, *Sale1*, has become a Skolem constant, and the variable standing for the exchange will be bound to that symbol.

Antecedent 5   With respect to the terms of a proposed exchange, the Restatement contains a particularly vague definition: "A term of a promise or agreement is that portion of the intention or assent manifested which relates to a particular matter" (Restatement of Contracts, Second, sec. 5(1)). In the program, finding the described terms of an exchange is one of the tasks done procedurally. Consider the description of an exchange given in figure 5.3, modified to describe a proposed exchange as shown in figure 5.5. The hypothetical world created to test antecedent 4 contains exactly the formulas of figure 5.3. For antecedent 5 the procedure starts with the name of the exchange (already bound to *Sale1*) and views it as, roughly, the root of a directed graph whose edges are slot names and whose nodes are fillers. Finding the terms is then a matter of traversing the graph. In figure 5.3 all the formulas shown would be included in the terms.

Antecedent 6   Suppose the current event says, "Joe said, 'My brother sold his house.'" Nothing in antecedents 1 through 5 would cause the offer rule to fail. Antecedent 6 does, but it leaves "Joe said, 'I

sold my house'" still in the running. That will be excluded by antecedent 7.

Antecedent 7   Antecedent 7, which checks whether the speaker "may
be willing to enter" the exchange, serves a screening function. Only
if an event is not screened out here as a possible offer does it become
worthwhile to test the Restatement's further qualification, that the
manifestation be "so made as to justify another person in understanding that his assent to that bargain is invited and will conclude it."

There are some significant points as to how an antecedent like 7
should be tested. It does not necessarily call for trying to reconstruct
the speaker's actual state of mind. For most cases the legally relevant
knowledge is knowledge about kinds of action that an observer
would normally interpret as indicating willingness to do something
and, in particular, as indicating willingness to enter a bargain.[14]

To make such knowledge available, one possible approach would
be to try to catalog all the kinds of action that might do, analyze the
results, and incorporate the analysis into the initial knowledge base
of the program. Such an approach seems not only infeasible but
mistaken. Its tendency would be to impose on the rule a sharper
meaning than its framers originally gave it. What is needed instead
is to allow the meaning to develop over time, as new cases arise and
force its clarification.

A better approach is to take "manifestation of willingness" or "may
be willing" initially as a mere gesture, in the general direction of
some kinds of situations where we would all agree that the actor has
indicated willingness to do something. The gesture is represented,
in the logical formula of the antecedent, by a predicate that serves
as a mere placeholder—here, *may-be-willing-to-enter*. The situation
types are represented as examples, not as rules; this was the proposal
of chapter 3. By using examples, one may be able to avoid prejudging
situations that the examples do not cover; one can add to the knowledge base gradually as new examples turn up; and one can retain
the possibility of analyzing the accumulated store of examples at
some later time, to see whether they reveal a common structure. If
so, it might prove appropriate to restate some of the example-based
knowledge in the form of rules. But this would be an a posteriori
analysis, and it could be expected to cover many data that one might
not have thought up in advance.

Antecedent 8   Antecedent 8, regarding the certainty with which the exchange is described, does not have a direct counterpart in the Restatement's definition of an offer. It reflects a subsequent Restatement section: "Even though a manifestation of intention is intended to be understood as an offer, it cannot be accepted so as to form a contract unless the terms of the contract are reasonably certain" (Restatement of Contracts, Second, sec. 33(1), Certainty). The entire Restatement treatment of certainty takes two sections (secs. 33–34) and about nine pages of commentary.

In the program, the predicate used is *reasonably-certain*, another placeholder. Because of the great variety of terms that one might need to specify in different contracting situations, the program is never able to conclude that it is clear that the terms have been stated certainly enough. It may sometimes be able to say that the terms are clearly too uncertain.

Antecedent 9   The test of antecedent 9, which corresponds to the "so made" clause of the Restatement definition, has three subparts, grouped together in a separate rule. It is not until this rule is invoked that the offeree is identified.

Parts a and b of the rule require an offeree to have appropriate roles with respect to the offeror's act of manifesting something and to the exchange being proposed. The reason for breaking off a separate rule here is the same reason, apparently, that the Restatement uses the indefinite phrase, "so made as to justify *another person* . . ." Not every offer is directed to an individual already identified; alternative rules could be added to cover these cases.[15] Some knowledge of agency relationships would also be needed for full coverage of the possibilities.

For the predicate of antecedent 9, *invites-acceptance*, to be satisfied, one more condition must be met. According to part c of the subrule, the prospective offeror must appear ready to be bound to a contract without doing anything more. Again, *apparently-ready-to-be-bound* is a placeholder for examples. While the program is usually unable to judge whether someone seems ready to be bound, there is one situation in which it can do so. An utterance early in a conversation may fail to qualify as an offer; the ATN therefore remains in state 0; and there is a reply such as "I accept your offer." In trying to construe

the reply as itself an offer, the program does find the speaker ready
to be bound.

Antecedents 10 and 11   With antecedent 9, the offer rule succeeds.
There are still two secondary antecedents that check facts about the
offer in advance of the time they will be needed. For both of these,
as for many other antecedents, much more knowledge could be filled
in about the kinds of situations they are meant to cover.

The Acceptance Rule
The offer rule is typical of most of the declarative legal rules used by
the program. There is one addition, however, that first arises in
connection with the acceptance rule. The acceptance rule begins by
retrieving facts about the pending offer. It checks for an act producing
a manifestation, as in the offer rule; that the act is done by the offeree;
and that it is addressed to the offeror. Again as in the offer rule, it
checks whether the content of the manifestation has something to
do with an exchange, and it finds any terms describing the exchange.
Next, the terms just found (possibly nil) must be matched against
the terms of the offer. The match is done procedurally. It produces
both a new set of terms, constructed from the terms on which the
offer and the reply are taken to agree, and a set of mismatches. The
new element arises from the fact that a mismatch need not be fatal
to finding an acceptance.

Ordinarily any terms stated in an acceptance should match the
terms of the offer exactly, but there are exceptions. Accordingly the
acceptance rule next tries to explain any mismatches. One kind of
explanation is that what the acceptance said was already implied by
the offer, perhaps with the help of an additional premise supplied
by usage or by law. In the sample problem of section 1.2.1, such an
additional premise is needed to explain an apparent mismatch between the first two telegrams: the first is silent about the time of
payment, while the second calls for cash on delivery. The Restatement provides a version of the premise needed: "Valid contracts are
often made which do not specify the time for performance. Where
the contract calls for a single performance such as the rendering of
a service or the delivery of goods, the time for performance is a
'reasonable time.' . . . *Payment is due when the service is completed or
the goods received*" (Restatement of Contracts, Second, sec. 33, com-

ment d; emphasis added). In the program, the rule used states in effect:

In an exchange,
> if $time1 is the time of payment and
>> $time2 is the time of completion of the transfer of goods,
>> and if $time1 and $time2 cannot be shown to be different,

then $time1 = $time2.

The rule is written as an MRS expression, similar in form to the rules of the abstraction hierarchy:

```
(if (and (exchange $x)
         (event1 $x $tr)
         (event2 $x $pay)
         (time $pay $time1)
         (completion $tr $del)
         (time $del $time2)
         (thnot (not (= $time1 $time2))))
    (= $time1 $time2))
```

Such rules are stored in an MRS theory called *Interpretation-rules*, which is activated only for the purpose of explaining mismatches between two sets of terms.

The remaining requirements for success of the acceptance rule are as follows: the offeree must, by some speech act, express willingness to enter the exchange; communication of the offer must have been completed (so that the speech act can be understood as a response to the offer); the act of purported acceptance must be timely; the act must meet any requirements for acceptance that were stated in the offer; the offer must be one that permits acceptance by a speech act (rather than requiring some nonverbal performance); and the speech act of acceptance must be unconditional. The last three of these requirements have been only partially implemented.

6.4.3 The Grammar of Formulas

The formulas of antecedents may use, but are not restricted to, the lexicon that is available for stating problems. The antecedents use a number of predicates, like *may-be-willing-to-enter* and *apparently-ready-to-be-bound*, about which the program's only knowledge is expressed in the form of examples. Unlike the predicates that occur in the abstraction hierarchy, they are not forced into a class name-slot name format and therefore are not restricted to taking only one or two arguments. They can be thought of as stating constraints on objects that do have a place in the hierarchy. Only if these extra constraints hold will an instance of a legal act be found.

Logical Connectives
The formulas of an antecedent need not be atomic; the connectives *and*, *or*, *not*, and *if* are all available. The connective *and* might have been omitted since the conjuncts could also be written as separate antecedents. It does, however, permit formulas to be grouped in a visually convenient way. In the acceptance rule, for example, the first antecedent looks up the symbol used for the pending offer (to which to bind the variable $o), and the second antecedent retrieves the fillers of its slots:

```
(and (offeree $o $offeree)
     (offeror $o $offeror)
     (obj $o (prop exist $x1 (exchange $x1)))
     (terms $o $tname1))
```

A good example of the use of *or* and *not* occurs in the rule that recognizes a defective acceptance as a counteroffer. The following antecedent looks for any of five ways in which the acceptance rule might have failed:[16]

```
(or (not (communication-completed $o $offeree))
    (requires-acceptance-by-performance $o $req)
    (conditional $sa-acc)
    (not (timely $act))
    (not (meets-any-requirements-in-offer $act)))
```

Because the analysis tree may branch as the result of testing an atomic formula, the connectives require a corresponding implementation. In figure 6.5, suppose that the antecedent to be tested at node 1 has the form

```
(or (P A)
    (not (Q B)))
```

and that the truth of both *(P A)* and *(Q B)* turn out to be hard questions. Then a list of three nodes will be returned, two (nodes 2

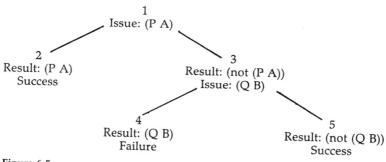

Figure 6.5
Branching possibilities for an antecedent of the form *(or (P A) (not (Q B)))*

and 5 of the figure) marked as analyses on which the antecedent succeeds and the third (node 4 of the figure) marked as a failure. To test *(not (Q B))*, the program simply tests *(Q B)* and then, at each node returned, reverses the marked findings of success and failure.

The use of *if* as a connective serves a special purpose. Ordinarily, when a formula contains an unbound variable and more than one binding can be found, the program investigates each binding separately, in parallel parts of the analysis tree. Sometimes, however, the treatment is not appropriate, and what is needed instead is to consider the bindings serially. For example, the need arises in trying to explain any mismatches between the terms of an offer and the terms stated in a potential acceptance. The connective *if*, as implemented, forces serial consideration of any bindings for the variable $mis:

(if (member $mis <mismatches>)
    (explainable $mis <terms that matched>))

Thus, supposing there are two mismatches of which the first is clearly explainable and the second clearly not, the following findings would both be entered at the same node of the analysis tree:

(explainable <mismatch-1> <terms that matched>)
(not (explainable <mismatch-2> <terms that matched>))

In effect, $mis is a variable local to the antecedent.

Metalevel Operators
There is an important extension to the syntax of formulas, beyond the elements discussed so far. Any such formula may be prefixed by a *metalevel operator* that specifies which parts of the data base are to

be used in testing the formula. These operators can be used to say any of the following:

1. In testing the formula, do not use the data base at all. Instead check a register of the ATN.

2. In testing the formula, use only those assertions belonging to certain MRS theories.

3. In testing the formula, use the assertions belonging to certain MRS theories in addition to any others that would normally be available.

These statements use the operators *currently*, *in*, and *using*, respectively.

Expressions using the operators have the following formats:

(currently <formula>)
(in <world list> <formula>)
(using <world list> <formula>)

For a *currently* expression, the predicate of <*formula*> determines which register is to be tested. In the others, <*world list*> is a Lisp expression that evaluates to a list of MRS theories, or worlds. The <*formula*> is assumed not to contain another metalevel operator.

The metalevel operators serve two rather different purposes: to prevent irrelevant inferences and to enable reasoning from propositions that have not been asserted to be true, especially propositions representing what the actors in a problem have said. To make these uses clear, it will be necessary to review the structure of MRS theories that the program uses and the default set of theories that are active when an antecedent is tested.

MRS Theories   The assertions of an input problem are partitioned into several MRS theories, named *Event1, Event2, . . . , Event-n.* There may also be a theory, here called *Time-independent-facts,* to hold input assertions not naturally associated with any particular event. When the processing of an event has been completed, the program's findings about that event are asserted in one or more newly created MRS theories; the number of theories is the same as the number of distinct legal interpretations of the event. Each such theory is asserted to include the event itself. For example, the processing of the first two events in a problem might lead to the structure of theories shown in figure 6.6. Here *"I"* in a theory name is mnemonic for "interpretation."

When processing of the third event begins, the top-level output graph might then have the structure shown in figure 6.7. This is in fact a more detailed version of the output graph of figure 1.1.

During the processing of an event at a node of the top-level graph (called a *context*), an additional structure of MRS theories is created. The detailed tree that records the processing is made up of nodes called *trace records;* each trace record has a field called *new-findings,* which holds the name of another MRS theory. Inclusion relations among these theories mirror the structure of the tree. Therefore, activating the theory at the trace record currently in focus makes available all the findings so far about the event being analyzed, along one path of the detailed tree.

An antecedent of a rule is always tested at a trace record in a context. Normally the MRS theories whose contents are accessible during testing are (1) the event being analyzed, (2) the findings about this event so far (from the new-findings field of the trace record), (3) conclusions about previous events, including the events themselves

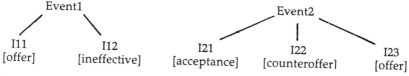

Figure 6.6
Structure of MRS theories showing alternate interpretations of events that have been fully processed

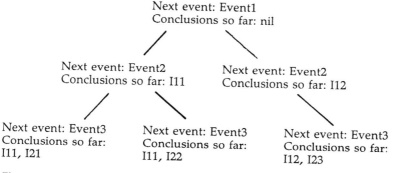

Figure 6.7
Relation of upper-level output graph to MRS theory structure

(from the context), and (4) any *general theories*—namely, the CSK rules of section 5.3 and, if present, *Time-independent-facts*. These are the defaults, which may be changed by a metalevel operator.

Reducing Irrelevant Inferences   For the reduction of irrelevant inferences, the appropriate operators are *in* and *currently*. At the beginning of the acceptance rule, for example, the first step is to determine what offer (or offers) are available to be accepted:

(currently (pending-offer $o)).

This antecedent could have been written as simply

(offer $o),

without the *currently* and with an empty predicate expansion. If the acceptance rule were to succeed on any offer found, a condition on the ATN arc would still check for the presence of this offer in the *Pending-offers* register. After a series of offers and counteroffers, however, this version would result in pointless effort to find acceptances of offers long since terminated.

   Besides the fact that *currently* causes testing of a register, antecedents using it are treated specially in one other way. Ordinarily when an antecedent succeeds (other than by direct lookup in the data base), the instantiated formula is asserted as part of the new findings of the current trace record. A formula containing *currently*, however, may become false later and therefore is never asserted. This distinguishes such formulas from those using the general MRS form of procedural attachment.

   Once the relevant offer is determined, no restrictions on retrieval are needed to ensure finding only the right bindings for the fillers of its slots. Thus the second antecedent of the acceptance rule is this:

(and (offeree $o $offeree)
     (offeror $o $offeror)
     (obj $o (prop exist $x1 (exchange $x1)))
     (terms $o $tname1))

This antecedent provides an example of the need for access to conclusions about previous events in the course of interpreting the current one.

   For another antecedent, present in most rules, it is important that previous events and their interpretations not be available for retrieval. To find an instance of any legal event, the program must find that some act was performed. Here, only acts reported in the current event are relevant:

(in (list current-fact 'commonsense) (act $act)).

The inclusion of *Commonsense* in the list of theories makes the abstraction hierarchy available for recognizing, for instance, that *(send Send1)* does report an act.

Using Propositions Hypothetically   The second use for the metalevel operators was to make available the content of propositions not asserted to be true. The operators serving this purpose are *in* and *using*. As a simple example, suppose the current event of the problem states that Joe said to Bill, "I want to buy your car." Asserted as facts will be that Joe uttered a sequence of sentences to Bill, say *(seq S1)*; that *S1* is a sentence with a certain presupposition and propositional content, say *P1* and *P2*, respectively; and furthermore that Joe asserted *P2*. Not asserted are the propositions themselves, which would be roughly as follows:

P1 (presupposition): Bill has a car—call it *Car-1*.

P2 (propositional content): Joe wants *P3*.

P3 (embedded proposition): Joe buys *Car-1*.

Any of these propositions might be false, but obviously they have to be used in deciding whether Joe said something about an exchange and whether he indicated willingness to enter such an exchange.

One way to use the propositions would be to inspect them as data structures. To be able to derive general results, however, one would also need to recode a great deal of built-in knowledge as declarative knowledge about operations on data structures—for example, as in Weyhrauch's metatheorems (1980).

A simpler method, and the one used here, is to assert the propositions hypothetically—that is, in their own MRS theories—and to see what follows from them. For anything of interest to follow, it is usually necessary for the theory containing the CSK rules to be active at the same time.

To carry out this approach, several functions are defined that may be used in the *<world list>* argument of an *in* or *using* expression. The basic function is called *world*:

(world <proposition>)

returns the name of an MRS theory in which just <*proposition*> has been asserted. Usually <*proposition*> is an existential statement. In that case the existential variables become, in the new theory, Skolem constants. When the theory is created, the function also asserts, in a special theory called *Vars*, a statement of the form

(skolem <variable name> <theory name>)

for each such variable. Variables from different utterances are assumed to be named disjointly.

The other functions, which build on *world*, take an argument that is either a sentence or a sequence of sentences. In the example in which Joe said he wanted to buy Bill's car, suppose *(world P1) = W1*, *(world P2) = W2*, and *(world P3) = W3*. Then

(worlds 'S1)

would return the list *(W1 W2)*, that is, the theories for the propositional content and the presupposition of the sentence. Similarly,

(embedded-worlds 'S1)

would return *(W1 W2 W3)*, that is, a list including worlds for any embedded propositions. Also available is *cworlds: (cworlds 'S1) = (commonsense W1 W2)*. Finally, for a sequence of sentences, these functions return the union of their values for the member sentences.

The function *embedded-worlds* must obviously be used with caution. In the example, it gives rise to a hypothetical world in which Joe buys Bill's car. That world would also arise if Joe had said, "I doubt that I will buy your car." One appropriate use for the function is in deciding whether something has been said about an exchange. This antecedent is written as follows. Here *$c* has been bound to a sequence of sentences, such as the content of a document:

(in (cons 'commonsense (embedded-worlds '$c)) (exchange $x)) .

Finally, consider antecedents such as the one that tests whether the speaker *may-be-willing-to-enter* the exchange. Such predicates are mere placeholders for examples. There is a question of what hypothetical worlds should be made available for matching to the examples. It turns out, because of the need to consider embedded propositions in context (such as a context of "I want" versus "I doubt"), that the question is better answered from within the examples themselves. Thus antecedents like *may-be-willing-to-enter* are written without a metalevel operator:

(may-be-willing-to-enter $offeror $x $c $sa).

6.5 Examples

6.5.1 Functions of Examples

The third level of legal knowledge in the program, below the network level and the rule level, is knowledge of examples of the kinds of things that are and are not covered by the predicates used in the rules.

The background for using examples was given in chapter 3. It was proposed there that a fully developed legal reasoning program would need to be able to use examples in two different forms. For one form, there would be a one-to-one correspondence between examples and court decisions. These would be large and complicated data structures in which could be sought similarities and dissimilarities with the case at hand. Such comparisons could yield arguments about how to resolve the issues in the case at hand; rarely would they yield definite conclusions. A procedure for seeking such comparisons should clearly be used selectively. One does not want elaborate analogical arguments about points that humans would find entirely obvious.

The second form of examples is aimed at providing heuristic knowledge sufficient to resolve the points that are obvious while leaving open those issues worth further attention. Only this second form is used in the current program. These examples are relatively simple patterns to be matched in the facts of the case at hand.

The patterns, or examples, function in two different ways. First, where the other knowledge available to the program is insufficient to derive either that a formula is true or that it is false, they help fill in gaps in this other knowledge. There are both legal and common-sense perspectives on this function.

The predicate used in the formula may be a legal abstraction, whose boundaries of application are unknown. Here the examples represent, at the level of commonplace fact, some of the central kinds of things the predicate has been used to cover. Adding new examples can change the performance of the program, as, for humans, reading more cases can add to their understanding of a legal concept, and as the decision of new cases can make more definite the meaning of the concept.

The predicates used in legal rules are not purely legal abstractions. The rules are, after all, written in English, and most words or phrases in the rules are not defined by further legal rules. The program, though, may have no knowledge at all of the predicate as an ordinary nontechnical word or phrase; only for predicates occurring in the CSK rules does it have any information whatever. From this viewpoint, the examples fill in commonsense knowledge otherwise missing. So long as legal knowledge and ordinary usage are not in disagreement, there is no conflict between these two perspectives.

The second function of examples is to allow for disagreement between technical meaning and ordinary meaning and also for disagreement among the cases on the technical meaning. An algorithm for using the examples, in a way that accommodates both of these functions, was sketched in section 3.4.2. It will be described in more detail below. First, however, some concrete illustrations of the examples will be shown.

6.5.2 Some Examples of Examples

The examples used in the program are for the most part rather simple. Consider the antecedent of the offer rule that checks whether an act, already found, produces a manifestation with some symbolic content. The formula is written as

(produces-manifestation-with-content $act $m $c)

and has two attached examples:

(and (send $act) (obj $act $m) (content $m $c))
(and (utter $act) (utter $m) (= $act $m) (obj $act $c)) .

If the first example succeeds, the manifestation *$m* will be bound to a document; this happens because, in the generalization hierarchy, only documents have a *content* slot. In the second example, the manifestation is taken to be the utterance act itself; *$c* will be the sequence of sentences that was the object of the utterance.

Somewhat more complicated are the examples for whether a prospective *$offeror*, by means of the symbolic content *$c*, has indicated willingness to enter the exchange $x. The formula of this antecedent is written

(may-be-willing-to-enter $offeror $x $c $sa) .

The fourth argument is to be bound to a speech act, and the examples give some of the kinds of speech acts that will do. They include requesting that the exchange take place, asserting that one wants the exchange to take place, and declaring that one accepts an offer for the exchange. These examples are written as shown in figure 6.8. Many more could be added.

Each of the examples in the figure begins by looking for a speech act of the appropriate class; then identifies the sentence *$s* by which the speech act was performed; and checks, by *(member $s $c)*, that the sentence is part of the current utterance or document. In the first

```
(and                        ; $offeror requests that $x exist
 (request $sa)
 (or (literal-force $s $sa) (effective-force $s $sa))
 (member $s $c)
 (obj $sa $prop)
 (world $prop $w)
 (true (skolem $x $w) vars))

(and                        ; $offeror asserts that he wants $x to
 (assertion $sa)            ; exist
 (or (literal-force $s $sa) (effective-force $s $sa))
 (member $s $c)
 (cworlds $s $ws)
 (true (and (want $w)
            (subj $w $offeror)
            (obj $w $prop2))
       $ws)
 (world $prop $w2)
 (true (skolem $x $w2) vars))

(and                        ; $offeror declares that he accepts an
 (declaration $sa)          ; offer for $x
 (or (literal-force $s $sa) (effective-force $s $sa))
 (member $s $c)
 (cworlds $s $ws)
 (true (and (acceptance $acc)
            (agent $acc $offeror)
            (obj $acc $o2)
            (obj $o2 (prop exist $x (exchange $x))))
       $ws))
```

Figure 6.8
Examples of indicating willingness to enter an exchange

example, covering a request, the next question is what was requested. The object of any request will be a proposition describing some state of affairs; *(obj $sa $prop)* retrieves this proposition. The last two clauses check that the symbol to which the exchange *$x* is bound is an existential variable in this proposition—that is, that whatever the speech act requests, it includes a request that the exchange exist. In the final clause of the example, the form *(true <formula> <theory>)* is an MRS expression, which causes *<theory>* to become the only accessible MRS theory while *<formula>* is being tested. The operator *true*, in MRS, is thus similar to the operator *in* of section 6.4.3; *true*, however, does not evaluate the argument *<theory>*.

The second and third examples in figure 6.8 illustrate the handling of embedded propositions. The second example, rather than looking for a request that *(exist <x> . . .)*, looks instead for an assertion that *(<offeror> wants (exist <x> . . .))*. Here the want, *$w*, must be found at the outermost propositional level, and the symbol to which *$x* is bound must be an existential variable in the proposition representing what is wanted. In the third example, the exact form of the embedded proposition is known because, by convention, the object of an offer always has the form *(prop exist <x> (exchange <x>))*.

The role of negative examples in the program varies according to whether, in the antecedent to which the examples are attached, the formula has been fully instantiated at the time it is tested. Consider the secondary antecedent of the offer rule that checks whether the situation is one of instantaneous communication:

(instantaneous-communication $m) .

Here *$m* is guaranteed to be bound already, and the types of possible bindings are known. In this situation, the examples serve to partition the possible bindings:

(ex (utter $m))
(negex (telegram $m) (document $m)).[17]

The partitioning does not have to be complete. If the program were given knowledge about the possibility of hand delivering a document, the negative examples could be revised to require finding a *send* of the document. This would leave previous results intact while leaving open the question whether, when a document is hand delivered, its contents are legally considered to have been communicated at the moment of delivery.

Examples can also check more complicated properties of the existing bindings. One interesting negative example concerns the requirement in the acceptance rule that a purported acceptance not be conditional. That is, if someone says, "I accept your offer for X provided you will also do Y and Z," he has not accepted the offer at all. The program is not yet able to recognize that an acceptance is conditional, but it has one negative example enabling it to say that some purported acceptances are not conditional. The assumption is that the internal representation of a conditional acceptance would have to use the symbol *if* or *or* (the latter since *(if P Q)* could also be written *(or (not P) Q)*). The negative example in effect inspects the entire content of the utterance or document and succeeds if no such symbol can be found. This is one of the few situations where it is more useful to inspect the form of propositions than to assert them hypothetically.

Negative examples also can be used with antecedents that may still contain unbound variables. The examples may or may not produce a binding. In either case, what does this mean? A good illustration comes from the rule that looks for a proposal to modify a contract. As in the offer rule, there is an antecedent that checks whether the speaker (*$offeror*) has, by what he said (*$c*), performed some speech act (*$sa*) indicating willingness to enter the exchange (*$x*). In one problem, what the speaker had actually said at this point amounted to, "I reject your offer."

As the rule is written, the antecedent has a negative example causing *$sa* to be bound to the speech act of declaring a rejection. Because the example is negative, the antecedent fails. In failing, it has identified a near miss.

The rule could have been written in several other ways. One would retain the example in exactly the same form except that the input variable *$sa* is replaced in the example by some local variable, say *$sa-rej*. Now the antecedent fails for want of a binding for *$sa*. But the negative example has still been matched, and in effect it gives a reason why no binding could be found.

Another alternative is to omit the negative example entirely. Again the antecedent fails for want of a binding, but this time no explanation has been given. In this version, saying "I reject your offer" is treated indistinguishably from saying something completely irrelevant.

Finally, the antecedent could be broken into two: one to find bindings for the speech act $sa and another to test for any given binding whether that speech act indicates willingness to enter the exchange. A disadvantage is that several irrelevant speech acts may be retrieved, which must then be considered individually. An advantage is that the second antecedent will always be instantiated before it is tested, so that the examples again have the role of partitioning the classes of possible bindings.

The current rules experiment in different places with all of these alternatives. Further work will be needed before generalizing about which should be used when.

6.5.3 Testing an Antecedent with Examples

The procedure for using examples was sketched in section 3.4.2. When it is invoked, the program is trying to test an atomic formula that occurs in an antecedent of some legal rule. The formula may be part of some larger expression. It has no attached legal rules and no attached procedure; thus the predicate of the formula is one that is viewed as open textured.

Conceptually, testing the formula requires asking three questions:

1. Can a tentative truth value for the formula be derived?

2. If so, is anything known that would defeat the tentative conclusion?

3. If a ground for defeat is known, does it support reversing the tentative conclusion, or does it just convert the truth of this conclusion to a hard question?

In the case of a formula containing no unbound variables, looking for a tentative truth value has four substeps, which are done in order until one of them succeeds or all have failed:

a. Try to prove <*formula*> directly.

b. Try to prove (*not* <*formula*>).

c. Try to prove a positive example of <*formula*>.

d. Try to prove a negative example of <*formula*>.

At each step, trying to prove something is a matter of invoking the proof procedures of MRS. The relevant MRS function, called *truep*, basically operates by database lookup and backward chaining.

If no tentative truth value can be derived, the program concludes that the truth of <*formula*> is a hard question. Otherwise it proceeds to step 2, looking for something that would defeat the conclusion. This is a matter of matching an example that would lead to the opposite conclusion. If none is found, the tentative conclusion becomes definite.

If step 3 is reached, there is support for saying that <*formula*> is true and other support for saying that it is false. On at least one side, the support is a matched example. There may still be untried examples on the other side. If so, step 3 tries them. Deciding what to do about <*formula*> then requires considering the nature of the support found. If examples matched on both sides, the interpretation is that there are conflicting legal precedents; accordingly the truth of <*formula*> is considered a hard legal question. If an example matched on only one side, the interpretation is that there is a precedent according to which the predicate of <*formula*> has a special legal meaning, different from its ordinary meaning. In this situation the legal meaning prevails, and no hard question is raised.

This description concerns the testing of a ground formula. If the formula contains unbound variables, the idea is the same, but its realization is more complicated. The main differences are the following:

1. A more general MRS function is used. Above, *(truep <formula>)* succeeded after finding only one proof. Here, *(trueps <formula>)* returns as many binding lists as it can find that make <*formula*> true.

2. In step 1b, the attempt to have MRS prove *(not <formula>)* is omitted. The reason is that, if MRS had a complete proof procedure and if the CSK rules contained complete axioms, trying to prove a formula like *(not (act $act))* would result in many irrelevant bindings: *Buyer* is not an *act*, *Telegram1* is not an *act*, and so on. That is, MRS treats the query *(not (act $act))* as if it said *(exist $act (not (act $act)))* rather than the desired interpretation *(all $act (not (act $act)))* or, equivalently, *(not (exist $act (act $act)))*.

3. Relevant bindings can be identified by matching examples, as well as by trying to prove <*formula*> directly. Furthermore, different

examples may generate different binding lists. For this reason the program tries to match all the positive examples and all the negative examples. If distinct binding lists are generated, a branch point is entered in the analysis tree, with a different set of bindings at each new node. At each such node, <*formula*> is then treated like a ground formula. Since all the examples have already been tried by this point, most of the work required to test a ground formula has already been done.

4. If no bindings at all can be found, then <*formula*> is considered false; the possible existence of some unknown object to which a variable could be bound is not considered a hard question. This limited application of the closed-world assumption can also be given a legal interpretation: a judge or jury is not to speculate about what might be the case without some basis in the evidence presented.

The use of the program so far has not produced any situations in which a tentative truth value is defeated. The most important reason seems to be that in the vast majority of cases, legal meaning is not at odds with ordinary meaning. The possibility that it may be, however, is always in the background. As the discussion of hard and easy questions tried to bring out, providing a way in which seemingly obvious conclusions can be defeated remains essential to the theoretical adequacy of any legal reasoning program.

7   Program Performance

The last two chapters have described a knowledge representation, a small knowledge base, and a program that uses them. The program was developed using the problem of section 1.2.1 as a test case. It has been tested on several additional problems. This chapter presents some illustrative results.

Section 7.1 traces through the program's analyses of two events of the test problem. Also covered in this section is one additional element of the program, which is the way the detailed analysis of an event is summarized before going on to the next event. Section 7.2 then summarizes the analysis of the test problem as a whole; this includes nine different legal interpretations of the whole event sequence. Finally section 7.3 presents the program's results on five other problems. These last are all taken from a well-known study aid for law students (Eisenberg 1982), which has the advantage of including published solutions with which the program's results can be compared. Some of these problems bring out aspects of the program that the test problem did not illustrate. On one problem, the program uncovers a real issue that the authors of the study aid seem to have overlooked.

7.1 Analyzing an Event and Summarizing the Analysis

Chapter 6 gave three different reasons for branching in the detailed tree that records the program's analysis of a single event. There may be competing rules, raising the legal question of which rule should be followed; there may be alternate bindings for variables; and there may be open-textured predicates, whose satisfaction in the case at hand appears to raise a hard question. Given these possibilities, an analysis tree for an event can become a rather large object. To control the combinatorics of problems, it is essential to prune and summarize this tree before going on to the next event. This section shows how two representative analysis trees are developed and how they are condensed in the upper-level context tree. Both illustrations are taken from the processing of the test problem in section 1.2.1.

7.1.1 Looking for an Offer

The first illustration is the processing of the first event in the test problem. Its English statement is as follows: "On July 1 Buyer sent the following telegram to Seller: 'Have customers for salt and need carload immediately. Will you supply carload at $2.40 per cwt?'" When the processing of this first event begins, the root of the context tree looks like this:

ID: C0002
Conclusions so far: NIL
ATN:
  State: 0
  Regs: ((PENDING-OFFERS) (CURRENT-BARGAIN)) ;registers
                                             ;are empty
  Pending transitions: NIL
Unprocessed events: (*EVENT1* *EVENT2* *EVENT3* *EVENT4*
                     EVENT5 *EVENT6* *EVENT7* *EVENT8*
                     EVENT9)
Tree: NIL
Children: NIL

As the result of processing the first event, both the detailed *tree* and the *children* of the context will be filled in.

The branching structure of the detailed tree is shown in figure 7.1.[1] The analysis of the first event begins at its root. At the start, the program determines that no transitions are pending. It retrieves the outgoing arcs from the ATN state, which in this case are only "offer" and "ineffective event." It looks for a stipulated offer by invoking MRS on the arc predicate, *(offer $0)*. When this fails, it is time to try any legal rules saying how an offer may be found. In the root node, this point is marked by filling in the *issue* field with the arc label, "offer," and creating one child node (node 2 of figure 7.1), at which application of the rule set now begins.

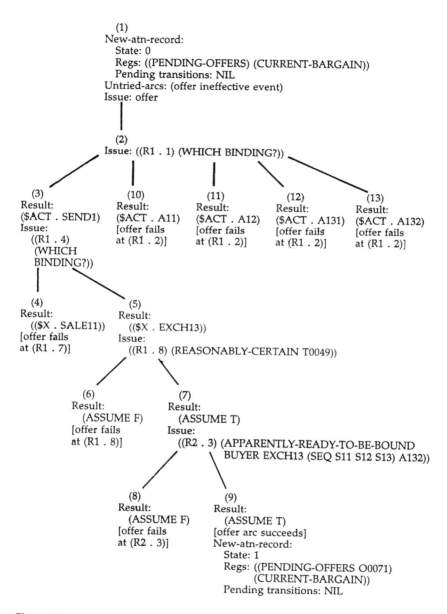

Figure 7.1
Detailed analysis tree for event 1

There is only one offer rule, *R1*. Its English statement was shown in figure 6.4. The first antecedent, *(R1 . 1)*, calls for finding an act:

(in (list current-fact 'commonsense) (act $act)) .

As the branching below node 2 of the figure indicates, five acts are found. These are, left to right, as follows:

Send1: The sending of the telegram.
A11: A speech act of asserting that Buyer has customers for salt.
A12: A speech act of asserting that Buyer needs salt.
A131: A speech act of asking whether Seller will supply salt.
A132: A speech act of requesting that Seller supply salt.[2]

The choice point is marked by filling in the *issue* field of the current node, node 2, and by placing one of the alternatives in the *result* field of each child. Trying the rule will now continue separately from each leaf.

As it turns out, the next antecedent fails for each act except *Send1*. This is the antecedent that asks whether the act produces a manifestation:

(produces-manifestation-with-content $act $m $c) .

At node 3 of the figure, *Send1* is pursued with *Telegram1* as the manifestation. Here a further issue of variable binding arises. The question is whether *Telegram1* concerns an exchange, x, and the program finds two exchanges. One (*Exch13*) is based on the sentence "Will you supply carload at $2.40 per cwt?" The other (*Sale11*) is based on "Have customers for salt." As before, the analysis tree branches. The next two antecedents, which find the description of the exchange and check that the speaker would be a party to the exchange, are both satisfied at each of the resulting nodes.

Then, antecedent *(R1 . 7)* asks whether the speaker, Buyer, may be willing to enter the exchange, according to some speech act performed by means of some sentence of the telegram:

(may-be-willing-to-enter $offeror $x $c $sa) .

At node 4, where *Sale11* is being considered, no example matches, and so no such speech act can be found. At node 5, where *Exch13* is being considered, an example does match, and the speech-act variable, sa, is bound to the request, *A132*, that Seller supply salt.[3]

The only live analysis of event 1 is now at this node, node 5. The next antecedent asks whether the terms of the exchange, *Exch13*, are reasonably certain. A proposition representing the terms was constructed, and given a name, by an earlier antecedent, so the formula of the current antecedent, *(reasonably-certain $tname)*, is already instantiated. MRS cannot prove the formula or its negation, and no example matches. The issue is marked by placing the instantiated antecedent in the *issue* field of the current node and, in the *result* field of its two new children, *(assume F)* or *(assume T)*.

At the node where *(assume T)* was entered, node 7, the program finds one last hard question about event 1: when Buyer requested Seller to supply salt, did he appear ready to be bound to a contract without doing anything more? This question arises at the third antecedent of the subsidiary offer rule, as shown in figure 6.4. The branch point created is similar to the previous one, with *(assume F)* entered at node 8 and *(assume T)* at node 9. At node 9, where the antecedent succeeds, the secondary antecedents of the offer rule are now tested, and its consequent is executed. With the latter, the existence of an offer is asserted in the *new-findings* of node 9 (not shown in the figure). The corresponding ATN arc is followed, and an updated ATN record is added to the node. At all the other leaves of the tree, by default, the "ineffective event" arc is taken.

Throughout the testing of the offer rule, the program was making other assertions as part of the *new-findings* of the nodes in the tree. For instance, when *(reasonably-certain $tname)* was tested, the program not only put *(assume F)* or *(assume T)* in the nodes' *result* fields but also asserted either *(not (reasonably-certain T0049))* or *(reasonably-certain T0049)* in the nodes' new findings. In general, at a node where a rule succeeds, the new findings along the path from this node back to the root will include assertions corresponding to the formula of each antecedent. There will also be assertions corresponding to examples that were matched along the way. Similarly, at a node where an antecedent fails, the negation of the formula will be entered. An exception is made if the finding required only database lookup and so was not really new.[4]

The detailed tree analyzing event 1 has eight terminal nodes. There is one path to success on the offer arc, and there are seven ways of failing. Clearly the program should not analyze event 2 in eight different contexts; the combinatorial explosion would occur long before the problem ends with event 9. But it cannot ignore the failures entirely. Some of the legal questions that a human would need to consider in analyzing the problem arise only on the assumption that event 1 is not an offer.

The program has several heuristics for condensing the leaves of a detailed tree into a smaller number of contexts at the upper level. As applied here, they lead to the following line of reasoning:

1. There is at least one path to success on a nontrivial arc.

2. Five of the paths to failure used variable bindings inconsistent with the bindings on any successful path. Probably these bindings were so inappropriate that a human (or a smarter program) would not have considered them at all. Therefore these paths can be ignored.

3. Two of the paths to failure (those ending at nodes 6 and 8) have binding lists that are subsets of the bindings along some path to success, and they both lead, by way of the "ineffective event" arc, to the same new ATN configuration. Therefore these two failures can be combined into a single new context.

4. Along these same two paths, the bindings used are consistent with each other. In the new context, therefore, the reasons for failure can be stated as a disjunction of the reasons for failure along the two paths.

As a result of this condensation step, the eight leaves of the detailed tree are reduced to two new contexts at the upper level. The contexts that result are shown in figures 7.2 and 7.3.[5]

7.1.2 Looking for a Response to an Offer

The second detailed illustration of the program's analysis of an event is also taken from the sample problem in section 1.2.1. The event to be treated here is Buyer's sending a purchase order to Seller. It is chosen because it is the most complex event of the problem.

To set the context, it will be helpful to summarize what has happened up to the point where the purchase order is considered. The events so far in the problem are as follows:

Event 1: On July 1, Buyer wires Seller (by *Telegram1*), ". . . Will you supply carload at $2.40 per cwt?"

Event 2: On July 1, Seller receives *Telegram1*.

```
ID:                          C0073
Parent:                      C0002
Source-records:              [node 9 of figure 7.1]
Conclusions so far:
     ((I0072
       (ACT SEND1)
       (PRODUCES-MANIFESTATION-WITH-CONTENT SEND1 TELEGRAM1 (SEQ S11 S12 S13))
       (IN (COMMONSENSE W0034 W0035 W0036 W0037) (EXCHANGE EXCH13))
       (IN (W0034 W0035 W0036 W0037)
           (TERMS
            EXCH13
            (PROP EXIST EXCH13 SUP13 TRANS13 MON13 DOL13 TIME13 SALT13 VOL13
                  (AND (FOLLOWS TIME13 T1) (NUMBER VOL13 1) (CARLOADS VOL13)
                       (QUANTITY SALT13 VOL13) (SALT SALT13) (OBJ SUP13 SALT13)
                       (TIME SUP13 TIME13) (BEN SUP13 BUYER)
                       (AGENT SUP13 SELLER) (SUPPLY SUP13) (DOLLARS DOL13)
                       (QUANTITY MON13 DOL13) (MONEY MON13) (OBJ TRANS13 MON13)
                       (TRANSFER TRANS13) (EVENT2 EXCH13 TRANS13)
                       (EXCHANGE EXCH13) (EVENT1 EXCH13 SUP13)))
            T0049))
       (PARTY-TO BUYER EXCH13 (SEQ S11 S12 S13))
       (TRUE (AND (EVENT1 EXCH13 SUP13)
                  (OR (AGENT SUP13 BUYER) (BEN SUP13 BUYER)))
             (COMMONSENSE W0034 W0035 W0036))
       (MAY-BE-WILLING-TO-ENTER BUYER EXCH13 (SEQ S11 S12 S13) A132)
       (REQUEST A132)
       (OR (LITERAL-FORCE S13 A132) (EFFECTIVE-FORCE S13 A132))
       (MEMBER S13 (SEQ S11 S12 S13))
       (OBJ A132 PROP13)
       (WORLD PROP13 W0036)
       (REASONABLY-CERTAIN T0049)
       (ADDRESSED-TO BUYER TELEGRAM1 SELLER)
       (IS-INVITED-TO-FURNISH-CONSIDERATION SELLER EXCH13 (SEQ S11 S12 S13))
       (CWORLDS (SEQ S11 S12 S13) (COMMONSENSE W0034 W0035 W0036))
       (TRUE (AND (EVENT1 EXCH13 SUP13)
                  (OR (AGENT SUP13 SELLER) (BEN SUP13 SELLER)))
             (COMMONSENSE W0034 W0035 W0036))
       (APPARENTLY-READY-TO-BE-BOUND BUYER EXCH13 (SEQ S11 S12 S13) A132)
       (INVITES-ACCEPTANCE (SEQ S11 S12 S13) BUYER EXCH13 SELLER)
       (NOT (INSTANTANEOUS-COMMUNICATION TELEGRAM1))
       (OFFER 00071) (OFFEROR 00071 BUYER) (OFFEREE 00071 SELLER)
       (ACT 00071 SEND1) (EMBODIMENT 00071 TELEGRAM1)
       (CONTENT 00071 (SEQ S11 S12 S13))
       (OBJ 00071 (PROP EXIST EXCH13 (EXCHANGE EXCH13))) (TERMS 00071 T0049)))
ATN:
     State: 1
     Regs: ((PENDING-OFFERS 00071) (CURRENT-BARGAIN))
     Pending transitions: NIL
Unprocessed events: (*EVENT2* *EVENT3* *EVENT4* *EVENT5* *EVENT6*
                     *EVENT7* *EVENT8* *EVENT9*
Children:                    NIL
```

Figure 7.2
Context interpreting event 1 as an offer

```
ID:                        C0075
Parent:                    C0002
Source-records:            [nodes 6 and 8 of figure 7.1]
Conclusions so far:
   ((I0074 (OR (NOT (APPARENTLY-READY-TO-BE-BOUND
                    BUYER EXCH13 (SEQ S11 S12 S13) A132))
               (NOT (REASONABLY-CERTAIN T0049))))))
ATN:
   State: 0
   Regs: ((PENDING-OFFERS) (CURRENT-BARGAIN))
   Pending transitions: NIL
Unprocessed events: (*EVENT2* *EVENT3* *EVENT4* *EVENT5* *EVENT6*
                     *EVENT7* *EVENT8* *EVENT9*)
Children:                  NIL
```

Figure 7.3
Context interpreting event 1 as not an offer

Event 3:   On July 12, Seller replies (by *Telegram2*), "Accept your offer carload of salt, immediate shipment, terms cash on delivery."

Event 4:   On July 12, Buyer receives *Telegram2*.

Event 5:   On July 13 Buyer sent by Air Mail its standard form "Purchase Order" to Seller. On the face of the form Buyer had written that it accepted "Seller's offer of July 12" and had written "One carload" and "$2.40 per cwt." in the appropriate spaces for quantity and price. Among numerous printed provisions on the reverse of the form was the following: "Unless otherwise stated on the face hereof, payment on all purchase orders shall not be due until 30 days following delivery." There was no statement on the face of the form regarding time of payment.

The program has found that the sending of *Telegram1* may or may not be an offer. Where the requirements for an offer are otherwise met, it has proved convenient for several reasons to let the offer arc be taken immediately on sending, rather than to enter a pending transition for confirmation by the telegram's receipt. Therefore, whether or not event 1 is an offer, event 2 causes no significant state transition.

At event 3, along the path where an offer was found, the program finds that the sending of *Telegram2* may or may not be an acceptance. This turns only on whether *Telegram2* was sent within a reasonable time of the offer; the program finds that all the other requirements for an acceptance are clearly met. Among these other requirements are that communication of the offer has been completed (satisfied by the receipt of *Telegram1* in event 2) and that there is no unexplainable mismatch between the descriptions of the exchanges as stated in the two telegrams. In reaching this last conclusion, the program finds a mismatch concerning the time of payment and then explains it using the interpretation rule shown at the end of section 6.4.2. Further, the program concludes that if the second telegram created an acceptance, the acceptance was effective when sent. Accordingly it makes an immediate transition along the acceptance arc, and the receipt of *Telegram2* in event 4 has no further legal effect.

On the opposing assumption—that *Telegram2* was sent too late to be an acceptance—the program has to consider what other legal effect it might have. By the time it has reached the question of timeliness, it has already eliminated most of the arcs representing the other possibilities. In particular, the sending of *Telegram2* is known not to be an acceptance with proposal to modify (since no real change of terms was found), a rejection (since Seller expressed willingness to enter the exchange he described), a revocation or modification of the offer (since the actor is the offeree, not the offeror), or a death. The possibility of a counteroffer is still open. The rule saying that a defective acceptance is a counteroffer succeeds, with lateness of the acceptance as the particular defect recognized.

It is along this last path that the program has the most alternatives available for characterizing the sending of the purchase order in event 5. The beginning context is as follows:

ID: C0250
Parent: C0163
Conclusions so far: ((I0249 (ACT RECEIVE4)) I0162 I0092 I0072)
ATN:
   State: 1
   Regs: ((PENDING-OFFERS O0159) (CURRENT-BARGAIN))
   Pending transitions: NIL
Unprocessed events: (*EVENT5* *EVENT6* *EVENT7* *EVENT8*
                              EVENT9)
Tree: NIL
Children: NIL

The *pending offer, O0159,* refers to the counteroffer made by *Telegram2.* The *conclusions so far* name the MRS theories containing the interpretations of events 1 through 4 along the current path in the context tree. The contents of only the most recent theory are shown.

Figure 7.4 shows the structure of the analysis of the purchase order in this context. The root of the detailed tree, node 1 of the figure, shows the eight arcs available for characterizing the event. As always, the acceptance arc is tried first.

The first two antecedents of the acceptance rule identify the pending offer and the fillers of its slots. The third looks for an act in the current event, and the tree branches as in figure 7.1. Four of the acts found are speech acts, which fail to produce a manifestation in the required sense. There is one nontrivial arc not requiring a manifestation: the arc representing termination of an offer by virtue of the death of the offeror or offeree. Accordingly the program checks at four of the nodes whether the act is one resulting in death. At each, it fails.

The focus, then, is on node 3 of figure 7.4, and the question is whether the sending of the purchase order (*Send5*) created an acceptance. The actor and the addressee are the appropriate people; the document concerns an exchange; the described terms of the exchange are found; and the speaker appears willing to enter the exchange. The terms must now be matched with the terms of the offer.

There is a mismatch. Both the offer and the purchase order contain terms saying that there is some time point at which the salt will be delivered and some time point when it will be paid for. In the matched terms, these become:

(time Del34 Tdel34)
(time Pay332 Tpay34) .

The purchase order, harmlessly, adds symbols for the numeric values of the time points:

(value Tdel34 N1)
(value Tpay34 N2) .

But the offer calls for payment on delivery, whereas the purchase order delays payment by thirty days. After substitution of corresponding variable names, the conflicting terms become:

(= Tpay34 Tdel34)
(not (< N2 (+ N1 30))) .

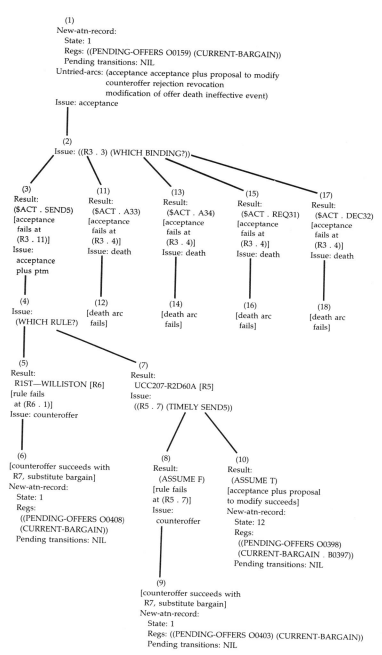

Figure 7.4
Delailed analysis of event 5 as a response to a counteroffer

The mismatch is found using a CSK rule saying that equal time points have equal values. Since the program has no way to explain it away, the acceptance rule fails.

In the light of the findings so far, the arcs still worth trying at this point have been reduced to those for an acceptance with proposal to modify the contract, a counteroffer, and an ineffective event. The arc for an acceptance with proposal to modify is tried next; in the figure, its processing begins by filling in the *issue* field of node 3 and creating a child node, node 4. The arc being considered has a competing rule set. In the tree the choice is marked at node 4 with the issue "which rule?" The result fields of the two children give symbolic names for the competing rules. In the *new-findings* of the children, statements of the form *(rule <rulename>)* also are asserted.

At one child, node 5, the rule fails immediately because it always fails. This is the rule, identified with Williston and the first Restatement, that says in effect "you can't do that"; an acceptance must be a mirror image of the offer. Accordingly, at node 5 the program goes on to consider the purchase order as a possible counteroffer, and this arc succeeds, at node 6, using the rule that looks for a proposal for a substitute bargain.

At the node using the other competing rule, node 7, the antecedents for an acceptance with proposal to modify all succeed easily—until the question of timeliness is reached. It is reasonable for the program to leave this question open. The offer was sent and received on July 12, and Buyer is replying on July 13. The Restatement says, as a positive rule, only that acceptance of an offer sent by mail is normally timely if the acceptance is mailed by midnight on the day of receipt.[6] For an offer made by telegram, as is the case here, it also adds that a reasonable time for acceptance may or may not be shorter than if the mail were used.[7]

Finally, then, the program adds one more branch point to the tree, with opposite assumptions about whether the purchase order was sent within a reasonable time. On one branch (node 10), the arc for an acceptance with proposal to modify succeeds. On the other (nodes 8 and 9), a counteroffer is found in the same way as before.

The tree for event 5, as a response to an earlier counteroffer, ends with seven terminal nodes. They are reduced to two new upper-level contexts, with the help of one new heuristic. This heuristic says that different paths to success on the same nontrivial arc can be combined, provided they lead to essentially the same new configuration of the network. Here the two ways of finding a counteroffer qualify.

A remaining question is what should be asserted about the event in the new context formed by combining the paths to a counteroffer. Any new findings that occur on both paths of the detailed tree may of course be included, but these do not explain why more than one path was present at all. In the current version of the program, the remaining findings along each path are conjoined; the conjunctions are disjoined; and the disjunction is asserted. One assertion about event 5 as a counteroffer, therefore, is in part as follows:

```
(OR (AND . . .
          (RULE UCC207-R2D60A)
          (NOT (TIMELY SEND5)))
    (AND . . . (RULE R1ST-WILLISTON))) .
```

The assertion says that, on this analysis, it is unnecessary to decide which of the competing rules should be followed.

7.2 Full Analysis of the Salt Problem

7.2.1 Results at the Summary Level

Altogether the program produces nine analyses of the test problem; that is, the context tree contains nine paths from the root to a terminal node. The shape of the tree is shown in figure 7.5. Along each path the general result is given by the final state of the ATN: in state 2 there is a contract; in state 0 or 1 there is not. In the figure the actual tree has been condensed slightly by consolidating adjacent events of sending and receiving a document into a single level.

A more detailed version of the tree, listing the nine analyses separately and expanding the abbreviations of figure 7.5, is given in figures 7.6 and 7.7. In these figures each entry shows the network state before and after the corresponding event is analyzed. At entries left blank, the event was found to be legally ineffective.

As figure 7.5 indicates, the nine analyses result from the program's finding eight major branching points, each with a two-way choice. The first three of these were discussed in the previous section. The full list of choices, corresponding to the numbered nodes in the tree, is as follows:

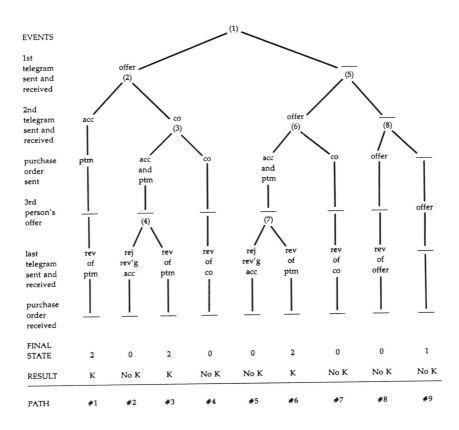

EVENTS

1st telegram sent and received									

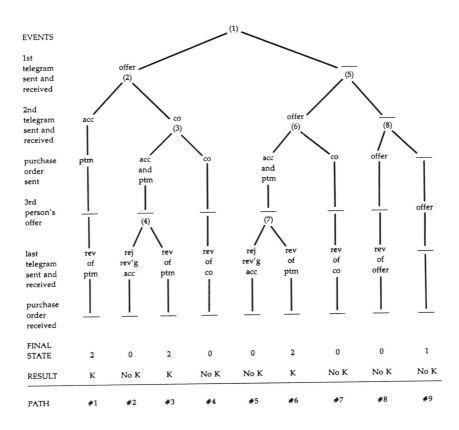

Abbreviations:
  acc - acceptance
  co - counteroffer
  ptm - proposal to modify the contract
  rev - revocation
  rej - rejection
  rej rev'g acc - rejection of offer, revoking a previous acceptance of the offer
  K - contract

Figure 7.5
Condensed version of summary-level decision tree

1. Is the first telegram an offer, or is it only a preliminary inquiry?

2. Assume the first telegram is an offer. Is the second telegram an acceptance, or is it a counteroffer?

3. Assume the first telegram is an offer and the second a counter-offer. Is the purchase order an acceptance of the counteroffer, with a concomitant proposal to modify the contract, or is the purchase order a further counteroffer?

4. Assume the first telegram is an offer, the second telegram is a counteroffer, and the purchase order is an acceptance (with proposal to modify). Did the final telegram revoke the acceptance and reject the offer?

5. Assume the first telegram is not an offer. Is the second telegram an offer?

6 and 7. Assume the first telegram is a preliminary inquiry but the second one is an offer. The same questions arise as in 3 and 4.

8. Assume neither of the first two telegrams is an offer. Is the purchase order an offer?

This list of choices is somewhat larger than a human lawyer would be likely to consider explicitly. Section 1.2.2 suggested four analyses, not nine. On the other hand, the transition network has an average branching factor of 5.25, so that the space of possible analyses for a nine-event problem is on the order of 5^9, even ignoring such complications as the possibility of finding multiple reasons for taking the same arc.

   Of the extra analyses generated by the program, three arise because the program is not yet able to conclude that treating the first telegram as an offer that expired is equivalent in this problem to treating it as a preliminary inquiry. With some additional knowledge, expansion of the tree could be discontinued below node 6 of figure 7.5 on the ground of its similarity to node 3. The other two extra analyses reflect the possibility that the second telegram, as well as the first, is only preliminary negotiation. There is a plausible legal foundation for recognizing this possibility.

7.2.2 Additional Reasoning in Characterizing the Nine Events

Section 7.1 followed the program's reasoning through choices 1, 2, and 3 of figure 7.5. Where the description there stopped, the program was following a path on which the first telegram created an offer;

EVENT	PATH #1	#2	#3	#4
1st telegram sent	0 offer 1	0 offer 1	0 offer 1	0 offer 1
1st telegram received				
2nd telegram sent	1 acceptance 2	1 counteroffer 1	1 counteroffer 1	1 counteroffer 1
2nd telegram received				
purchase order sent	2 proposal to modify (ptm) 12	1 acceptance plus ptm 12	1 acceptance plus ptm 12	1 counteroffer 1
3rd person's offer				
last telegram sent	12 provisional revocation of ptm 12	12 provisional rejection of counteroffer, revoking acceptance 12	12 provisional revocation of ptm 12	1 provisional revocation of counteroffer 1
last telegram received	12 revocation confirmed 2	12 rejection confirmed 0	12 revocation confirmed 2	1 revocation confirmed 0
purchase order received				
CONCLUSIONS	State 2: Contract	State 0: No contract	State 2: Contract	State 0: No contract

Figure 7.6
Analyses 1 through 4 of test problem

PATH

#5	#6	#7	#8	#9
0 offer 1	0 offer 1	0 offer 1		
1 acceptance plus ptm 12	1 acceptance plus ptm 12	1 counteroffer 1	0 offer 1	
				0 offer 1
12 provisional rejection of offer, revoking acceptance 12	12 provisional revocation of ptm 12	1 provisional revocation of counteroffer 1	1 provisional revocation of offer 1	
12 rejection confirmed 0	12 revocation confirmed 2	1 revocation confirmed 0	1 revocation confirmed 0	
State 0: No contract	State 2: Contract	State 0: No contract	State 0: Contract	State 1: No contract

Figure 7.7
Analyses 5 through 9 of test problem

the second telegram, a counteroffer; and the purchase order, either a further counteroffer or an acceptance with proposal to modify the contract. This section will review more briefly the reasoning in the other parts of the tree. In particular the treatment of the final telegram has not yet been discussed.

The Final Telegram
To take the simpler case first, assume that the purchase order has been found to be a further counteroffer. The program is now on the path numbered 4 in figures 7.5 and 7.6, and the network is in state 1. The next event is the third person's offer:

Event 6:   Later on July 13 another party offered to sell Buyer a carload of salt for $2.30 per cwt.

Although event 6 stipulates that there is an offer, the program looks for such a stipulation only in state 0. In state 1 the program tries to construe the event as an action on the offer already pending. Correctly, it fails, and the "ineffective event" arc is taken. Still in state 1, the program considers the final telegram:

Event 7:   Buyer immediately wired Seller: "Ignore purchase order mailed earlier today; your offer of July 12 rejected."

Event 8:   This telegram was received by Seller on the same day (July 13).

Event 9:   Seller received Buyer's purchase order in the mail the following day (July 14).

Because the agent of event 7, Buyer, is the offeror of the pending offer, the arcs worth trying are quickly reduced to those for revocation or modification of the offer. The revocation rule succeeds, with the declaration of rejection as the needed expression of unwillingness to enter an exchange. Since the telegram gives no description of this exchange, a match with the exchange proposed by the offer is assumed. The consequent of the revocation rule then uses the result from a secondary antecedent: sending a telegram does not count as instantaneous communication; therefore the revocation should not take effect until (and unless) it is received. Accordingly the rule returns a result of provisional success rather than full success. Event 7 is concluded with the transition network still in state 1 but with a transition pending for the revocation. At event 8 the receipt of the telegram confirms the transition, back to state 0. Event 9, receipt of the purchase order, has no effect.

Now consider the other case below node 3 of figure 7.5. Buyer, by sending the purchase order, has accepted an offer and also has proposed a modification of the contract with respect to the time of payment. The transition network is in state 12, with both the existing bargain and the proposed modification represented in the registers. The set of arcs available is somewhat different from those in the previous case. In particular it includes an arc for revocation of an acceptance, rejecting the previous offer instead. This arc has the second example of a competing rule set.

On one branch of the detailed tree, the rule allowing such an act is tried. The rule succeeds after checking, among other things, that Seller has not yet received the purchase order informing him of the acceptance. Since a rejection, like a revocation, is not effective until received, the result is again a pending transition, later confirmed by event 8. As an incidental effect, the proposal to modify the contract is also revoked.

On the other branch, the competing rule says in effect that an acceptance can never be undone. On this branch, the program goes on to consider whether the telegram could be a revocation of the proposal to modify the contract, and the revocation rule succeeds. If the program knew about breaches of contract, then it would be able to reach a stronger conclusion here: that the final telegram repudiated the existing contract. But the program deals only with contract for-mation, and revocation of the proposal to modify is therefore the strongest conclusion available about event 7 if withdrawal of one's acceptance is not permitted.

Other Choice Points

There are four choice points, those labeled 5 through 8 in figure 7.5, that remain to be discussed.

Choices 6 and 7   At nodes 6 and 7 the choices are similar to those at nodes 3 and 4. Their presence, however, points up an element that is missing from the current program and that should be supplied in a future version. This element is a representation of the state of the discourse, separate from the representation of the legal state.

On the paths considered earlier—those on the left-hand side of the tree of figure 7.5—the need for such a distinction was not obvious.

On these paths every document has some legal effect. The characterization of each document in terms of its legal effect, along with the findings made in the course of reaching that characterization, preserves most of the relevant information about what the document contributes to the conversation.

On the right-hand side of the tree, on the other hand, the first document exchanged is found not to be an offer. With the network still in state 0, the program considers the second document as if it were the beginning of the conversation. This means that at node 6, where the second telegram is found to be the initial offer, the terms of this offer are computed without cumulating them with what went before. Thus its terms are not identical with those of the counteroffer found at node 3. For this reason, terminating expansion of the tree at node 6 would require a significant conceptual addition to the program.

Choices 5 and 8   With the addition just mentioned, the tree would still contain the choice points labeled 5 and 8 in figure 7.5. Along this path, the first telegram has failed to create an offer for either of two reasons: its terms may be uncertain, and its author, Buyer, may not be ready to be bound to a contract by just a positive reply. When the second telegram is considered at node 5, the program leaves open the same question about the certainty of terms. In contrast with the earlier telegram, however, it is here able to use the phrase *accept your offer* to conclude that the author, Seller, does appear ready to be bound.

On the path where the terms of the second telegram are also too uncertain, the final choice point is whether the purchase order could be an initial offer. Again there is an issue as to certainty of terms. The issue seems to be a reasonable one despite the detailed provisions on the reverse of the form. How do we know that they know what kind of salt they are talking about?

Indeed they might not. A relevant case, in which the subject matter was described as *chicken,* rather than *salt,* was mentioned in note 1 to chapter 5. Cases of this sort are commonly explained as involving misunderstanding between the parties, not as involving uncertainty of the contractual terms. The relationship between misunderstanding and uncertainty, however, is left rather unclear in most legal writing. The results from the program suggest that perhaps the relationship should be explored.

7.3 Analyses of Other Problems

The program has been used to analyze several more problems. The problems and their published solutions are given for reference in figures 7.8 and 7.9.

The first is a case where the offer specifies a time limit for acceptance. In the long problem considered above, no such time limits were stated, so that the period for acceptance always defaulted to a "reasonable time."

The second and third problems, numbered 23a and 23b in the figure, call for distinguishing a counteroffer from an acceptance with proposal to modify the contract and from a mere inquiry about the offer. The first distinction points up a bug, not in the program but in the legal definition of an acceptance with proposal to modify. Problem 23a is not a strong enough case to force the issue. A slight variation on the problem, however, would present a first real example of the need for a nonliteral reading of a legal rule.

In both problems 23a and 23b, the negotiation is apparently conducted by direct conversation, not by mail. In 23b the offeree

22. On March 1, A wrote to B offering to sell her house for $40,000. The letter stated that the offer would remain in effect for only five days.

   a. Assume B received the letter on March 3, and sent an acceptance letter on March 7. Has a contract been formed?

23. A offers to sell B a parcel of land for $5,000.

   a. Assume B replies "I will pay you $4,800 for the parcel." Later that day, B says, "OK, I'll pay the $5,000," but A now refuses to sell. Is there a contract?

   b. Assume B's first reply was, "Will you accept $4,800?" Would B's subsequent "acceptance" of the $5,000 offer form a contract?

   c. Assume that B mailed a rejection to A, but later the same day B changed her mind and telegraphed an acceptance to A. The acceptance was in fact received by A prior to the rejection. Is there a contract?

   d. Suppose B had mailed an acceptance to A, but later that day changed her mind and telegraphed a rejection, and the rejection was received by A *prior* to the acceptance. Is there a contract?

Figure 7.8
Additional problems. Source: *Gilbert Law Summaries: Contracts* (Eisenberg 1982, p. 148)

22. a. YES   An offer terminates by operation of law after expiration of the period of time specified in the offer. The period commences to run on the date of actual *receipt* of the offer or on the date it would normally be received. Since the offer was received on March 3 and there does not appear to be an unreasonable delay in the transmission, the five-day acceptance period would commence to run on March 3. As the acceptance was dispatched within five days, a contract was formed. [Secs. 180, 311]

23. a. NO   B's $4,800 counter-offer terminated her power of acceptance. B's "acceptance" thereafter did not form a contract. [Sec. 190]

    b. YES   B's question is neither a rejection nor a counter-offer, but an inquiry. A's offer would therefore still be open, and B's acceptance would create a contract. [Sec. 191]

    c. YES   Generally, an acceptance is effective on dispatch *unless* there has been a *previous* rejection. In such event, acceptance is effective only on *receipt*. However, since A in fact received the acceptance prior to the rejection, a contract was formed. (But if A regards the later-arriving rejection as a repudiation of the acceptance, and relies on it, B will be estopped from enforcing the contract.) [Secs. 339–340]

    d. YES   Under the *Adams v. Lindsell* rule, the contract was formed on dispatch of the acceptance, even though A *learned* of the rejection first. (If, however, A relied on the rejection and contracted to sell the property to C, B should be *estopped* to assert the contract.) [Secs. 344–345]

Figure 7.9
Published answers to the additional problems. Source: *Gilbert Law Summaries: Contracts* (Eisenberg 1982, p. 170)

responds to an offer by asking whether the offeror would accept a lower price. Later—how much later is not stated—the offeree tries to accept the original offer. According to the published solution, the acceptance is effective because the first reply, falling short of a counteroffer, did not terminate the power to accept. The program finds an additional issue here: whether the attempted acceptance was given within a reasonable time. The issue seems to be a good one because, according to the Restatement, "Where the parties bargain face to face or over the telephone, the time for acceptance does not ordinarily extend beyond the end of the conversation unless a contrary intention is indicated" (Restatement of Contracts, Second, sec. 41, comment d).

The fourth and fifth problems, numbers 23c and 23d, both involve an offeree's change of mind about whether to accept or reject an offer. In 23c a rejection is sent first, but the acceptance arrives first. This situation yields a case in which the program enters two pending transitions. Receipt of the acceptance then confirms one transition and defeats the other.

In problem 23d the order of events is reversed, with an acceptance sent first but arriving later. Here the situation is like that in the salt problem. The published answer to 23d does not mention the possibility of a rejection that revokes a prior acceptance. The text sections to which the answer refers, however, do mention that the cases are split as to what rule should be followed in this situation.

In the remainder of this chapter, the program's treatment of the first two of these problems, which are conceptually the most challenging, will be reviewed in more detail.

7.3.1 A Stated Time Limit for Acceptance

The representation for the first problem, 22a, was discussed in section 5.4.2. The first event is a stipulated offer, *O1*, whose content includes propositions according to which the offer will expire five days after it becomes effective:

(prop exist TO1 N1 (and (effective-time O1 TO1) (value TO1 N1)))
(prop exist TO2 (and (expiration-time O1 TO2)
                     (value TO2 (+ N1 5)))).

The offer is sent on March 1, received by the offeree on March 3, and the offeree sends an acceptance letter on March 7:

(time-line TL1)
(points TL1 (seq Start-March1 Tsend1
                 Start-March2
                 Start-March3 Trec2
                 Start-March4
                 Start-March7 Tsend3
                 Start-March8)) .

The program finds, as does the published solution, that a contract has clearly been formed.

The important antecedent of the acceptance rule is the one that checks for timeliness of sending the acceptance letter:

(timely Send3) .

A similar antecedent was shown in the discussion of the salt problem (figure 7.4) but in simplified form. In fact the predicate *timely* has an attached rule set. One rule succeeds if the offer does not state a time limit and the acceptance is given within a reasonable time. The other rule, as applied here, succeeds by finding that the time of the acceptance letter, *Tsend3*, is earlier than the expiration time stated in the offer, *TO2*.

If a particular date of expiration had been stated, this step would be simple. Here, however, *TO2* is defined in terms of the effective time of the offer, which the offer called *TO1*. The program finds that the default effective time of the offer is the time of its receipt, *Trec2*; that the offer does nothing to change the default;[8] and that therefore *TO1* is the same as *Trec2*. Once this identification is made, the program can use known values of points on the time line,

(value Start-March3 303)
(value Start-March8 308) ,

to find that the interval from *Trec2* to *Tsend3* is under five days.

7.3.2 Counteroffers and the Meaning of "Definite Expression of Acceptance"

The next problem, number 23a of figures 7.8 and 7.9, appears to be very straightforward. It has three events:

Event 1:   A offers to sell B a parcel of land for $5,000.
Event 2:   B replies, "I will pay you $4,800 for the parcel."
Event 3:   Later that day, B says, "OK, I'll pay the $5,000."

According to both the program and the published answer, event 2 is clearly a counteroffer, and it becomes the only offer pending. Thus event 3 cannot be an acceptance. The program goes on to give a positive characterization of event 3: that it is a modification of the counteroffer. With or without this last characterization, no contract is formed.

The interesting aspect of the problem emerges because of the ordering of arcs to be tried in the transition network. In dealing with event 2, the program tries the acceptance arc and the arc for an acceptance with proposal to modify before it reaches the counteroffer arc. In the associated rules, each category has slightly different requirements for an expression of willingness to enter the described exchange. The basic requirement appears in the acceptance rule:

(is-willing-to-enter $offeree $x2 $sa-acc $c2) .

For an acceptance with proposal to modify, something more is required:

(definite-expression-of-acceptance $offeree $x2 $sa-acc) .

For a counteroffer proposing a substitute bargain (in this problem, with a substitution as to the price of the land), there is a different extra requirement:

(apparently-ready-to-be-bound $offeree $x2 $sa-acc) .

The predicate *definite-expression-of-acceptance* is taken from the Restatement, which in turn takes it from the Uniform Commercial Code. The predicate *apparently-ready-to-be-bound* is taken from the offer rule, since a counteroffer must itself qualify as an offer.

For the counteroffer rule to succeed in this problem, it is necessary to find that B's saying "I will pay you $4,800 for the parcel" does express willingness to enter an exchange, does not qualify as a definite expression of acceptance, but does show him ready to be bound to a contract if A says something like "I agree." All of these conclusions are reached by way of an example, which is positive for the first and third predicates and negative for the second: the offeree asserts that he will do an act that constitutes his half of the exchange he is describing. For this particular problem, the conclusions are reasonable.

The distinctions among these predicates still seem tenuous, with good reason. As contracts scholars are well aware, the trouble is in the rule permitting an acceptance, despite mismatching terms (which become proposed modifications), if there is a definite expression of acceptance. Suppose B had said, "I accept your offer, and I will pay you $4,800 for the parcel." If the rule is applied literally, it produces the conclusion that B has bound himself to pay $5,000.

This conclusion is nonsensical, but it is not clear how the legal rule should be changed to avoid it. One suggestion (Eisenberg 1982, p. 48) is that a definite expression of acceptance should not be found if there are major mismatches in the terms. Listed as examples of major mismatches are differences as to quality, price, quantity, delivery, and payment (ibid.). Another suggestion (White and Summers 1980, p. 37) is that a definite expression of acceptance should not be found if there are mismatches in bargained-for terms as opposed to terms merely printed on a form. If the courts follow some such suggestion, the phrase *definite expression of acceptance* will have acquired a special technical meaning rather different from its ordinary meaning.

At present the meaning is still unsettled. This openness of meaning can be treated within the framework of the present program, either with competing rules or with negative examples attached to the predicate *definite-expression-of-acceptance*. Such an addition to the knowledge base would affect the analysis of the salt problem. When Buyer's purchase order is considered as a possible acceptance with proposal to modify, the program could find both that there was a definite expression of acceptance, since Buyer said he accepted, and that there was not, since the mismatch concerned the time for payment, which Seller had expressly mentioned. Satisfaction of the predicate would thus become a hard question. Whether it ought to be a hard question is a good point for lawyers to think about as they try to reach a satisfactory reformulation of the rule.

8   Conclusion

This book has presented a computational framework for modeling legal reasoning. Broadly viewed, the task requires the drawing together of two disparate sources. One is AI work on automated reasoning in general—ranging from abstract theorem-proving to narrowly focused expert systems and including the knowledge representations that support such reasoning. If this work were the only important source, law would be just another domain for knowledge engineering.

But law is more than that, as is shown by the other source, legal philosophy. Legal philosophy tells us that legal rules do not dictate legal outcomes; there is more going on in the decision of a case than ordinary deduction. One extra element is that there is often room for choice about which of several possible decisions is to be preferred. Another is that the choice, once made, sets a precedent, which may change the space of choices available in later cases. Sometimes precedents have their effect by giving new meaning to the language of old rules. And finally, despite these qualifications, there still are some cases that are perceived by all sides as cases in which only one decision is available.

In most previous computational work on legal reasoning, legal issues have been treated as if they were all alike. In some work the program is presented with a case raising a single major issue, which is assumed not to have a clear-cut answer, and is expected by some means to weigh the factors favoring a decision either way. In other work it is assumed that deduction from the rules is sufficient, perhaps supplemented by asking the user what choice would be made on some points. That the user may not know, and may wrongly assume that he or she does know, is usually not taken into full account.

Within the framework of this study, different kinds of issues can each be treated in the appropriate way. On some issues the program reaches an answer deductively, determines that it knows nothing that might defeat the answer, and jumps to the conclusion that on this issue the result is certain. On other issues the program concludes that the human decision maker has some room for choice. Reasoning about which would be the better choice remains a major research area for the future. Equally important is the development of a broader knowledge base on which to refine the present heuristics for jumping to conclusions.

What promise is there in this line of work? For AI, bringing the program even to its present state has required making a beginning on several open problems. One is the need in expert systems to allow for disagreement among the experts. In this research the problem has been addressed by using competing rules and by allowing for positive and negative examples that may both be matched in the facts of a particular case. Where a conflict is found and makes a difference, the issue is left open for human judgment. The use of competing rules does require one expert to diagnose the disagreement and mark the rules as competing. The use of competing examples, while not yet illustrated in the current knowledge base, appears not to.

A second area in which the research does something new is in combining the use of legal rules and examples. The examples of the present program, of course, are still abstract patterns and not particulars, and the use of fuller case representations remains for future work. That universally quantified statements can be used as examples is itself cause for reflection. The next paper called "What's in an X?" (Woods 1975; Brachman 1977; Clancey 1983) could well consider what is in an example.

Underlying both the use of examples and the provision for expert disagreement is the idea that legal predicates have open texture. The phrase *open texture,* as used here (and in Hart 1961, from which it is drawn), has been a catchall. It has turned out, in the course of the work, to include several related phenomena. For some predicates there may be a clear prototype case with many possible variations. For others there may be a definition that looks analytic but is in fact defeasible. For still others the concept may be so abstract that its range can be worked out only piecemeal. But these are all phenomena of natural language, not just law. If a legal reasoning program can be made to behave appropriately in the face of these complications, there should be implications for knowledge representation and natural-language processing in general.

AI work on legal reasoning may be important for the law as well as for AI. Three levels can be distinguished. First is the level of legal philosophy. A computational approach here, as in other fields, may lead to the reframing of old questions and the opening up of new ones. Such a development would be helpful because current accounts of some important topics—such as clear cases, reasoning by example, and reasoning from the purposes of rules—are too imprecise to be very satisfying.

The second level is the development and criticism of the substantive law. Creating a legal knowledge base for an AI program requires systematizing legal materials; so do the traditional enterprises of writing treatises and Restatements. But in the course of trying to write rules and examples that make sense computationally, one may uncover difficulties that natural-language treatments leave hidden. Some rules might be formulated rather differently if an AI program had tested them on a stored set of problems, which was not limited to the problems the rule's draftsman had in mind.

Finally, there is the question of practical applications for AI systems in the everyday workings of the law. It is widely predicted that legal reasoning programs will revolutionize the practice of law (e.g., Grossman and Solomon 1983), but similar predictions were made twenty years ago. Chapter 4 reviewed objections to using programs as in any way a substitute for human judgment. There may still be a role for programs as a new form of textbook or treatise. The quality of such efforts may be expected to range, as with the traditional forms, from excellent to abominable. As the ideal, one might think of being able to ask a modern Corbin how he sees the issues in your case. One would also like to be able to browse through this computerized work, to use it for orientation in unfamiliar areas and as an entry point to the relevant decisions. One would even like the program to read new decisions as they come out, updating and reorganizing its knowledge base as appropriate. For any readers outside the AI community, it should be pointed out that this is all just as much science fiction as it always has been.

It is worth suggesting some feasible directions for near-term research. First, the set of constructs available for representing problems needs to be enlarged. Of particular interest are constructs needed to represent mistakes and misunderstandings between the contracting parties—as in the classic case where each used the name *Peerless* to mean a different ship. Handling a range of such cases will call for an explicit representation of beliefs. Closely related is the need for an express representation of the discourse state, since this depends on what is within the awareness of each party. Also needed is knowledge, almost nonexistent in the present knowledge base, about human institutions and practices. In the salt problem, for instance, the program is not now able to infer that Buyer and Seller are both merchants. With only a little more legal knowledge, that inference would become critical.

Next, the scope of the legal knowledge base should be enlarged—both in breadth, by way of more rules, and in depth, by more examples. The ideas presented here will not have had a fair test until this is done. In particular the current heuristics for recognizing easy questions are known to be inadequate. What extensions are necessary remains to be seen.

Third, it is possible to make some beginning steps with respect to the argument of hard questions. Legal arguments are not all alike, and an early step is to try to identify classes of arguments that a program should be able to find. Some of these will require use of detailed representations of precedents. Constructing those case representations and comparing the program's analysis of the cases with the actual decisions should be a revealing way to begin.

Finally, there is the question of program input and output. The program's output graph was originally envisioned as a structure that a student, writing an essay answer to an examination question, would need to traverse. In its present form the graph does highlight the important questions to be addressed, and it includes findings supporting the conclusions drawn. Still, the material is presented in a form that is inconvenient for humans to read and that assumes the reader to be familiar with the internal representation for rules and examples. More should be done to make the program's results easily understandable.

On the input side, manual encoding of the facts of cases is not convenient. So far it has been necessary to concentrate on designing the target representation, not on producing it automatically. Automatic encoding appears to require abilities not found in current natural-language programs. For instance, for some of the sentences translated in chapter 5, it was necessary to use legal knowledge, as well as knowledge of language, to select an appropriate reading.

Giving a principled account of the translation, with due attention to what knowledge is used when, is another substantial task for the future.

These extensions to the program are worth pursuing. Artificial intelligence and legal theory are at only the beginning of discovering what they can learn from each other.

Notes

Chapter 1

1. In some usages, open texture is distinguished from other kinds of indeterminacy of meaning. Waismann distinguished it from vagueness; Hart does not. Here the more inclusive sense is intended.

2. The program's actual results on the problem, which include these analyses, are described in chapter 7.

Chapter 2

1. Personal communication.

2. See Restatement of Contracts, Second, sec. 23, comment b, "Unintended appearance of mutual assent."

3. See ibid., sec. 21, comment a, "Intent to be legally bound."

Chapter 3

1. For this sense of *intentionality,* see Searle (1983).

2. People v. Hall, 4 Cal. 399 (1854).

3. Good arguments in support of this treatment are made by Simpson (1964).

4. Even the use of full text provides only a second-hand description of the facts. There is no guarantee that the court's opinion will state the facts clearly and without significant omissions.

5. Consequently the program does not have a good way of representing, as an assertion in ordinary language, that an action

was done "immediately." The proposal that an action described as immediate would be a good example of an action done within a reasonable time has therefore not been implemented.

Chapter 4

1. There are other programs, done from a political science viewpoint rather than a legal one, in which the data concern legally irrelevant matters such as the ideology and social background of individual judges. See Schubert (1975); Goldman and Sarat (1978).

2. 316 U.S. 455 (1942).

3. 372 U.S. 335 (1963).

4. "Judgment Day: The Thinking Computer Arrives," *Wall Street Journal*, 3 September 1982.

5. "Of Sound Mind and Software: Computer Wills," *San Francisco Sunday Examiner and Chronicle*, 3 July 1983, p. D3.

Chapter 5

1. For example, one famous case involved a contract to send cargo by the ship *Peerless*, but there turned out to be two ships named *Peerless*, which left port three months apart (Raffles v. Wichelhaus, 2 Hurl. & C. 906 (1864)). Another case concerned a contract for the sale of chicken: the seller, who said that *chicken* named a genus, sent stewing chickens; the buyer, who wanted broilers and fryers, said that *chicken* meant young birds (Frigaliment Importing Co. v. B.N.S. Int'l Sales Corp., 190 F. Supp. 116 (1960)). Cases involving other kinds of ambiguity, as well as ambiguity of reference and word sense, could undoubtedly be found.

2. An extreme example is Sherwood v. Walker, 66 Mich. 568, 33 N.W. 919 (1887). Walker contracted to sell a particular cow, Rose, in the belief that she was barren. Before the buyer took delivery, Rose was found to be with calf. The court, holding that Rose need not be turned over to the buyer, explained that the buyer had also believed she was barren and that therefore the object contracted for did not exist. A breeding cow, it was said, differs from a barren one not just "in some quality or accident" but in substance. This case and those of the preceding note are all included in Fuller and Eisenberg (1981).

3. More precisely, a half-open interval such as [701, 702).

4. Of course more complicated kinds of sales are possible, which this representation does not accommodate.

5. For example: "An offer is a promise which is in its terms conditional upon an act, forbearance or return promise being given in exchange for the promise or its performance" (Restatement of Contracts, 1932, sec. 24, Offer Defined).

6. Contracts texts find it necessary to explain why acceptance of such a proposal is not legally binding. For example, the Restatement of Contracts says, "In some situations the normal understanding is that no legal obligation arises, and some unusual manifestation of intention is necessary to create a contract" (Restatement of Contracts, Second, sec. 21, comment c, "Social engagements and domestic arrangements").

Chapter 6

1. Compare Restatement of Contracts, Second, sec. 29, To Whom an Offer is Addressed.

2. Compare Restatement of Contracts, Second, sec. 50, Acceptance of Offer Defined; Acceptance by Performance; Acceptance by Promise; sec. 19, Conduct as Manifestation of Assent; and sec. 69, Acceptance by Silence or Exercise of Dominion.

3. See Restatement of Contracts, Second, sec. 59, comment a, "Qualified acceptance"; Uniform Commercial Code, sec. 2-207.

4. A partial exception to this generalization is discussed in section 6.2.3.

5. See Restatement of Contracts, Second, sec. 63, comment c.

6. See Dick v. U.S., 113 Ct. Cl. 94, 82 F. Supp. 326 (1949), summarized in Fuller and Eisenberg (1981, p. 414).

7. See Restatement of Contracts, Second, sec. 39.

8. The interpretation of $o here is as an existentially quantified variable, rather than a universal, because the expression is used as a query to the data base rather than an assertion. See Nilsson (1980).

9. Compare Restatement of Contracts, Second, sec. 40, Time When Rejection or Counter-offer Terminates the Power of Acceptance; sec.

42, Revocation by Communication from Offeror Received by Offeree; sec. 63, Time When Acceptance Takes Effect.

10. See Restatement of Contracts, 1932, sec. 59; Williston, 1957 ed., sec. 73.

11. See Restatement of Contracts, Second, sec. 59, comment a; Uniform Commercial Code, sec. 2-207.

12. Compare Restatement of Contracts, Second, sec. 39, Counter-offers, and sec. 70, Effect of Receipt by Offeror of a Late or Otherwise Defective Acceptance.

13. Compare Restatement of Contracts, Second, sec. 64, Acceptance by Telephone or Teletype, which speaks of media of "substantially instantaneous two-way communication."

14. The Restatement says, for example, "The phrase 'manifestation of intention' adopts an external or objective standard for interpret-ing conduct; it means the external expression of intention as distinguished from undisclosed intention. A promisor manifests an intention if he believes or *has reason to believe* that the promisee will infer that intention from his words or conduct" (Restatement of Contracts, Second, sec. 2, comment b; emphasis added).

15. Compare Restatement of Contracts, Second, sec. 29, To Whom an Offer is Addressed, and sec. 52, Who May Accept an Offer.

16. The corresponding Restatement sections are as follows: sec. 23, Necessity That Manifestations Have Reference to Each Other; sec. 32, Invitation of Promise or Performance; sec. 59, Purported Acceptance Which Adds Qualifications; sec. 41, Lapse of Time; and sec. 60, Acceptance of Offer Which States Place, Time or Manner of Acceptance.

17. Since a telegram is a kind of document, the first negative example could have been omitted. Including it speeds up the match a bit in most problems.

Chapter 7

1. Throughout this section, nodes of trees are shown with some fields omitted and the content of some fields simplified.

2. The program does not have enough knowledge of speech acts to determine for itself that a yes-no question may be a request. In the internal representation of the problem, the question, *A131*, is shown as the *literal-force* of the sentence "Will you supply . . . ?" and the request, *A132*, as its *effective-force*.

3. For the examples that are available, see figure 6.8.

4. Another exception, as mentioned in section 6.4.3, is made for antecedents containing the operator *currently*.

5. In figure 7.2 some terms of the exchange are missing:
(quantity Salt13 Weight13)
(cwt Weight13)
(number Weight13 N13)
(number Dol13 (* 2.40 N13))

The reason concerns the procedure that matches two sets of terms, such as those from an offer and those from a possible acceptance. A straightforward extension to this procedure is needed to enable it to handle one-to-many relations, like *quantity*.

6. Restatement of Contracts, Second, sec. 41(3).

7. Ibid., comment e, "Offers made by mail or telegram."

8. As the published solution points out, the default effective time might also be changed by delay in communication of the offer. The program's current rule does not check for this possibility.

References

Allen, James F. 1981. What's Necessary to Hide? Modeling Action Verbs. In *Proceedings, Nineteenth Annual Meeting, Association for Computational Linguistics*, Stanford, pp. 77–81.

Allen, James F. 1983a. Maintaining Knowledge about Temporal Intervals. *Communications of the ACM* 26, 832–843.

Allen, James F. 1983b. Recognizing Intentions from Natural Language Utterances. In Brady and Berwick 1983, pp. 107–166.

Allen, Layman E. 1957. Symbolic Logic: A Razor-Edged Tool for Drafting and Interpreting Legal Documents. *Yale Law Journal* 66, 833–879.

Allen, Layman E. 1963. Beyond Document Retrieval toward Information Retrieval. *Minnesota Law Review* 47, 713–767.

Allen, Layman E. 1980. Language, Law and Logic: Plain Drafting for the Electronic Age. In Bryan Niblett, ed., *Computer Science and Law*, pp. 75–100. Cambridge: Cambridge University Press.

Allen, Layman E., and Engholm, C. Rudy. 1978. Normalized Legal Drafting and the Query Method. *Journal of Legal Education* 29, 380–412.

Anscombe, G. E. M. 1958. On Brute Facts. *Analysis* 18, no. 3 (n.s. no. 63), 69–72.

Artificial Intelligence 13, nos. 1–2. 1980. Special Issue on Non-Monotonic Logic.

Ashley, Kevin D. 1985. Reasoning by Analogy: A Survey of Selected A.I. Research with Implications for Legal Expert Systems. In Charles Walter, ed., *Computing Power and Legal Reasoning*. St. Paul: West.

Austin, John. 1885. *Lectures on Jurisprudence*. 2 vols. 5th ed., revised and edited by Robert Campbell. London: John Murray.

Austin, J. L. 1962. *How to Do Things with Words*. 2d ed. Cambridge: Harvard University Press, 1975.

Baade, Hans W., ed. 1963. *Jurimetrics*. New York: Basic Books. Originally published in *Law and Contemporary Problems* 28 (1963), 1–270.

Baker, G. P. 1977. Defeasibility and Meaning. In P. M. S. Hacker and J. Raz, eds., *Law, Morality, and Society*, pp. 26–57. Oxford: Clarendon Press.

Bench-Capon, Trevor, and Sergot, Marek. 1985. Toward a Rule Based Representation of Open Texture in Law. Technical Report, Department of Computing, Imperial College of Science and Technology, London.

Bing, Jon. 1980. Legal Norms, Discretionary Rules and Computer Programs. In Bryan Niblett, ed., *Computer Science and Law*, pp. 119–136. Cambridge: Cambridge University Press.

Bing, Jon, and Harvold, Trygve. 1977. *Legal Decisions and Information Systems*. Oslo: Universitetsforlaget.

Bobrow, Daniel G., and Winograd, Terry. 1977. An Overview of KRL, A Knowledge Representation Language. *Cognitive Science* 1, 3–46.

Borchgrevink, Mette, and Hansen, Johannes. 1980. SARA: A System for the Analysis of Legal Decisions. In J. Bing and K. S. Selmer, *A Decade of Computers and Law*, pp. 342–375. Oslo: Universitetsforlaget.

Boyd, William E., and Saxon, Charles S. 1981. The A-9: A Program for Drafting Security Agreements under Article 9 of the Uniform Commercial Code. *American Bar Foundation Research Journal* 1981, 637–669.

Brachman, Ronald J. 1977. What's in a Concept: Structural Foundations for Semantic Networks. *International Journal of Man-Machine Studies* 9, 127–152.

Brachman, Ronald J. 1978. A Structural Paradigm for Representing Knowledge. BBN Report No. 3605, Bolt Beranek and Newman Inc., Cambridge, Mass.

Brady, Michael, and Berwick, Robert C., eds. 1983. *Computational Models of Discourse*. Cambridge: MIT Press.

Braucher, Robert. 1964. Offer and Acceptance in the Second Restatement. *Yale Law Journal* 74, 302–310.

Buchanan, Bruce G. 1982. New Research on Expert Systems. In J. E. Hayes, Donald Michie, and Y-H Pao, eds., *Machine Intelligence 10*. New York: Halsted Press, John Wiley.

Buchanan, Bruce G., and Headrick, Thomas E. 1970. Some Speculation about Artificial Intelligence and Legal Reasoning. *Stanford Law Review* 23, 40–62.

Buchanan, Bruce G., and Mitchell, Tom M. 1978. Model-Directed Learning of Production Rules. In D. A. Waterman and Frederick Hayes-Roth, eds., *Pattern-Directed Inference Systems*, pp. 297–312. New York: Academic Press.

Buchanan, Bruce G., and Shortliffe, Edward H. 1984. *Rule-based Expert Systems: The MYCIN Experiments of the Heuristic Programming Project*. Reading, Mass.: Addison-Wesley.

Buchanan, Bruce G.; Sutherland, G. L.; and Feigenbaum, E. A. 1970. Rediscovering Some Problems of Artificial Intelligence in the Context of Organic

Chemistry. In B. Meltzer and D. Michie, eds., *Machine Intelligence 5*, pp. 253–280. New York: American Elsevier.

Buchanan, Jack R. 1981. Technology Comes to the Legal System. *Perspectives in Computing* 1, 29–34.

Buchanan, Jack R., and Fennell, Richard D. 1977. An Intelligent Information System for Criminal Case Management in the Federal Courts. In *Proceedings, Fifth International Joint Conference on Artificial Intelligence*, Cambridge, Mass., pp. 901–902.

Cardozo, Benjamin N. 1921. *The Nature of the Judicial Process*. New Haven: Yale University Press.

Cardozo, Benjamin N. 1924. *The Growth of the Law*. New Haven: Yale University Press.

Charniak, Eugene, and McDermott, Drew. 1985. *Introduction to Artificial Intelligence*. Reading, Mass.: Addison-Wesley.

Clancey, William J. 1983. The Epistemology of a Rule-based Expert System—A Framework for Explanation. *Artificial Intelligence* 20, 215–251.

Corbin, Arthur L. 1914. The Law and the Judges. *Yale Review*, n.s. 3, 234–250.

Corbin, Arthur L. 1928. The Restatement of the Law of Contracts. *American Bar Association Journal* 14, 602–605.

Corbin, Arthur L. 1929. The Restatement of the Common Law by the American Law Institute. *Iowa Law Review* 15, 19–41.

Corbin, Arthur L. 1950. *Corbin on Contracts: A Comprehensive Treatise on the Working Rules of Contract Law*. 12 vols. St. Paul: West, 1950–64.

Corbin, Arthur L. 1961. The Judicial Process Revisited. *Yale Law Journal* 71, 195–201.

Corbin, Arthur L. 1963. *Corbin on Contracts* (above), vol. 1, 1963 ed.

Corbin, Arthur L. 1964. Sixty-Eight Years at Law. *University of Kansas Law Review* 13, 183–195.

D'Amato, Anthony. 1977. Can/Should Computers Replace Judges? *Georgia Law Review* 11, 1277–1301. Reprinted in D'Amato, *Jurisprudence: A Descriptive and Normative Analysis of Law*. Dordrecht: Martinus Nijhoff, 1984.

Davidson, Donald. 1967. The Logical Form of Action Sentences. In Davidson, *Essays on Actions and Events*, pp. 105–122. Oxford: Clarendon Press, 1980.

Davis, Randall. 1979. Interactive Transfer of Expertise: Acquisition of New Inference Rules. *Artificial Intelligence* 12, 121–157.

deBessonet, Cary G., and Cross, George R. 1985. An Artificial Intelligence Application in the Law: CCLIPS, a Computer Program That Processes Legal Information. Technical report, Louisiana State Law Institute.

Dewey, John. 1924. Logical Method and Law. *Cornell Law Quarterly* 10, 17–27.

Dias, R. W. M. 1979. *A Bibliography of Jurisprudence*. 3d ed. London: Butterworths.

Dickinson, John. 1931. Legal Rules: Their Application and Elaboration. *University of Pennsylvania Law Review* 79, 1052–1096.

Dworkin, Ronald. 1977a. *Taking Rights Seriously*. Cambridge: Harvard University Press.

Dworkin, Ronald. 1977b. Seven Critics. *Georgia Law Review* 11, 1201–1267. Reprinted as "A Reply to Critics" in Dworkin 1977a (paperback ed., 1978).

Dworkin, Ronald. 1978. No Right Answer? *New York University Law Review* 53, 1–32. Reprinted as "Is There Really No Right Answer in Hard Cases?" in Dworkin, *A Matter of Principle*. Cambridge: Harvard University Press, 1985.

Eisenberg, Melvin A., ed. 1982. *Gilbert Law Summaries: Contracts*. 10th ed. New York: Harcourt Brace Jovanovich Legal and Professional Publications.

Erman, Lee D.; Hayes-Roth, Frederick; Lesser, Victor R.; and Reddy, D. Raj. 1980. The Hearsay-II Speech Understanding System: Integrating Knowledge to Resolve Uncertainty. *Computing Surveys* 12, 213–253.

Feigenbaum, Edward A. 1977. The Art of Artificial Intelligence: I. Themes and Case Studies of Knowledge Engineering. In *Proceedings, Fifth International Joint Conference on Artificial Intelligence*, Cambridge, Mass., pp. 1014–1029.

Frank, Jerome. 1930. *Law and the Modern Mind*. New York: Brentano's.

Frank, Jerome. 1949. *Courts on Trial*. Princeton: Princeton University Press.

Friedland, Peter, ed. 1985. Special Section on Architectures for Knowledge-Based Systems. *Communications of the ACM* 28, 902–941.

Fuller, Lon L. 1940. *The Law in Quest of Itself*. Chicago: Foundation Press.

Fuller, Lon L. 1946. Reason and Fiat in Case Law. *Harvard Law Review* 59, 376–438.

Fuller, Lon L. 1958. Positivism and Fidelity to Law: A Reply to Professor Hart. *Harvard Law Review* 71, 630–672.

Fuller, Lon L. 1966. Science and the Judicial Process. *Harvard Law Review* 79, 1604–1628.

Fuller, Lon L. 1967. *Legal Fictions*. Stanford: Stanford University Press.

Fuller, Lon L. 1969. *The Morality of Law*. Rev. ed. New Haven: Yale University Press.

Fuller, Lon L., and Eisenberg, Melvin A. 1981. *Basic Contract Law*. 4th ed. St. Paul: West.

Gaines, B. R. 1976. Foundations of Fuzzy Reasoning. *International Journal of Man-Machine Studies* 8, 623–668.

Gaines, B. R., and Kohout, L. J. 1977. The Fuzzy Decade: A Bibliography of Fuzzy Systems and Closely Related Topics. *International Journal of Man-Machine Studies* 9, 1–68.

Gallie, W. B. 1956. Essentially Contested Concepts. *Proceedings of the Aristotelian Society*, n.s. 56, 167–198.

Genesereth, Michael R.; Greiner, Russell; Grinberg, Milton R.; and Smith, David E. 1984. The MRS Dictionary. Memo HPP-80-24, Stanford Heuristic Programming Project, Stanford University. December 1980; revised January 1984.

Genesereth, Michael R.; Greiner, Russell; and Smith, David E. 1980. MRS Manual. Memo HPP-80-24, Stanford Heuristic Programming Project, Stanford University.

Gilmore, Grant. 1961. Legal Realism: Its Cause and Cure. *Yale Law Journal* 70, 1037–1048.

Gilmore, Grant. 1974. *The Death of Contract*. Columbus: Ohio State University Press.

Gilmore, Grant. 1977. *The Ages of American Law*. New Haven: Yale University Press.

Goldman, Sheldon, and Sarat, Austin. 1978. *American Court Systems: Readings in Judicial Process and Behavior*. San Francisco: W. H. Freeman.

Greiner, Russell, and Lenat, Douglas B. 1980. A Representation Language Language. In *Proceedings, First Annual National Conference on Artificial Intelligence*, Stanford, pp. 165–169.

Grossman, Garry S., and Solomon, Lewis D. 1983. Computers and Legal Reasoning. *American Bar Association Journal* 69, 66–70.

Haar, Charles M.; Sawyer, John P., Jr.; and Cummings, Stephen J. 1977. Computer Power and Legal Reasoning: A Case Study of Judicial Decision Prediction in Zoning Amendment Cases. *American Bar Foundation Research Journal*, 651–768.

Hafner, Carole D. 1981. *An Information Retrieval System Based on a Computer Model of Legal Knowledge*. Ann Arbor: UMI Research Press.

Harris, J. W. 1979. *Law and Legal Science: An Inquiry into the Concepts Legal Rule and Legal System*. Oxford: Clarendon Press.

Hart, H. L. A. 1949. The Ascription of Responsibility and Rights. *Proceedings of the Aristotelian Society*, n.s. 49 (1948–49), 171–194. Reprinted in Antony Flew, ed., *Logic and Language: First and Second Series*, pp. 151–174. Garden City: Anchor Books, 1965.

Hart, H. L. A. 1958. Positivism and the Separation of Law and Morals. *Harvard Law Review* 71, 593–629. Reprinted in Hart, *Essays in Jurisprudence and Philosophy*. Oxford: Clarendon Press, 1983.

Hart, H. L. A. 1961. *The Concept of Law.* Oxford: Clarendon Press.

Hart, H. L. A. 1967. Problems of Philosophy of Law. In P. Edwards, ed., *The Encyclopedia of Philosophy,* vol. 6, pp. 264–276. New York: Macmillan and Free Press. Reprinted in Hart, *Essays in Jurisprudence and Philosophy.* Oxford: Clarendon Press, 1983.

Hart, Henry M., Jr., and Sacks, Albert M. 1958. *The Legal Process: Basic Problems in the Making and Application of Law.* Tentative ed. Cambridge: [Harvard Law School].

Hayes, Patrick J. 1979a. The Logic of Frames. In Dieter Metzing, ed., *Frame Conceptions and Text Understanding,* pp. 46–61. Berlin: Walter de Gruyter. Reprinted in Bonnie Lynn Webber and Nils J. Nilsson, eds., *Readings in Artificial Intelligence,* pp. 451–458. Palo Alto: Tioga Publishing, 1981.

Hayes, Patrick J. 1979b. The Naive Physics Manifesto. In Donald Michie, ed., *Expert Systems in the Micro-electronic Age.* Edinburgh: Edinburgh University Press.

Hayes-Roth, Frederick; Waterman, Donald A.; and Lenat, Douglas B., eds. 1983. *Building Expert Systems.* Reading, Mass.: Addison-Wesley.

Hobbs, Jerry R., and Moore, Robert C., eds. 1985. *Formal Theories of the Commonsense World.* Norwood, N.J.: Ablex.

Holmes, Oliver Wendell. 1881. *The Common Law.* Edited by Mark DeWolfe Howe. Boston: Little, Brown, 1963.

Holmes, Oliver Wendell. 1897. The Path of the Law. *Harvard Law Review* 10, 457–478. Reprinted in O. W. Holmes, *Collected Legal Papers.* New York: Harcourt Brace, 1921.

Hustler, Allen. 1982. Programming Law in Logic. Research Report CS-82-13, Department of Computer Science, University of Waterloo.

Hutcheson, Joseph C., Jr. 1929. The Judgment Intuitive: The Function of the "Hunch" in Judicial Decision. *Cornell Law Quarterly* 14, 274–288.

Johnson, Paul E.; Johnson, Michael G.; and Little, Raleigh K. 1984. Expertise in Trial Advocacy: Some Considerations for Inquiry into Its Nature and Development. *Campbell Law Review* 7, 119–143.

Jones, Edgar A., Jr., ed. 1962. *Law and Electronics: The Challenge of a New Era.* Proceedings of the First National Law and Electronics Conference, Lake Arrowhead, California, October 21–23, 1960. New York: Matthew Bender.

Jones, Gareth, ed. 1973. *The Sovereignty of the Law: Selections from Blackstone's "Commentaries on the Laws of England."* Toronto: University of Toronto Press.

Joshi, Aravind K.; Webber, Bonnie L.; and Sag, Ivan A. 1981. *Elements of Discourse Understanding.* Cambridge: Cambridge University Press.

Karlgren, Hans, and Walker, Donald E. 1983. The Polytext System: A New Design for a Text Retrieval System. In Ferenc Kiefer, ed., *Questions and Answers,* pp. 273–294. Dordrecht, Netherlands: D. Reidel.

Kelso, Louis O. 1946. Does the Law Need a Technological Revolution? *Rocky Mountain Law Review* 18, 378–392.

Kort, Fred. 1963. Content Analysis of Judicial Opinions and Rules of Law. In Glendon Schubert, ed., *Judicial Decision-Making*, pp. 133–197. Glencoe: Free Press.

Langdell, C. C. 1879. *A Selection of Cases on the Law of Contracts.* 2 vols., plus separately bound Summary. 2d ed. Boston: Little, Brown.

Langdell, C. C. 1886. Address delivered November 5, 1886. Reprinted in *Law Quarterly Review* 3 (1887), 123–125.

Lasswell, Harold D. 1955. Current Studies of the Decision Process: Automation versus Creativity. *Western Political Quarterly* 8, 381–399.

Lawlor, Reed C. 1963a. Foundations of Logical Legal Decision Making. *Modern Uses of Logic in Law* 1963, 98–114.

Lawlor, Reed C. 1963b. What Computers Can Do: Analysis and Prediction of Judicial Decisions. *American Bar Association Journal* 49, 337–344. Reprinted in Glendon Schubert, ed., *Judicial Behavior: A Reader in Theory and Research*, pp. 492–505. Chicago: Rand McNally, 1964.

Lawlor, Reed C. 1972. Excerpts from "Fact Content of Cases and Precedent—A Modern Theory of Precedent." *Jurimetrics Journal* 12, 245–270.

Lawlor, Reed C. 1980. Computer Analysis of Judicial Decisions. In Bryan Niblett, ed., *Computer Science and Law*, pp. 219–232. Cambridge: Cambridge University Press.

Lehnert, Wendy G. 1978. Representing Physical Objects in Memory. Research Report 131, Department of Computer Science, Yale University.

Lehnert, Wendy G.; Dyer, Michael G.; Johnson, Peter N.; Yang, C. J.; and Harley, Steve. 1983. BORIS—An Experiment in In-Depth Understanding of Narratives. *Artificial Intelligence* 20, 15–62.

Levi, Edward H. 1949. *An Introduction to Legal Reasoning.* Chicago: University of Chicago Press.

Lindsay, Robert K.; Buchanan, Bruce G.; Feigenbaum, Edward A.; and Lederberg, Joshua. 1980. *Applications of Artificial Intelligence for Chemistry: The DENDRAL Project.* New York: McGraw-Hill.

Llewellyn, Karl N. 1930. *The Bramble Bush: On Our Law and Its Study.* 1960 ed. Dobbs Ferry, N.Y.: Oceana Publications.

Llewellyn, Karl N. 1938. On Our Case Law of Contract: Offer and Acceptance. *Yale Law Journal* 48, 1–36 (1938), 779–818 (1939).

Llewellyn, Karl N. 1960. *The Common Law Tradition: Deciding Appeals.* Boston: Little, Brown.

Loevinger, Lee. 1949. Jurimetrics: The Next Step Forward. *Minnesota Law Review* 33, 455–493.

Loevinger, Lee. 1961. Jurimetrics: Science and Prediction in the Field of Law. *Minnesota Law Review* 46, 255–275.

Loevinger, Lee. 1963. Jurimetrics: The Methodology of Legal Inquiry. *Law and Contemporary Problems* 28, 5–35.

McCarthy, John. 1977. Epistemological Problems in Artificial Intelligence. In *Proceedings, Fifth International Joint Conference on Artificial Intelligence*, Cambridge, Mass., pp. 1038–1044.

McCarthy, John. 1980. Circumscription—A Form of Non-Monotonic Reasoning. *Artificial Intelligence* 13, 27–39.

McCarthy, John. 1984. Some Expert Systems Need Common Sense. In H. R. Pagels, ed., *Computer Culture: The Scientific, Intellectual, and Social Impact of the Computer*, pp. 129–137. New York: New York Academy of Sciences.

McCarthy, John, and Hayes, P. J. 1969. Some Philosophical Problems from the Standpoint of Artificial Intelligence. In B. Meltzer and D. Michie, eds., *Machine Intelligence 4*, pp. 463–502. New York: American Elsevier.

McCarty, L. Thorne. 1977. Reflections on TAXMAN: An Experiment in Artificial Intelligence and Legal Reasoning. *Harvard Law Review* 90, 837–893.

McCarty, L. Thorne. 1980a. The TAXMAN Project: Towards a Cognitive Theory of Legal Argument. In Bryan Niblett, ed., *Computer Science and Law*, pp. 23–43. Cambridge: Cambridge University Press.

McCarty, L. Thorne. 1980b. Some Requirements for a Computer-based Legal Consultant. In *Proceedings, First Annual National Conference on Artificial Intelligence*, Stanford, pp. 298–300.

McCarty, L. Thorne. 1983. Permissions and Obligations. In *Proceedings, Eighth International Joint Conference on Artificial Intelligence*, Karlsruhe, 287–294.

McCarty, L. Thorne, and Sridharan, N. S. 1980. The Representation of Conceptual Structures in TAXMAN II: Part One: Logical Templates. LRP-TR-4, Laboratory for Computer Science Research, Rutgers University. A shorter version is McCarty and Sridharan, "The Representation of an Evolving System of Legal Concepts: I. Logical Templates," in *Proceedings, Third Biennial Conference of the Canadian Society for Computational Studies of Intelligence*, Victoria, B.C. (1980), pp. 304–311.

McCarty, L. Thorne, and Sridharan, N. S. 1982. A Computational Theory of Legal Argument. LRP-TR-13, Laboratory for Computer Science Research, Rutgers University. A shorter version is McCarty and Sridharan, "The Representation of an Evolving System of Legal Concepts: II. Prototypes and Deformations," in *Proceedings, Seventh International Joint Conference on Artificial Intelligence*, Vancouver (1981), pp. 246–253.

McCarty, L. Thorne; Sridharan, N. S.; and Sangster, Barbara C. 1979. The Implementation of TAXMAN II: An Experiment in Artificial Intelligence and Legal Reasoning. LRP-TR-2, Laboratory for Computer Science Research, Rutgers University, January 16, 1979.

McCoy, Richard Whitfield. 1976. Improving Legal Service Delivery with Computer Technology. Ph.D. dissertation, University of Wisconsin.

McCoy, Richard W., and Chatterton, William A. 1968. Computer-Assisted Legal Services. *Law and Computer Technology* 1 (November 1968), 2–7.

Mackaay, Ejan, and Robillard, Pierre. 1974. Predicting Judicial Decisions: The Nearest Neighbor Rule and Visual Representation of Case Patterns. *Datenverarbeitung im Recht* 3, 302–331.

Maggs, Peter B., and deBessonet, Cary G. 1972. Automated Logical Analysis of Systems of Legal Rules. *Jurimetrics Journal* 12, 158–169.

Meldman, Jeffrey A. 1975. A Preliminary Study in Computer-Aided Legal Analysis. MAC-TR-157, MIT.

Michaelson, Robert H. 1982. A Knowledge-based System for Individual Income and Transfer Tax Planning. Ph.D. dissertation, University of Illinois.

Michaelson, Robert H. 1984. An Expert System for Federal Tax Planning. *Expert Systems* 1, 149–167.

Michener [Rissland], Edwina R. 1978. Understanding Understanding Mathematics. *Cognitive Science* 2, 361–383.

Moore, Michael S. 1981. The Semantics of Judging. *Southern California Law Review* 54, 151–294.

Moore, Robert C. 1981. Problems in Logical Form. In *Proceedings, Nineteenth Annual Meeting, Association for Computational Linguistics,* Stanford, pp. 117–124.

Mostow, Jack. 1983. 1983 International Machine Learning Workshop: An Informal Report. *Sigart Newsletter,* no. 86, 24–31.

Nagel, Donna. 1983. Concept Learning by Building and Applying Transformations between Object Descriptions. LRP-TR-15, Laboratory for Computer Science Research, Rutgers University.

Newell, Allen; Shaw, J. C.; and Simon, H. A. 1957. Empirical Explorations with the Logic Theory Machine: A Case Study in Heuristics. In E. A. Feigenbaum and J. Feldman, eds., *Computers and Thought,* pp. 109–133. New York: McGraw-Hill, 1963.

Newell, Allen, and Simon, H. A. 1972. *Human Problem Solving.* Englewood Cliffs, N.J.: Prentice-Hall.

Nii, H. Penny, and Aiello, Nelleke. 1979. AGE (Attempt to Generalize): A Knowledge-Based Program for Building Knowledge-Based Programs. In *Proceedings, Sixth International Joint Conference on Artificial Intelligence,* Tokyo, 1979, pp. 645–655.

Nilsson, Nils J. 1980. *Principles of Artificial Intelligence.* Palo Alto: Tioga Publishing.

Pitman, Kent M. 1983. The Revised Maclisp Manual. MIT/LCS/TR-295, Laboratory for Computer Science, MIT.

Pople, Harry. 1977. On the Knowledge Acquisition Process in Applied A. I. Systems. In *Proceedings, Fifth International Joint Conference on Artificial Intelligence*, Cambridge, Mass., pp. 998–999.

Popp, Walter G., and Schlink, Bernhard. 1975. JUDITH, a Computer Program to Advise Lawyers in Reasoning a Case. *Jurimetrics Journal* 15, 303–314.

Pound, Roscoe. 1908. Mechanical Jurisprudence. *Columbia Law Review* 8, 605–623.

Putnam, Hilary. 1970. Is Semantics Possible? In Howard E. Kiefer and Milton K. Munitz, eds., *Language, Belief and Metaphysics*, pp. 50–63. Albany: State University of New York Press. Reprinted in H. Putnam, *Philosophical Papers*, vol. 2, *Mind, Language and Reality*, pp. 139–152. Cambridge: Cambridge University Press, 1975.

Putnam, Hilary. 1975. The Meaning of 'Meaning'. In Keith Gunderson, ed., *Language, Mind, and Knowledge*. Minnesota Studies in the Philosophy of Science, vol. 7, pp. 131–193. Minneapolis: University of Minnesota Press. Reprinted in H. Putnam, *Philosophical Papers*, vol. 2, *Mind, Language and Reality*, pp. 215–271. Cambridge: Cambridge University Press, 1975.

Reiter, Raymond. 1978. On Reasoning by Default. In *TINLAP-2: Theoretical Issues in Natural Language Processing-2*, Urbana, pp. 210–218.

Restatement of the Law of Contracts. 1932. 2 vols. St. Paul: American Law Institute Publishers.

Restatement of the Law, Second: Contracts 2d. 1981. 3 vols. St. Paul: American Law Institute Publishers.

Restatement of the Law, Second: Torts 2d. 1965–1979. 4 vols. St. Paul: American Law Institute Publishers.

Rissland, Edwina L. 1978. See Michener 1978.

Rissland, Edwina L. 1982. Examples in the Legal Domain: Hypotheticals in Contract Law. In *Proceedings, Fourth Annual Conference, Cognitive Science Society*, Ann Arbor, pp. 96–99.

Rissland, Edwina L. 1983. Examples in Legal Reasoning: Legal Hypotheticals. In *Proceedings, Eighth International Joint Conference on Artificial Intelligence*, Karlsruhe, pp. 90–93.

Rissland, Edwina L. 1985. Argument Moves and Hypotheticals. In Charles Walter, ed., *Computing Power and Legal Reasoning*. St. Paul: West.

Rissland, Edwina L.; Valcarce, Eduardo M.; and Ashley, Kevin D. 1984. Explaining and Arguing with Examples. In *AAAI-84, Proceedings, National Conference on Artificial Intelligence*, Austin, Texas, pp. 288–294.

Russell, Stuart. 1985. The Compleat Guide to MRS. Report KSL-85-12, Stanford Knowledge Systems Laboratory, Computer Science Department, Stanford University.

Sacerdoti, Earl D. 1974. Planning in a Hierarchy of Abstraction Spaces. *Artificial Intelligence* 5, 115–135.

Sacerdoti, Earl D. 1980. Problem Solving Tactics. *AI Magazine* 2, no. 1, 7–15 (1980–81).

Schank, Roger C. 1975. *Conceptual Information Processing.* New York: American Elsevier.

Schank, Roger C. 1982. *Dynamic Memory: A Theory of Reminding and Learning in Computers and People.* Cambridge: Cambridge University Press.

Schank, Roger C., and Abelson, Robert P. 1977. *Scripts, Plans, Goals and Understanding.* Hillsdale, N.J.: Lawrence Erlbaum.

Schubert, Glendon. 1968. The Importance of Computer Technology to Political Science Research in Judicial Behavior. *Jurimetrics Journal* 8, no. 3, 56–63. Reprinted as "On a Computer Court" in Schubert 1975, pp. 13–20.

Schubert, Glendon. 1975. *Human Jurisprudence: Public Law as Political Science.* Honolulu: University Press of Hawaii.

Schwartz, Stephen P., ed. 1977. *Naming, Necessity, and Natural Kinds.* Ithaca: Cornell University Press.

Searle, John R. 1969. *Speech Acts.* London: Cambridge University Press.

Searle, John R. 1975a. Indirect Speech Acts. In Peter Cole and Jerry Morgan, eds., *Syntax and Semantics,* vol. 3, *Speech Acts,* pp. 59–82. New York: Academic Press. Reprinted in Searle, *Expression and Meaning: Studies in the Theory of Speech Acts.* Cambridge: Cambridge University Press, 1979.

Searle, John R. 1975b. A Taxonomy of Illocutionary Acts. In Keith Gunderson, ed., *Language, Mind, and Knowledge.* Minnesota Studies in the Philosophy of Science, vol. 7, pp. 344–369. Minneapolis: University of Minnesota Press. Reprinted, with a change in terminology, in Searle, *Expression and Meaning: Studies in the Theory of Speech Acts.* Cambridge: Cambridge University Press, 1979.

Searle, John R. 1983. *Intentionality.* Cambridge: Cambridge University Press.

Sergot, Marek J. 1985. Representing Legislation as Logic Programs. Technical Report, Department of Computing, Imperial College of Science and Technology, London.

Sergot, Marek J.; Sadri, F.; Kowalski, R. A.; Kriwaczek, F.; Hammond, P.; and Cory, H. T. 1986. The British Nationality Act as a Logic Program. *Communications of the ACM* 29, 370–386.

Shortliffe, Edward H. 1976. *Computer-Based Medical Consultations: MYCIN.* New York: American Elsevier.

Simpson, A. W. B. 1964. The Analysis of Legal Concepts. *Law Quarterly Review* 80, 535–558.

Slayton, Philip. 1974. Radical Computer Use in Law. Report prepared for the Department of Communications of the Government of Canada. June 1974. Photocopied typescript.

Sprowl, James A. 1976. *A Manual for Computer-Assisted Legal Research*. Chicago: American Bar Foundation.

Sprowl, James A. 1979. Automating the Legal Reasoning Process: A Computer That Uses Regulations and Statutes to Draft Legal Documents. *American Bar Foundation Research Journal* 1979, 1–81.

Sprowl, James A., and Staudt, Ronald W. 1981. Computerizing Client Services in the Law School Teaching Clinic: An Experiment in Law Office Automation. *American Bar Foundation Research Journal* 1981, 699–751.

Sridharan, N. S. 1978. AIMDS User Manual—Version 2. CBM-TR-89, Department of Computer Science, Rutgers University.

Stefik, Mark. 1979. An Examination of a Frame-Structured Representation System. In *Proceedings, Sixth International Joint Conference on Artificial Intelligence*, Tokyo, pp. 845–852.

Stevens, Robert. 1971. Two Cheers for 1870: The American Law School. *Perspectives in American History* 5, *Law in American History*, 403–548.

Stone, Julius. 1964. *Legal System and Lawyers' Reasonings*. Stanford: Stanford University Press.

Stone, Julius. 1966. *Law and the Social Sciences in the Second Half Century*. Minneapolis: University of Minnesota Press.

Stratman, James F. 1984. Studying the Appellate Brief and Opinion Composing Process. *Juris* 19, no. 1, 9–14 (1984) and no. 2, 12–19 (1985).

Sussman, Gerald; Winograd, Terry; and Charniak, Eugene. 1971. Micro-Planner Reference Manual (revised). A.I. Memo 203A, Artificial Intelligence Laboratory, MIT.

Szolovits, Peter, and Pauker, Stephen G. 1978. Categorical and Probabilistic Reasoning in Medical Diagnosis. *Artificial Intelligence* 11, 115–144.

Tapper, Colin. 1973. *Computers and the Law*. London: Weidenfeld and Nicolson.

Thomas, Bart T. 1979. Unauthorized Practice and Computer Aided Legal Analysis Systems. *Jurimetrics Journal* 20, 41–51.

Turow, Scott. 1978. *One L: An Inside Account of Life in the First Year at Harvard Law School*. New York: Penguin.

Tyree, Alan L. 1980. Can a "Deterministic" Computer Judge Overrule Himself? *Rutgers Journal of Computers, Technology and the Law* 7, 381–384.

Tyree, Alan L. 1981. Fact Content Analysis of Case Law: Methods and Limitations. *Jurimetrics Journal* 22, 1–33.

Uniform Commercial Code. 1978. 9th ed. Philadelphia: American Law Institute; Chicago: National Conference of Commissioners on Uniform State Laws.

Van Melle, W.; Scott, A. C.; Bennett, J. S.; and Peairs, M. A. S. 1981. The EMYCIN Manual. Report STAN-CS-81-885, Department of Computer Science, Stanford University.

Waismann, Friedrich. 1945. Verifiability. *Proceedings of the Aristotelian Society,* supp. 19, 119–150. Reprinted in Antony Flew, ed., *Logic and Language: First and Second Series,* pp. 122–151. Garden City: Anchor Books, 1965.

Walker, Donald E. 1981. The Organization and Use of Information: Contributions of Information Science, Computational Linguistics and Artificial Intelligence. *Journal of the American Society for Information Science* 32, 347–363. Another version is Walker, "Computational Strategies for Analyzing the Organization and Use of Information," in Spencer A. Ward and Linda J. Reed, eds., *Knowledge Structure and Use: Implications for Synthesis and Interpretation,* pp. 229–284. Philadelphia: Temple University Press, 1983.

Wambaugh, Eugene. 1894. *The Study of Cases.* 2d ed. Boston: Little, Brown.

Waterman, D. A., and Peterson, Mark A. 1980. Rule-Based Models of Legal Expertise. In *Proceedings, First Annual National Conference on Artificial Intelligence,* Stanford, pp. 272–275.

Waterman, D. A., and Peterson, Mark A. 1981. Models of Legal Decision-making. Report R-2717-ICJ, Rand Corporation, Institute for Civil Justice.

Waterman, D. A., and Peterson, Mark A. 1984. Evaluating Civil Claims: An Expert Systems Approach. *Expert Systems* 1, 65–76.

Weizenbaum, Joseph. 1976. *Computer Power and Human Reason: From Judgment to Calculation.* San Francisco: W. H. Freeman.

Weyhrauch, Richard W. 1980. Prolegomena to a Theory of Mechanized Reasoning. *Artificial Intelligence* 13, 133–170.

White, James J., and Summers, Robert S. 1980. *Handbook of the Law under the Uniform Commercial Code.* 2d ed. St. Paul: West.

Wiener, Frederick Bernays. 1962. Decision Prediction by Computers: Nonsense Cubed—and Worse. *American Bar Association Journal* 48, 1023–1028.

Wiener, Norbert. 1948. *Cybernetics.* 2d ed. New York: MIT Press and John Wiley, 1961.

Wilks, Yorick. 1977. Good and Bad Arguments about Semantic Primitives. Research Report 42, Department of Artificial Intelligence, University of Edinburgh.

Williams, Glanville. 1939. *Liability for Animals.* Cambridge: Cambridge University Press.

Williams, Glanville. 1945. Language and the Law. *Law Quarterly Review* 61 (1945), 71–86, 179–195, 293–303, 384–406; *Law Quarterly Review* 62 (1946), 387–406.

Williston, Samuel. 1957. *A Treatise on the Law of Contracts.* Vol. 1. 3d ed. by Walter H. E. Jaeger. Mount Kisco, N.Y.: Baker, Voorhis.

Winograd, Terry. 1976. Towards a Procedural Understanding of Semantics. *Revue internationale de philosophie* 30, 260–303.

Winograd, Terry. 1980a. What Does It Mean to Understand Language? *Cognitive Science* 4, 209–241.

Winograd, Terry. 1980b. Extended Inference Modes in Reasoning by Computer Systems. *Artificial Intelligence* 13, 5–26.

Winograd, Terry. 1983. *Language as a Cognitive Process.* Vol. 1, *Syntax.* Reading, Mass.: Addison-Wesley.

Wisdom, John T. 1945. Gods. *Proceedings of the Aristotelian Society,* n.s. 45 (1944–45), 185–206. Reprinted in Antony Flew, ed., *Logic and Language: First and Second Series,* pp. 194–214. Garden City: Anchor Books, 1965.

Wittgenstein, Ludwig. 1958. *Philosophical Investigations.* Translated by G. E. M. Anscombe. 3d ed. New York: Macmillan.

Woods, William A. 1975. What's in a Link: Foundations for Semantic Networks. In Daniel G. Bobrow and Allan Collins, eds., *Representation and Understanding,* pp. 35–82. New York: Academic Press.

Zadeh, L. A. 1965. Fuzzy Sets. *Information and Control* 8, 338–353.

Index